Stubborn Theological Questions

Stubborn Theological Questions

John Macquarrie

scm press

© John Macquarrie 2003

British Library Cataloguing in Publication data

A catalogue record for this book is available
from the British Library

0 334 02907 4

First published in 2003 by SCM Press
9–17 St Albans Place, London N1 0NX

www.scm-canterburypress.co.uk

SCM Press is a division of
SCM-Canterbury Press Ltd

Typeset by Rowland Phototypesetting Ltd,
Bury St Edmunds, Suffolk
Printed and bound in Great Britain by
Biddles Ltd, *www.biddles.co.uk*

To
Maurice Wiles

Friend, Colleague
and Fellow Struggler with the
Stubborn Questions

Contents

Preface

Teachers of theology, and presumably of other subjects, are often requested to write short pieces to mark special occasions. It may be to write a chapter for a *Festschrift* honouring a colleague who has reached the age of retirement, or the centenary of a university, or even the appearance of a controversial book. These pieces may be published at the time of composition, though they reach only a very limited readership, or they may simply accumulate unpublished over the years. I have accumulated quite a large number of such essays and lectures myself, and think that some of them might be interesting to a larger readership.

As I looked over possible items for inclusion in this collection, I was struck by the fact that certain questions seem to come up again and again. These are the so-called 'stubborn questions' mentioned in the title of the book. I find there are three that seem to have dogged me.

The first is the question of how we are to think and speak of God in a changing and nowadays largely secularized world. Maybe God himself is unchanging, but our images and conceptions of God have frequently changed. One could even say that there have been revolutionary changes in the way that men and women have thought of God. The most revolutionary and influential change of all was effected by Jesus Christ and the movement which he founded. Before his time, God was imagined as an all-powerful monarch in the skies, a celestial counterpart of an earthly emperor, to be feared rather than loved. This was true in large measure even of the God of Israel. But the God whom Christians believed they had learned about from the teaching and the life of Jesus was, we could say, a creature-friendly God. This change in human thinking about God was so revolutionary that we are still catching up with it, and the older images of the arbitrary, punishing, nationalistic God keep coming back, so that we need from time to time to rethink our understanding of God. I believe that in the past fifty years or so there has been a movement among Christian theologians to lay more stress on the closeness and immanence of God, in various forms of panentheism.

Although I am writing as a Christian theologian, I am not saying that only in the Christian tradition is there a true (though imperfect) understanding of God, but the whole human race has at least some inkling of this God, in whose image we are said to be made. It is because of this universal impact of God on the creation that I have included in the first chapter not only a brief account of the life and teaching of Jesus, but a parallel account from classical pagan civilization of the career of Socrates.

The second of our 'stubborn questions' concerns the person of Jesus Christ. His teaching about God and the example of his life combined to bring a new image of God to Jesus' followers, and this eventually developed into a belief that, in a special way, God was in Christ, and so to a doctrine of incarnation, the doctrine that in Christ the Word of God had become flesh and had lived on earth among the events and trials of historical human existence. As soon as this doctrine took shape, it became a matter of controversy and has probably given rise to more 'heresies' than any other Christian doctrine, with now the divinity of Christ, now the humanity, being exaggerated at the expense of the other. In 451 the Council of Chalcedon attempted to reconcile the factions by declaring Jesus Christ to be fully man and fully God, but in modern times the questions has come back, and again in the past fifty years or thereabouts, there has been a fresh concern to be more realistic in recognizing the humanity of Christ. An accompanying development has been the recognition that the idea of incarnation, however difficult it may be, is not something peculiarly Christian. Something close to it appears in Indian religion, for instance, in the figure of Krishna, and this can be seen as a convergence of Indian and Christian aspirations, whereas formerly language about the 'only-begotten Son', Jesus Christ, tended to restrict incarnation exclusively to Christianity.

The third and more general 'stubborn question' relates to the problem of religious knowledge, and is perhaps inevitable in an age of science. Since the Renaissance and Enlightenment, the success of the sciences had led to a widespread prejudice that only through the methods of the natural sciences can we gain any reliable knowledge of the natural world or of the human world or of the cosmos of which human beings and nature are parts or aspects. So the theologian has to return to the question of how we know about God and human destiny. Are there ways of knowing other than the scientific way? He must ask about knowledge of other people, knowledge of the human self, about mysticism, revelation, spirituality and so on. Are those who claim a monopoly of knowledge for the empirical sciences blind to other avenues of knowledge? That is perhaps the most stubborn of all the questions confronting the contemporary theologian.

Of the eighteen chapters in this book, 1 to 6 discuss questions relating to God; 7 to 12, questions relating to incarnation and the person of Christ; 13 to 18, questions about the sources of religious knowledge, all question which overlap and intertwine with one another.

I wish to thank the many friends and colleagues with whom I have discussed these questions; my wife who has given me much help with the preparation of this book; and those who invited me to give the lectures or write the articles from which the chapters have been developed and who have now consented to their publication in the present volume. They are named in the notes to each chapter.

John Macquarrie
Oxford, June 2002

Jesus and Socrates: Spiritual Vision versus Political Power

The Greek scholar Plutarch (46–120 CE) wrote a series of biographies which he called *Parallel Lives*. He chose this name because the biographies are arranged in pairs, one telling the story of a famous Greek and the other that of a famous Roman. This suggested to me a pattern for this essay. I am setting side by side two lives, which might, I think, be called parallel. One is the life of the Greek philosopher, Socrates; the other is not the life of a Roman, but of a Jew living in the Roman Empire more than four hundred years after the time of Socrates – Jesus of Nazareth. Both Socrates and Jesus were men of outstanding moral and spiritual vision, who devoted their lives to bettering the condition of the people among whom they lived. But both of them met with rejection, and were eventually put to death by the civil authorities. As we study their careers, we shall find that there are many parallels, though also differences. Although they lived many centuries ago, I hope we shall find also in both of them, in their teachings and in their examples, some things that can help us as we shape our lives in the world today.

We do not know much about the childhood and youth of either Jesus or Socrates. We can be sure, however, that each of them received a reasonably good education. Josephus tells us that there were quite good provisions for education in the Palestine of the first century. The earliest education was given at home, followed by instruction in the synagogue, and then, in the case of bright children, by tuition from some learned rabbi.

This education was mostly in the Scriptures, history and culture of the Jewish people. We can be sure that Jesus received some such education, for in his arguments with the Pharisees and others, we see that he was familiar with the traditional lore of his people, and also well skilled in argumentation.

So when the question is asked, 'Could Jesus read and write?', the answer is probably affirmative. According to Mark's Gospel, when Jesus returned to his home town of Nazareth, he taught in the synagogue there (Mark 6.1–6). Luke adds further details, telling us that Jesus read from the prophet Isaiah, and then closed the book, and proceeded to expound the passage (Luke 4.16–21). Of course, it is possible that someone with a retentive memory and a keen interest in what he was hearing, would take it all in, even if he himself could not read or write. We may get a glimpse of this, also in Luke's Gospel, when Jesus, still a boy of twelve, was found by his parents in the Temple, 'sitting among the wise men, listening to them and asking them questions; and all who heard him were amazed at his understanding and his answers' (Luke 2.46–7).

Socrates was probably more fortunate in the matter of education. His parents seem to have been well off, and when he grew up, he did not even have to work for a living but was able to devote himself to the pursuit of knowledge. He had also a mystical side to his nature, and heard an inner voice which he believed to be a sign from God.[1] Jesus, on the other hand, was a *tekton*, a skilled worker in wood, and the son of a *tekton*. But our records do not tell of him working in his father's business. Rather, he seems to have left his home and livelihood, and had taken up the eschatological ideas circulating at that time, according to which the history of Israel was coming to an end when the whole people would be restored as a united kingdom. At some point he fell under the influence of John the Baptist. John was a visionary in the tradition of the old Hebrew prophets. He condemned the greed and the materialism of the society he saw around him, and urged the people to change their ways of life. This change was symbolized by a rite of baptism, which John administered in the Jordan River. Jesus was among those who accepted John's baptism, and he may for a time have belonged to the company of John's disciples. But Jesus had his own ideas, apparently less austere and more affirmative than John's, and he began to gather his own disciples round him, including some who had previously followed John. Socrates, for his part, had, to begin with, an interest in the natural sciences, but like Jesus he was distressed by the state of the society of his time, and embarked on a mission for its improvement.

Both Jesus and Socrates, when still young men, had profound experiences of vocation. For Jesus, this was his baptism, already mentioned. As he came out of the Jordan, he heard an inner voice, which he took to be the voice of God, declaring 'You are my beloved Son, in whom I am well pleased' (Mark 1.11) and felt the Spirit of God descending on him like a dove. From then on, he spent his time in proclaiming the kingdom of God, a kingdom which he felt himself responsible for inaugurating. What did he mean by this kingdom of God? No doubt his ideas developed, and he may have begun by thinking that his mission was to gather the tribes of Israel into a new unified kingdom on the traditional territory, but as time went on, it became clear that this kingdom of God was not a political kingdom and there was nothing about it that would necessarily confine it to Israel. It was to be a kingdom for all who would live under the rule of God as brothers and sisters under their one Father. He gave descriptions of what he had in mind in his parables. The kingdom would begin like a tiny mustard seed and grow into a great tree; it would be a society in which the humble and meek would be honoured rather than the wealthy and powerful, a kingdom in which war and violence would be set aside and the peacemakers would be called the 'children of God' (Matt. 5.9). He taught many other things about the kingdom, but he also acted as if the kingdom were already coming. The signs of its coming, derived from Hebrew prophecy and perhaps taking Elijah as a model, were his own acts of healing and of service toward people in various kinds of need.

Likewise, Socrates had his moment of vocation as a young man. It was a different experience from that of Jesus, but it was similar in the sense that it set the course for the rest of his life. Just as Jesus had been influenced by John the Baptist, so Socrates found his vocation through a friend named Chaerophon. This friend had gone to the ancient shrine of Delphi, where there was an oracle of the god Apollo. Chaerophon enquired of the oracle whether anyone was wiser than Socrates. He was told that no one was wiser than Socrates, and he went back to Athens and told Socrates himself what he had learned from the god. At first, Socrates could not believe it, for he was deeply conscious that there were many things which he did not know, and many matters about which he did not feel in the least wise. But surely Apollo had spoken the truth, for a god does not lie. Socrates decided to put the matter to the test. He would go to people who were supposed to be wise and ask them questions to which he himself did not know the answers. If he found that one or more of them could enlighten him on those questions, then indeed he would know that there were people wiser than himself in the world, and the oracle had been wrong. So he began by interrogating likely candidates; first, the politicians, then the poets, then the artisans. He would ask them apparently simple questions. What is courage? What is piety? What is justice? He got no satisfactory answers, and being a skilful debater, found himself exposing the ignorance of those men who were supposed to be so wise and learned. Those of us who have spent our lives teaching can understand that Socrates' questions must have been very embarrassing to the wise men of Athens!

Socrates soon came to see that the oracle had spoken truly. He was himself the wisest man in Athens because he at least knew his own ignorance, and therefore had the advantage over people who thought that they knew quite a lot, but were in fact the victims of ignorance and error. So Socrates, like Jesus, came to believe that he had been called to a divine mission. Apollo (whom he sometimes calls simply 'God') through the oracle reported by Chaerophon, had sent him to awaken his fellow Athenians to their true state of ignorance. Only when they recognized that ignorance was their true condition would they be ready seriously to pursue wisdom. It would be a mistake, however, to believe that Socrates' philosophical activity was merely negative and destructive. If he exposed ignorance and error, it was so that people would turn their minds to serious questions. He believed that what is important in human life is what he called the soul (*psyche*), perhaps nowadays we would call it 'person-hood' or 'personal being'. He wanted his fellow citizens to be more concerned with the virtues of the soul than with the profits of the market-place. At this point, we see how close his message came to one of Jesus' sayings: 'What shall it profit a man, if he shall gain the whole world, and lose his own soul?' (Mark 8.16).

Once embarked on their missions, both Socrates and Jesus soon ran into opposition, for both of them were taking a stance against the 'establishment' in their respective societies. We have already seen that exposing the ignorance of the supposedly wise men of Athens was bound to make Socrates unpopular. His mission was a dangerous one. The mission of Jesus was even more dangerous. Though his teaching was in the main affirma-tive, having the kingdom of God as its theme, he could not preach the kingdom without at the same time criticizing, either explicitly or implicitly, whatever stood in its way, above all hypocrisy, self-righteousness and pride. Especially the party in Israel called the Pharisees was in constant conflict with Jesus. They were for the most part earnest men, and a few of them became in fact Christian disciples, but the majority were too much satisfied with their own religiosity and too much lacking in sympathy for ordinary sinful human beings, for them to be able to make any significant response to Jesus.

So among the intellectual elite of Athens anger rose against Socrates, and among the spiritual elite of Jerusalem anger rose against Jesus. In both cases, the anger rose to a climax where it could be satisfied only by the destruction of those against whom it was directed. The climax came more quickly in the case of Jesus than in that of Socrates. Jesus carried on his mission for three years at the most – the Synoptic Gospels suggest an even shorter time. Then the authorities took action against him. He had gone up to Jerusalem for the feast of the Passover, and some of his sympathizers hailed him as the expected Messiah.

He was also involved in a disturbance, when he drove out some traders from the Temple precincts. These occasions were a sufficient pretext for action. He was arrested by the Jewish authorities, tried for blasphemy, and found guilty. He was then handed over to the Roman governor, Pontius Pilate. The governor was not interested in the blasphemy question, but was on the lookout for any political subversion. Had not Jesus been talking about a kingdom? Was he planning to raise a rebellion against Roman rule and to restore the old kingdom of David? Pilate was incapable of understanding what Jesus meant when the latter said, 'My kingdom is not of this world'. (The saying is taken from John's Gospel, and is likely to be a formulation of the evangelist rather than actual words of Jesus. But it is profoundly true.)

The trial of Jesus is not easy to decipher, partly because it began in a Jewish court and ended in a Roman one, but even more because the real motive behind the trial was concealed. To claim to be Messiah (if Jesus made that claim) was not in itself blasphemy, while to suppose that a wandering teacher, who preached non-violence and whose followers were not armed bandits, could be a dangerous revolutionary, was quite absurd. The real motive must have been that both the Jewish and Roman rulers felt threatened by the moral searchlight that had been turned on them and were worried about the popular support that Jesus seemed to have inspired. Like so many political powers in history, they had deluded themselves into thinking that their power was absolute. But now that delusion was challenged, and they realized that they were facing a more serious threat than even an armed rebellion would have been. This Jesus had demonstrated that there is a power beyond that of the state, a power that relativizes all human power; and that likewise there is a law beyond all human law, a moral law by which all human laws may be judged. John's Gospel, in particular, conveys these ideas, and John's report of the trial is a literary masterpiece, a supreme exercise in irony, for as we read it, we realize that the people on trial are Pilate and the Jewish leaders, while Jesus is himself the judge. But to return from irony to sober historical fact, Jesus was found guilty, sentenced to death by the barbarous method of crucifixion, and the sentence was carried out almost immediately.

The case of Socrates was, on the surface, rather different, though the underlying motivations were probably very similar. Socrates' mission of trying to awaken the Athenians to a more honest recognition of their real condition went on much longer than did the mission of Jesus. Socrates spoke of himself as a kind of gadfly in Athens,[1] and he may have filled this role for as long as thirty years. These were troubled years for Athens, for they were the years of the Peloponnesian War. Under the leadership of Sparta, several of the Greek city-states which were jealous of the power and wealth of Athens had formed a military alliance against that city, and eventually in 404 BCE the Athenians were brought to defeat. When a country is smarting under defeat, it often happens that those in authority look round for a scapegoat on whom to lay the blame and who can be made the target of the people's resentment. Socrates' enemies – and he must have made many during his years of philosophical activity – saw their chance. They believed that they could show that Socrates was an enemy of the state. So an accusation was made against him in the name of a citizen, a certain Meletus. According to Xenophon, there were two charges in the indictment. The first was a charge of impiety; it was claimed that Socrates did not believe in the gods recognized in the official religion of the state. The second charge was that he had corrupted the youth of Athens.

Like the two charges that more than four hundred years later would be brought against Jesus, these charges against Socrates were without substance, or so it would seem to any unprejudiced observer. As far as the charge of impiety is concerned, we have the evidence of Xenophon that Socrates was scrupulous in offering sacrifices,[2] and, of course, his entire mission had been inspired, as he believed, by the god Apollo. It may be that Socrates was moving away from the traditional belief in many gods towards a belief in one universal God, and this may have been in his mind when, at his trial, he declared in the face of his accusers that he believed in the gods 'in a higher sense' than they themselves believed.[3] Perhaps what he meant was that he believed in 'the Good' as the highest reality. In any case we get the impression of a man who was both devout and moral. So far was he from being guilty of impiety that one would say he had reached a level of religion beyond that of his accusers.

The charge that he had corrupted the youth seems equally groundless. He had indeed gathered about him a band of disciples, and probably he had taught them to follow his own example in asking awkward questions, but surely teaching young men to think and question for themselves could not possibly be described as corrupting them. Socrates himself claimed that he had sought 'to persuade every man among you that he must look to himself and seek virtue and wisdom before pursuing his private interests'.[4] To be perfectly fair to Socrates' accusers, it should be mentioned that one of his young admirers, Alcibiades, a brilliant but apparently irresponsible character, had behaved very badly. Among his misdeeds were putting on a burlesque of religious ceremonies, misconduct in military affairs, and finally defection to the enemy. He was already dead when Socrates was put on trial, but his faults were still remembered and were now laid at the door of his teacher. There is no reason to believe that Socrates had led him astray. It is more likely that the philosopher had been a good influence in trying to save a young man from his follies.

But although to us the charges brought against Socrates may seem just as weak as those brought against Jesus, the jury of Athenian citizens found him guilty. In the bitterness of defeat in war, men could easily be stirred to suspicion even if there were no solid evidence. In the legal system of Athens, the jury not only gave the verdict but also decided the penalty, if the accused was found guilty. The prosecutors asked for the death sentence, but in accordance with the city's custom, the jury invited the accused to propose an alternative punishment. Historians seem to be agreed that if Socrates had proposed exile from Athens as an alternative to death, that would have been accepted. But in spite of the urging of his friends, Socrates would not choose this way out. Did he then throw himself on death and martyrdom? I shall discuss this question in a moment. But now I quote his words to the jury, words making it clear that he would be loyal to his mission, even to the point of death:

> Men of Athens, I have the warmest affection for you; but I shall obey God rather than you, and while I have life and strength, I shall never cease from the practice and teaching of philosophy, exhorting anyone whom I meet and saying to him after my manner, 'You, my friend, a citizen of the great and mighty and wise city of Athens, are you not ashamed of devoting yourself to acquiring the greatest amount of money and honour and reputation, and caring so little about wisdom and truth and the greatest improvement of the soul, which you never regard or heed at all?'[5]

So Socrates, like Jesus, was condemned to death by a society which did not want him. In Socrates' case, the sentence was not carried out immediately, and he remained in prison for a month before the jailer brought him the cup of poison, which was the instrument of execution in Athens.

I come back to the question about the attitude to death that we find in Jesus and Socrates. There is a sense in which each of them died voluntarily. John's Gospel tells us that after the raising of Lazarus, 'Jesus walked no more openly among the Jews, but went thence into a country near to the wilderness, into a city called Ephraim, and there continued with his disciples' (John 11.34). It would have been easy for him and his disciples to have slipped off into the wilderness, far from the confines of Judaea, though in that case we would probably never have heard of him again. But after a short time he chose to return to Jerusalem openly to observe the Passover. Later still in John's Gospel – perhaps too late – it is suggested that Pilate might have been willing to make a deal with Jesus. Pilate says, confronted with the silence of Jesus who, unlike Socrates makes no speech in his defence: 'You will not speak to me? Do you not know that I have power to release you, and power to crucify you?' Jesus' answer is very significant, for it contrasts the civil power with the ultimate but different power of God: 'You would have no power over me, unless it had been given you from above' (John 19.10–11). Whether Pilate in fact offered a deal to Jesus or whether John is telling the story in such a way as to throw the blame on hostile factions among the Jews rather than on the Roman governor cannot be known, but he is confirming the fact that Jesus declined any way of escaping death.

We have already noted a parallel to this in Socrates' refusal to engage in bargaining with the jury by seeking to exchange a sentence of exile for the sentence of death. But in Socrates' case, as in that of Jesus, there were two moments when escape from death was presented as a possibility. The second arose a month after the trial, when he lay in prison in the early hours of the very day on which the death sentence was expected to be carried out. Before dawn, the door of his cell opened and there came in one of his closest friends, Crito by name. He had dramatic news. He had bribed the jailer and the way was open for escape.[6] Within hours, Socrates would be out of Attica and free to live the remainder of his life in one of the neighbouring states. But Socrates did not accept the offer. Though he might survive in some other city, he would do so as a lawbreaker, a fugitive from justice. I wonder too if the bribing of the jailer, the corruption of a human being, was something that he could not countenance. So he stayed in his cell, spent the day conversing with his friends, and at the appointed hour drank the poisoned chalice.

We usually think of death as an evil, and in some respects it always is an evil, something negative and destructive. But death is sometimes transfigured, so that it becomes the culmination, the summing up, the final expression of the life that has gone before it. This was the case with both Socrates and Jesus. Both were called to a mission, both gave to that mission all that they had to give. Both believed passionately in a moral order that is above all human laws, and they believed in God as the author of that moral order. Both explicitly taught that when the choice has to be made, we must obey God rather than men. Both sealed their teaching by dying for it, so that their deaths were not simply the termination of their lives but a witness to truth. Thus we return to them again and again, to study their lives, to listen to their words, and to seek to share in their moral wisdom.

But how is that vision to be realized? Or are we simply to say, with resignation, 'It is only a vision, and there is no place for it in the real world'? That would really amount to agreeing with those who brought about the deaths of Jesus and Socrates, the religious men of Jerusalem and the politicians of Athens, who had no room in their societies for such men as Jesus and Socrates. But here we must note that those who brought about the deaths of those two witnesses or martyrs for truth were not the great tyrants or dictators who appear from time to time in history, not Nero or Hitler or Stalin or any other of the notorious mass-killers. Even the leaders of those who attempted to silence for ever the voices of Jesus and Socrates were only relatively minor characters – Pilate, Caiaphas, Meletus. Their very names are remembered only because these characters appear briefly in the stories of Jesus and Socrates. It was the society as a whole which rejected Jesus and Socrates, the ordinary people of Jerusalem who shouted 'Crucify him! Crucify him!' and the respectable Athenian citizens, about five hundred of them, who sat on the jury which found Socrates guilty as charged, and condemned him to death. We can only conclude that sin is not the monopoly of the great villains of history, but is lurking to some degree in all human beings. Power and the desire for power and domination are not confined to the great tyrants, but found in all human life. Every human being has some power, however small, in a family, in a school, in a church, in a social group of one kind or another. At every level, political and social power must be subject to moral and spiritual power, as we believe it is in God himself. The things to be valued most are not power and the instruments of power, but love, justice, mercy, forgiveness, rationality. These, paradoxically, are the strongest powers of all. Power is to be understood as a gift, to be used in accordance with higher laws, not as an opportunity for self-aggrandisement. We in the twenty-first century are still far from having learned those truths. That is why we must still listen and respond to the voices of Jesus and Socrates and others who have borne similar witness, all in fact, known and unknown, who were the victims of irresponsible power in their own days, but who through their witness to the point of death left for us examples that can never perish and words that inspire now as always: 'We must obey God rather than men!' 'You would have no power over me, unless it had been given you from above.'

2

Wycliffe on Lordship, Divine and Human

In or about the year 1344 a new student arrived at the University of Oxford. He had come all the way from the north of England, from the parish of Wycliffe, near the ancient town of Richmond in Yorkshire. Like most of the entering students in those days, he was a mere youth of perhaps fifteen years. However, he was destined to spend most of the remainder of his life in Oxford, sometimes in studies, first for his master's degree, then for his doctorate, which he did not complete until 1372; sometimes holding official positions – he was for a short time Master of Balliol College and then Warden of the (no longer extant) Canterbury College; sometimes, apparently, simply engaging in controversy, drawing his income from benefices elsewhere in the country as an absentee rector or vicar.

This young man, John de Wycliffe, or John Wycliffe, as we now call him, made his way to Balliol College, which, then as now, had a special relation to the northern part of the country. The Oxford in which he took up residence was then very different from the Oxford we know today. It is true that many of the churches and some other famous buildings were already there, but for the most part the city consisted of dark narrow insanitary streets. Balliol College stands in Broad Street, which is today a noble and spacious thoroughfare. When Wycliffe arrived, it was not a street at all, but a broad ditch, and, moreover, a particularly foul-smelling one, as it was the dumping place for every conceivable kind of filth and garbage. Along the south side of the ditch ran the city wall, of which some parts still remain. It was pierced by the north gate, adjoining which was the prison, known as the Bokardo, where two centuries after Wycliffe's time Cranmer and his fellow bishops would be incarcerated, awaiting trial and execution. On the opposite side of the ditch, and therefore outside the city walls, stood Balliol College, St Mary Magdalene's church, and other buildings, forming together a northern outpost of Oxford.

Not only did the students of the fourteenth century see an Oxford very different in its outward appearance from the one we know today, they also had to face hazards which are unknown to the present generation. Wycliffe was still a student when, in the fateful year of 1349, after a blazing hot Oxford summer, the Black Death struck the city. This outbreak of bubonic plague, which is estimated to have killed about a third of the population of Europe, was particularly severe in Oxford. The outbreak was so devastating that the work of the University was disrupted for about four years. According to an Oxford historian, the school doors were shut, colleges and halls abandoned, and hardly enough people left to guard the buildings or even to bury the dead.

Scarcely had the University got back into its routine when there was a new interruption, the so-called 'Great Slaughter' of 1355. In those days there was great rivalry between the townspeople and the University. The townspeople had a sense of grievance, believing that the University had too many privileges. One day some swaggering University men went into the Swindlestock Tavern, the cellars of which are said to be still existing under a bank in the centre of town, and ordered drinks. When they were served, they complained about the quality of the wine. This led first to an altercation, then to a brawl, and next day there was a pitched battle between town and gown. The teachers and students of the University had to flee from the city, and sixty-three of them are said to have been killed in the disturbances. So, with distractions like these, we can perhaps find excuses for Wycliffe and others who at that time took so many years to complete their degrees.

However, we shall not pursue Wycliffe's life story any further.

In any case, we do not know very much about it, or what kind of man he was. Certainly, many of his writings have come down to us, but even from them it is not easy to form a picture of the author. That partially explains why, six hundred years after his death, he is still the subject of controversy.

What, for instance, are we to say of his intellectual standing? Clearly, he had considerable ability, and was one of the leading figures in the Oxford of his time. But though he was versed in both philosophy and theology, we would not reckon him as one of the great thinkers of the Middle Ages. He came at the end of the scholastic period, and by then scholasticism had lost whatever power it may once have possessed, and kept going over the same old problems with little new illumination. Thus, there is little that is original in Wycliffe. It is true as time went on he began to embrace more and more extreme positions on theological questions, and it may be for this reason that he failed to appeal to the moderate English mentality, so that his ideas found acceptance eventually not so much in the Church of England with its *via media*, as they did among the Puritans and nonconformists.

Again, what is one to say about his moral integrity? In some respects, he appears as the great opponent of some of the undoubted abuses which disfigured the late medieval Church. Yet he himself practised some of these very abuses, being able to spend so many years at Oxford because he drew the income from various ecclesiastical benefices without having to perform the duties incumbent on the holder. His sympathetic biographer, Dr Herbert Workman, was constrained to write: 'The historian must confess to a measure of inconsistency between Wycliffe's ideals and his conduct.'[1] The same writer, commenting on the unholy alliance between Wycliffe and John of Gaunt, Duke of Lancaster, says: 'That the reformer should have allowed himself to be made the tool of a man with whom he had scarcely anything in common is deplorable.'[2]

But even allowing for his lapses and ambiguities, one cannot deny the significance of Wycliffe in the development of Christianity in England and even beyond England. I have chosen for this memorial lecture a theme which, I think, shows Wycliffe at his best. It is on the theme of *dominium* or 'lordship', on which Wycliffe wrote two treatises. The first dealt with the lordship of God himself, *De Dominio Divino*; the second with lordship as exercised by human beings, *De Civili Dominio*.[3] Even in these writings, Wycliffe is not especially original, for many of the ideas contained in them had already been expressed by Archbishop Richard Fitzralph of Armagh in his treatise, *De Pauperie Salvatoris*, the text of which has in modern times been printed for ease of comparison in the same volume as *De Dominio Divino*.[4]

I think there are at least three good reasons for paying attention to these writings of Wycliffe on lordship. The first is that throughout the history of the Church there have been so many distortions of the idea of lordship, both theologically in the teaching about God and practically in the exercise of government and discipline within the Church, that we cannot spend enough time coming back to the distinctively Christian understanding of lordship, with its unique and paradoxical association of lordship with service. While some Christian thinkers (Kierkegaard and, more recently, Bonhoeffer are examples) have seen this as the very heart of the Christian revelation, many have been slow to get the message and, even after two thousand years, the monarchical conception of God, understood primarily in terms of power and sovereignty, keeps asserting itself, and this theological misunderstanding can in turn encourage authoritarian patterns of discipline. A second reason is that no academic study goes on in a vacuum, and certainly theology does not. If there is one element in the philosophy of Karl Marx that is likely to prove of permanent value, it is his theory of ideology, especially in the broader form which it has received at the hands of such neo-Marxists as Habermas.[5] On this view, theories are not purely academic, but reflect the interests of those who create them. When we remember that theology exists in the closest relation to a powerful institution, the Christian Church, we see at once that the discussion of theological issues cannot be separated from the influence of social factors operating in the churches. In view of what has just been said, my third reason for believing that Wycliffe's treatment of lordship is worthy of study will seem to some of my readers not a reason at all, or even a reason for staying away from it. I mean that, unlike the Marxists, Wycliffe does not confine his analysis of lordship to sociological and secular considerations, but probes the metaphysical foundations of lordship. In other words, he brings God into the picture. Here Wycliffe's treatment contrasts with that of modern philosophers who have also given attention to the meaning of lordship.

One of the most famous discussions of the problem is Hegel's analysis of the master–slave relationship,[6] a discussion so subtle and penetrating that commentators are still arguing over its interpretation. Modern discussions, in agreement with the canons of what we deem to be 'scientific' enquiry, confine themselves to the phenomena that are immanent in human society. The medievalist, on the contrary, viewed such questions within the broader framework provided by God and the creation. The importance of this, when one is discussing lordship, is obvious (as we have seen in our discussion of Jesus and Socrates in the preceding chapter) because, immediately God is introduced, every human form of lordship is relativized. But in the absence of God, human claims to lordship can and sometimes do acquire an absoluteness, which they cannot have, when the ultimate lordship of God is recognized.

In fairness to the modern secularist, it has to be added that sometimes the conception of God has been manipulated in such a way that he is used to invoke his ultimacy for a human lordship which, it is claimed, is derived from God. This is the kind of abuse that troubled Wycliffe and other reformers. Probably there were medieval Popes who really believed that their lordship was on a level with divine lordship, and probably there have been modern dictators who thought of themselves as men of destiny pursuing a divinely ordained course (Hitler) or who, having given up belief in God, have claimed the ultimate power for themselves or their political organization (Lenin, Stalin). But the correct solution is not to abolish God, equate him with a human power or leave him out of account, for then we have only the clash of human lordships. The right solution is the one for which Wycliffe was searching, that is to say, to determine the meaning of divine lordship and then ask about the consequences for human lordship. So far then am I from making excuses for going back to a medieval thinker in search of an understanding of lordship that I would say that only by going back in this way can we get the problem into its proper perspective. It is worth remembering that some of the best Christian social teaching of modern times went back to the Middle Ages for its guiding principles. William Temple (whom we shall be considering in the next chapter) was critical of the secular theories of both capitalism and communism, and found a more comprehensive treatment in Thomas Aquinas because the latter set limits to the concepts of property, ownership and the power that may be wielded by human agencies.[7] The sociological critique of ideology does not abolish the theological or metaphysical critique, but requires it for its completion. It was the American sociologist Peter Berger who wrote that 'the denial of metaphysics may be identified with the triumph of triviality'.[8]

It seems to have been the conflict between Church and state that first got Wycliffe interested in the concept of lordship. In 1365 Pope Urban V had demanded from the realm of England certain tributes which, he claimed, were due to him. His claims were resisted, and in 1366 Wycliffe wrote a short piece known as the *Determinatio*[9] in which he already argued that the duty of the Pope is to be the chief follower of Christ, and since Christ never claimed any temporal lordship or monetary tribute, but rather despised it, the Pope ought to follow his example in this. It is quite likely that when he wrote this, Wycliffe was already at work on his two treatises on lordship.

The earlier of the two, *De Dominio Dei*, may have been completed about 1372. Wycliffe had conceived the idea of writing a *Summa Theologiae*, and the treatise on divine lordship was to have formed the first part of the projected work. No doubt there are many topics that might serve as the starting-point for a systematic theology. Most theologians have thought it appropriate to begin with the doctrine of God, and that had been the way followed by St Thomas Aquinas. But Wycliffe tried to go behind the substance of the doctrine to ask about the forces influencing its formation. Thus, whereas St Thomas took off from the question, 'Does God exist?' Wycliffe's first question is whether there is such a thing as lordship. He simply assumes that lordship is an obvious fact of life and immediately passes on to the difficult and complicated question, 'What is lordship?' In the broadest and loosest sense, he defines lordship as that state of affairs in which one being is passively at the disposal of another. Wycliffe's own example is that human beings are at the disposal of death, but this would be an unusual and somewhat poetic way of speaking. Wycliffe seems to have recognized this, for he then narrows the definition by confining it to the lordship that is exercised by a rational subject. So lordship is defined as 'the habit of the rational nature in accordance with which it is said to be set over that which serves it'. (*Dominium est habitudo naturae racionalis secundum quam denominaturse prefici servienti.*)[10]

It may be objected that this definition is somewhat circular, but Wycliffe does go on to offer some explanations. The notion of 'being set over', for example, presupposes a world in which there are relations of superordination and subordination, and to be subordinate is to owe some service to one's superior. Already in his definition Wycliffe includes the claim that every creature owes service to God whom he calls the 'principal Lord', the Lord *par excellence*. In recognizing that there is a universal obligation of service to God, Wycliffe is also asserting that any obligation to a human superior can be only a limited obligation. In fact, he speedily introduces a distinction between *servitium* (service) and *servitudo* (servitude or slavery) and between *serviens* (servant) and *servus* (slave). Service is honourable, and is ennobled by Christ himself, who came not to be served, but to serve, and who is described as the 'most efficient servant of the Trinity'.[11] Slavery, on the other hand, is a degraded condition, springing from human sinfulness. It is significant that Wycliffe uses the words meaning 'servant' and 'service', not 'slave' and 'servitude', for the human relation of subordination to God, making it clear that man is a rational creature and therefore has some affinity to God, and so God's lordship can never be mere despotism or tyranny. It is important to remember this because in his writings Wycliffe seems sometimes to waver between his belief that God exacts from his human creatures a rational or reasonable service and the competing view of some theologians that God is to be understood on what I have called the 'monarchical' model, an arbitrary deity exercising his will in, for example, double predestination and strict determinism. Such a view of God seems to make a nonsense of human freedom and responsibility, and likewise of the idea that the creature could owe obedience to God. Wycliffe is striving for a better understanding of the divine lordship, though it may be questioned whether he ever achieves complete consistency or whether indeed it is possible to give a completely consistent account of the paradox of a lordship which is at the same time service. Let us examine more closely what he has to say on these difficult questions.

God's lordship, we have seen, is above all others. He is the 'principal Lord'. Yet God is also the supreme reason, so his lordship will be rational, not an arbitrary despotism. Furthermore, God's lordship is not only above all others, it is also the measure or model for all other lordships, and if the human being has also a share in rationality, the demand that human lordship should measure itself against the lordship of God is not impossible. 'The lordship of God is the measure, anterior and presupposed, of all other lordships that may be allotted.' (*Dominium Dei mensurat, ut prius et presuppositum, omnia alia assignanda.*)[12]

But we find Wycliffe saying other things which seem to imply different presuppositions about God's lordship. We are told that the divine lordship transcends all other lordships in three ways, which make it different and unique. (1) God does not need the service of the creatures. (2) The divine lordship is indestructible and inalienable. (3) The creature cannot help doing service to God, for even if he tries to serve the devil, the devil too is subject to God, whose providence turns all things to his own purposes.

There seems to be an inconsistency here. We have been told that the human creature has an obligation to obey God, then we are told that after all, it doesn't really matter, for God's will is going to be accomplished, whatever human beings or even the devil may do. Here the monarchical God seems to be returning. He is self-contained and self-sufficient, and his lordship, in spite of what Wycliffe has said, seems to be quite despotic. The human being has an obligation to do service to God, but there is no possibility of doing otherwise. We are called to find our true being in the paradox of a service which is perfect freedom. This presents one of the most stubborn problems in Christian theology, and in the next chapter we shall find it plaguing William Temple six hundred years after Wycliffe, but in very similar terms (see below, pp. 32–4).

Wycliffe was not unaware of the difficulties, but he was determined not to give up either the supremacy of the divine lordship or the freedom and responsibility of human life. Is it possible to reconcile them?

According to Wycliffe, God is the most exalted of Lords, yet it is also said that he is the easiest to please. (*Patet quod Deus inter omnes dominos sit facillimum complacere.*)[13] These words recall Jesus' saying, 'My yoke is easy and my burden is light' (Matt. 7.30). The reasons for this fresh approach to the problem become clearer later in the treatise. Wycliffe sets out three acts which are typical of the divine lordship.[14] The first of these is giving. 'God is supremely liberal, and therefore supremely giving.' (*Deus est summe liberalis, ergo maxime donativus.*)[15] God has given existence in creation, and to that he adds 'every good and perfect gift' (James 1.17). But God's giving does not mean that what he gives is alienated from his ultimate lordship, so that strictly speaking he does not give but entrusts (*non donat sed dispensat*), and man is not the ultimate owner of what is given, but a steward (*dispensator*).[16] So if he misuses the gift, he is guilty of sin and loses his right to that gift. Here Wycliffe is talking about the gifts of the created order, but goes on to say that God's greatest gift is the gift of himself. This gift of himself is identified with the Holy Spirit, bestowed upon the faithful. We now see the meaning of the claim that God is the easiest of all lords to please, for in giving his own Spirit to his creatures, he gives them the grace whereby they are able rightly to use all his gifts and to fulfil their obligations to him.

This brings us to the second action which Wycliffe holds to be typical of the divine lordship, namely, receiving. God receives his due from the creature, yet what he receives is what he has himself given, and even the human capacity to offer something to God arises from the gift of the Holy Spirit.[17] This leads Wycliffe to say that by receiving, God becomes no richer. Technically, this may be the case, yet once again the question of consistency arises. Wycliffe is anxious to portray God's lordship in terms of giving, even self-giving, and I have no objection to this. But I suspect that the motive is not so much gratitude to God as the persistence in the background of the idea of God as the absolute monarch, self-contained and self-sufficient. I think a simpler and more honest course would be to abandon these tortuous arguments and frankly acknowledge that there is a synergism between God and his rational creatures. If we follow the Wycliffe line beyond a certain point, then we would have to say (as some theologians have said) that God would not be in the slightest degree diminished by the annihilation of his creation.

The third action that is typical of God's lordship is lending,[18] but this does not seem to add any new idea, since the lending is simply the combination of the giving (strictly, the entrusting, see above, p. 21), and the receiving. The point is hammered home that any human lordship is relative to divine lordship, so that from a Christian point of view, the human being is a steward rather than an owner, Wycliffe is virtually anticipating by two hundred years Luther's teaching, that a 'Christian is a perfectly free lord of all, subject to none; a Christian is a perfectly dutiful subject of all, subject to all'.[19] But precisely how do such ideas relate to divine lordship?

The reasoning behind Wycliffe's claims is obscure, but I think it could be made explicit somewhat as follows. Jesus Christ, as we have seen from the earlier treatise, is the lord who is also servant, and who has exalted and dignified the whole notion of service. Jesus Christ was also called in that treatise 'the most efficient servant of the Trinity'. But he is also one of the coequal persons of the Trinity, and this implies that his servanthood has its place within the Trinity itself. That brings us back to Kierkegaard's insight that in Jesus Christ God revealed himself in servant form and that this was no mere disguise but his true form and inward nature.

In the later parts of *De Civili Dominio* Wycliffe deals with specific problems such as the limits of papal power, the conditions of a just war, the power of the state in relation to the Church (especially in matters of property), and so on. We need not go into these questions, for they are subject to the general principles already expounded. We may notice, however, that Wycliffe becomes increasingly extreme and one-sided in his applications. His attacks on ecclesiastical abuses of lordship led in the direction of an Erastian theory of the superiority of the civil power over the Church, and must have given great comfort to men like John of Gaunt, who were only too eager to find excuses for despoiling the Church. Even so, of course, this leaves untouched the just criticism of the preoccupation with wealth and property characteristic of many churchmen of the time.

I shall conclude this chapter by indicating three contemporary problems where Wycliffe's thoughts on lordship can still be useful to us. One is a problem of philosophical theology: the question of God and his relation to the world. The second is a question of moral theology: how ought human beings to handle the earth's resources, over which they have acquired such enormous power? The third problem is one of ecumenical authority: what kind of authority would be appropriate when and if the currently separated communions of Christendom come together in unity?

On the question of God, we note that at least since the time of the Enlightenment, there has been a growing revolt against what may be called the 'monarchical' idea of God. The drift toward atheism has been motivated not so much by intellectual dissatisfaction with theism as by an emotional rebellion against a celestial power which theologians often portrayed as in opposition to all human freedom and responsibility. Feuerbach, Nietzsche and Camus are classic instances of this rebellion. Modern theistic or quasi-theistic philosophies, such as those of Hegel, Whitehead and Jaspers, are attempts to meet these problems. Perhaps the best response is to go back into the resources of Christianity especially to the doctrine of incarnation, which is an adequate corrective to the idea of the monarchical God.

Now, Wycliffe is somewhat inconsistent in these matters. He hankers after the arbitrarily predestinating God, who really does make a nonsense of human freedom and responsibility. But in his treatises on lordship, we see him moving far in the direction of a fuller christianization of the idea of God. We know God in Jesus Christ, who is the second Person of the Trinity; but this Jesus is the Lord whose lordship has been manifested in service, or even the one in whom lordship and service are paradoxically identified. This means that God's lordship is conjoined with service, so that God is no arbitrary monarch and is no oppressor, but one who works with and for his creatures.

On the question of our attitude to the world's resources, the complaint has been made that, according to the Bible, God, after creating the human couple, commanded them to subdue the earth and exercise dominion over the other creatures – and the word used in the Vulgate to express this command is precisely the verb *dominari* (Gen. 1.28). So it has been alleged that the Bible and its doctrine of creation have encouraged that ruthless plundering of earth's resources that threatens the future of humanity. This complaint would hold only if we entertained a thoroughly un-Christian and unredeemed notion of dominion. If we learn from Wycliffe, Aquinas and other medieval thinkers that all human dominion derives from God and is therefore stewardship, and further that mutual service among the rational creatures demands a just sharing of earthly goods, then we see that the exercise of dominion as stewardship is highly rational and responsible, possibly the only solution to our problems.

There is a widespread sentiment that in any drawing together of the divided churches, a place must be found for the papacy, as a primary centre of Christian unity. Accredited theologians of the Anglican and Roman communions have already commended the idea of a universal primacy based on Rome, and they do not think of the holder of this office as a mere figurehead. What would Wycliffe have said?

He does not seem to have rejected the possibility of a Pope who would have been more obviously a follower of Jesus Christ than some of the medieval pontiffs, more obviously the 'servant of the servants of God', to recall a traditional title. I think we may now set aside his invective against the papacy, called forth by such a dubious successor to St Peter as Urban V, and learn from his sober thoughts on lordship, not only in determining the nature of a universal primacy but in reflecting on what kind of authority is generally appropriate within the Christian Church.

3

Temple on Transcendence
and Immanence

Born 1881, died 1944. Just to quote the dates of William Temple's life is to say quite a lot about him. In 1881, Queen Victoria was on the throne and only six years away from her Golden Jubilee, Mr Gladstone was Prime Minister for the second time, and the British Empire was in its full glory. In 1944, the Second World War had been raging for five years, the super-powers were the United States and the Soviet Union, and the England into which Temple had been born was in process of radical transformation. Temple's life spanned the period of transition from what had seemed the unshakable structures of late Victorian times to the uncertainties and anxieties of the modern world.

He himself was no mere spectator of the vast changes that were going on. He was an active participant. He was influential in the world of thought, particularly in philosophy and theology; he played a major part in ecclesiastical affairs, not only in the Church of England but also in the ecumenical movement; but perhaps he will be chiefly remembered on account of his work for society at large, in education, in politics, and in attempts to reshape the economic order. One gets the impression that in modern times very few churchmen ever attain to an influence over politicians, at least, in Britain. Temple was one of the few. Edward Heath has written about him:

The influence of Temple on my generation was immense . . . The reason was not far to seek. William Temple was foremost among the leaders of the nation, temporal and spiritual, in posing challenging, radical questions about the nature of our society. Most important of all, he propounded with lucidity and vigour his understanding of the Christian ethic in its application to the contemporary problems which engross us all.[1]

But let us go back briefly to 1881. Temple was born into the Establishment, with, let us say, a silver ecclesiastical spoon in his mouth. He saw the light of day in the episcopal palace at Exeter, where his father, Frederick Temple, had been appointed bishop, not without some controversy, a few years earlier. His father went on to be Bishop of London when William was four years old, and then to be Archbishop of Canterbury. William received the education considered proper for an Englishman of the upper class, that is to say, public school and ancient university, in his case, the impeccable credentials of Rugby and Balliol.

From then on, his career reads like the ecclesiastical success story *par excellence* – it would have been the envy of even the most ambitious dignitary of *Barchester Towers*. Fellow and Tutor in Philosophy in the Queen's College, Oxford, Headmaster of Repton, Canon of Westminster, Bishop of Manchester, Archbishop of York and finally Archbishop of Canterbury. It might seem a pity that he had to take in the industrial city of Manchester in his triumphal progress. Yet it may have been his eight years in Manchester that lay nearest to his heart.

If we look at some of the things he was doing 'on the side', so to speak, rather than at his list of official appointments, we get a somewhat different picture. Already while a layman he was active in the Workers' Educational Association. For seven years he was a member of the Labour Party, though he left it in 1925 and what he would have made of it today is hard to know. He organized conferences on social questions, especially a notable conference on 'Christian Politics, Economics and Citizenship', held at Birmingham in 1924. According to Edward Norman, this conference 'marked the rise of William Temple to ascendancy over the social teaching of the Church of England'.[2] Meanwhile he was also busy with ecumenical conferences on 'Faith and Order' and 'Life and Work'. Within the Church of England he was chairman for several years of a commission on doctrine. Its report, published in 1938, was one of the best things that have been done on this subject, and is still being quoted. Temple's relatively early death prevented him from ever presiding at a Lambeth Conference, but as Archbishop of York he was one of the most active figures in the Lambeth Conference of 1930, where after an unimpressive beginning he made major contributions, especially in the field of ecumenical relations.[3]

I have been dwelling on Temple's achievements as social reformer and churchman, but these were rooted in his theological and philosophical thinking, and it would be giving a misleading impression if he were represented as primarily a social activist. He would have despised those activists who distance themselves from theology and spirituality. He had, after all, begun his career as a philosopher. He wrote: 'Thought and action, if separated from one another, are abstractions and falsifications, the real fact is active rational life, and this is best expressed in rational activity, where thought and conduct are inextricably united.'[4] His devotion to learning is perhaps best attested by the story that he spent the night before his wedding finishing his philosophical book, *Mens Creatrix*.

The most striking thing about Temple's thought is its extraordinary range. He had a remarkable mastery of philosophy, theology, natural science and both English and classical literature. All of these elements flow together into his own synthesis – and 'synthesis' is the word, for Temple sought to bring things together and to see them in their unity and wholeness. This quest for unity was no doubt part of the legacy he had received from his philosophy teacher, the idealist Edward Caird, and even if he was later attracted to Whitehead, he continued to do philosophy on the grand scale. Temple's philosophy is the obvious place to begin in any account of his thought, though his philosophy incorporates his science and flows into his theology, so that it would be impossible to mark them off sharply from one another. Temple's idea of philosophy was virtually the opposite of the one which still prevails today in a large part of the English-speaking world. Contemporary philosophy is analytical and critical in its style; by contrast, Temple believed that it is the business of philosophy to show the unity and coherence of experience. He tells us that the standard of the mind in its search for truth is totality – 'the embrace of all relevant reality in a comprehensive unity', to quote his own words.[5] Of course, the presupposition of this belief is that the world is a rational whole, and that the principle of unity is graspable. It is perhaps a pity that although analytical philosophy was in the ascendant when Temple was at the height of his powers, he took little interest in it. It is perhaps even more a pity that he did not interest himself in Kierkegaard, who was being rediscovered in these same years. I believe myself that philosophy has always had two tasks, analysis and synthesis, but I should think that most contemporary philosophers, coming to Temple, would judge that there is too little critical analysis in his work, and that his claim to be building up a philosophy out of the facts discoverable in the various areas of human experience and investigation is strongly suspect. One critic, Owen Thomas, declares: 'He was a man of profound Christian faith, and what he actually has done is to arrange the facts so that they give support to his faith.'[6] Perhaps Thomas should not have used the word 'arranged', which contains a hint of artificiality or manipulation. But I think his general point is justified, namely, that Temple's philosophy is to be seen as a form of apologetics. There is a tacit assumption of the truth of Christian theism, and then an exposition of the facts of experience so as to show that they are highly compatible with the initial unspoken assumption. Of course, apologetics is a perfectly legitimate exercise and a necessary one at times when Christianity is under attack, and Temple's work is in many ways a model for apologetics, but we should be clear what he is doing.

How is the philosophy underlying Temple's synthesis to be characterized? It is usually said that he moved from idealism to realism – in particular, from the influence of such thinkers as

Caird, Bosanquet and Royce to the realism of Whitehead. Broadly speaking, this is true, but the terms 'idealism' and 'realism' are somewhat vague. Temple's move from the former to the latter was by no means complete, and his synthesis retains elements of both.

There is no doubt that he was an epistemological realist, that is to say, he believed that we know things and facts in the real world and not just ideas in our own minds. This is the point of his brilliant and justly famous criticism of Descartes: 'If I were asked what was the most disastrous moment in the history of Europe, I should be strongly tempted to answer that it was the period of leisure when René Descartes, having no claims to meet, remained for a whole day "shut up in a stove".'[7] That day began the 'turn to the subject' in western philosophy. Only two centuries later did we begin to escape from it, and Temple is in good company among modern philosophers in his rejection of Cartesianism. But we should notice that he also considered that Cartesianism constituted a 'necessary movement of thought'.[8] Temple is often said to have migrated philosophically from the idealism of Caird to the realism of Whitehead, but he retained from his idealist origins a firm belief in dialectic, especially in the history of ideas, viewed in a Hegelian way. The Middle Ages had been predominantly realist, thus realism is the thesis. Cartesian and post-Cartesian philosophy was the antithesis that corrected the defects in medieval realism. But Temple believed that in dialectics the weight of truth lies with the original thesis, that the antithesis is secondary and dependent in character, and that in the final synthesis we shall be closer to the original thesis, though suitably modified so as to take account of whatever was valid in the antithesis. Thus he believed that he was now moving into a phase that would resume the epistemological realism of the Middle Ages but would also incorporate the turn to the subject.

As well as epistemological realism, there is also a metaphysical realism, with metaphysical idealism as its correlate. And here it is harder to determine whether Temple really broke out of idealism. It may well have been his respect for the natural sciences that encouraged him toward epistemological realism in the first place. With that basis, he then had to accept the evolutionary scheme presented in the modern scientific picture of the world. This view implied that there was a time when mind had not appeared in the world, and matter existed independently of mind – at least, of any created mind. Temple accepts this as a refutation of any Berkeleian type of idealism, according to which what we call 'material things' are in fact percepts of mind – *esse est percipi*, their very existence is to be perceived. But then, as his argument develops, Temple tends to reverse this stance. Mind is said to be secondary and derivative in the process; it first manifests itself as the behaviour by which organisms cope with their environment, but then it is set free from biological needs, it begins to apprehend and even comprehend the process itself and it eventually transcends the process and becomes the clue to the nature of the whole. To quote his words: 'It achieves a certain superiority to, and independence of, the process – not indeed such as to endow it with a life wholly detached from the process, but such that the process falls within its grasp, not it within that of the process.'[9] Have we not gone back finally to a kind of metaphysical idealism in which mind is the creative source of everything? Temple is, of course, correct in his contention that a process, which brings forth minds capable of understanding and transcending it, is not ultimately explicable in reductionist terms. But if one then posits that mind – indeed a divine, creative and transcendent mind – has been there from the beginning, is it not misleading to claim that one is a metaphysical realist and to hold that the ultimate reality is the emergent process that has been going on for billions of years before mind appeared? C. D. Broad, a near contemporary of Temple, represents a genuinely realist position in his book, *The Mind and Its Place in Nature*, a kind of emergent materialism in which the mind does not have the privileged position which Temple gives it. It may be doubted that Temple ever moves from the metaphysical idealism expressed in the title of his early book, *Mens Creatrix*.

The difficulties of Temple's position become clearer when we

consider his ambiguous relation to Whitehead. The latter begins
from the processes of nature as interpreted by modern science,
but he is able to end with a metaphysic that finds room for
value, spirit, mind and even God. The attraction of this view
for Temple is obvious. Whitehead overcomes the bifurcation or
dualism so disastrously introduced into philosophy by Descartes. But Whitehead's metaphysic is rejected by Temple as
finally inadequate. Its highest category is that of organism and,
according to Temple, we must go beyond that to the category
of personhood or personal being. But this judgement means that
Whitehead's God is likewise bound to be inadequate, in the
sense that he is immanent in and correlative with the process of
the world. 'Personality,' declares Temple, 'is always transcendent in relation to process.'[10] Temple struggles long and hard
to work out a satisfactory conception of the relation between
God and the world, one that would avoid that correlation which,
to use his own words, 'we found to be the capital error of
Whitehead's philosophy'.[11]

In more than half a dozen passages scattered through his
Gifford Lectures, we find Temple wrestling with the God–world
problem. In most of these passages he is upholding the transcendence and independence of God, as against what he considers
to be the 'capital error' of Whitehead, yet in each case he qualifies what he has to say to allow some scope for divine immanence. He divides his Gifford Lectures into two parts, equal in
length, entitled, 'The Transcendence of the Immanent' and 'The
Immanence of the Transcendent'. On his own view of the superiority of thesis over antithesis, this seems to give a preference to
transcendence over immanence. He criticizes some analogies as
making God too external to the world, others for correlating
him with the world, but nowhere gives a clear statement of a
middle way which he obviously seems to be seeking. So we find
him saying that the world is dependent on God in a way in
which God is not dependent on the world. Yet he is not external
or indifferent to it, as a carpenter might be to a box which he
had hammered together or even as a poet who has composed a
poem. That second analogy, he says, is 'an improvement on the

first analogy of the carpenter and his box', but it leaves God too external to the world.[12] In another place, he makes a still stronger statement than the one about the carpenter and the box. He writes: 'Only by a doctrine of thoroughgoing transcendence is the world explicable or the religious impulse satiable. In the sense in which God is necessary to the world, the world is simply not necessary to God. Apart from him, it has no being; he is himself in plenitude of being. The world – God = o, God – the world = God.'[13] Perhaps he said this because of the wide influence which belonged at that time to Barth, but pushed to extremes such a formula ends in a kind of acosmism, and we find that Temple immediately modifies this view, because it would deprive history of meaning, and history is important in religion, especially in Christianity. Again, we find Temple saying, 'Upon God the world depends for its existence; in no sense does God depend on the world for his existence.'[14] This is true, if one accepts a doctrine of creation. But Temple further qualifies it by saying that the world's aspirations and heroisms have value for God, and especially the historical events associated with Jesus Christ. So it would seem that Temple rejects the Thomist view that the world is affected by God, but not God by the world, and this brings him closer to Whitehead and the panentheists.

So now we look at the other side of the balance sheet. He says that 'If all else but God were abolished, God himself would still be whole and entire', but he adds, 'capable of creating another world to take the place of the one that had gone out of existence.'[15] It seems to be implied here that God always has some world. The word 'necessary' is introduced a few pages further on: 'God is active in the world, and its process is his activity. Because he is, and is creative, he must create; therefore the universe is necessary to him in the sense that he can be himself only by creating it.'[16] I do not myself see much difference between what Temple says here and what he calls Whitehead's 'capital error' about the correlation of God and world, except that perhaps it rules out the notion that there is a power beyond God, some kind of fate, which dictates even the actions of God.

Temple also strongly denies that the body/mind analogy, used by many Whiteheadian theologians, is at all adequate to throw light on the relation of the world to God. So, on the one hand, Temple rejects the analogy of an artist to his or her work on the ground that it makes God too external to the world, while on the other hand he rejects the analogy of soul and body on the ground that it too closely identifies God and the world. The true analogy would seem to come somewhere between them, but what it might be is not said and is indeed hard to imagine.

The fundamental problem inherent in Temple's philosophy appears to me to be as follows. If one begins from the physical processes of a nature that is unfolding itself in space and time, and says that mind is an episode, that it is secondary and derivative (and Temple does say these things) then I do not believe that one can get beyond a strongly immanentist, even pantheistic, doctrine of God. It might, I suppose, be some form of panentheism. Perhaps there is no need to get beyond this point, for one might hold that panentheism is the form of belief in God that is both intellectually coherent and religiously satisfying, and, in particular, one that is close to the Christian doctrines of incarnation and atonement. But Temple feels that he has to go on to a fully transcendent conception of God, though I do not think he can consistently reach this position from his starting-point, not even by introducing what he calls a 'dialectical transition'. His dilemma is very similar to that of his almost exact contemporary, Pierre Teilhard de Chardin. The two men were born in the same year, but of course Temple never got to know Teilhard's work, which was published only after both of them had died. Clearly the two had much in common. Teilhard's appreciation for the potentialities and mysteries of matter would have strongly appealed to Temple, and the interest that each of them had in evolution together with the optimistic outlook which that interest tended to produce was another point in common. But they shared the same fundamental difficulty. When Teilhard announces at the beginning of *The Phenomenon of Man* that he proposes *only to see*, that is, to confine himself to phenomena,[17] he sets out on a path of immanence, from which he eventually breaks out only by a *tour de force*. It may be noted, however, that both Teilhard and Temple employ an idea that considerably eases some of their problems – I mean, the idea that everything that exists, even the most elementary particle or unit of energy has a mental as well as a physical pole (the language is Whitehead's), an inside as well as an outside. This is the doctrine called 'panpsychism'. It did not much commend itself to Temple, though it would cohere rather well with his teaching about value, according to which the mind discovers kinship with itself among the things of nature.

I have said that Temple's philosophy flows naturally into his theology, and that one might expect this result if, as we have seen reason to believe, the philosophy is largely determined by Christian apologetic motives. But the theology is not left unaffected by its philosophical substrate. There is a reciprocity between the two, as we shall see.

Temple, according to his biographer, was never a Protestant in the theological sense of the word. His theology could be broadly described as a kind of liberal catholicism. This again might have been expected because of his dialectical understanding of history. The catholic Christianity that developed into the medieval dogmatic system is the thesis, while the Reformation is the antithesis. Here Temple draws an explicit comparison between the development in theology and the development in philosophy, and in particular between Luther and Descartes. The relation between these two men, he holds, was 'neither superficial nor accidental: both express one great principle, the principle of private judgment'.[18] But since the synthesis is nearer to the thesis than to the antithesis, though it contains whatever valuable corrections find expression in the antithesis, modern theology will strive to preserve catholic truth in its integrity (and in fact Temple was a very orthodox theologian), but catholic truth as criticized and set free by the spirit that was born in the sixteenth century.

Two doctrines are especially present in Temple's theology; the doctrine of the incarnation and the doctrine of the sacraments. These doctrines are very much in accord with the catholic and Anglican tradition, but clearly they are in accord also with the tendency of Temple's philosophy and his stress on the reality of the physical and material. We may recall his often quoted assertion that Christianity 'is the most avowedly materialist of all the great religions ... its own most central saying is, "The Word became flesh", where the last term was chosen, no doubt, because of its specially materialistic associations'.[19]

Incarnation was a major concern of Temple throughout his career. 'The Divinity of Christ' was the title of a long essay he contributed in 1912 to the important symposium, *Foundations*, subtitled 'A Statement of Christian Belief in Terms of Modern Thought'. This essay was followed in 1924 by the full-length study of christology called *Christus Veritas*.

His Gifford Lectures of ten years later argue that the knowledge of God to be gained from our natural knowledge of the world demands completion in an act of incarnation. I remarked a few sentences back that Temple's concern with incarnation accords well with his philosophical interest in the material world, but again we have to notice that the relation of philosophy and religion in his mind was a reciprocal one, so that his choice of a philosophy reflects or may reflect his prior belief in incarnation. Already in *Christus Veritas* he was complaining that although idealism is a philosophy usually both theistic and spiritual, it cannot allow for a specific incarnation because it devalues concrete existence in the everyday world.[20] So again one might argue that his philosophical ideas were not so much an independent substructure from which he went on to theology, as an interpretation of the natural world made in the light of a prior commitment to the Christian faith. His actual working out of incarnational doctrine is inspired more by John's Gospel than by any philosophical system, though admittedly he sees St John, whom he called 'the most modern of theologians'[21] as the teacher of a comprehensive, if mainly implicit, philosophy. No doubt he had to some extent been influenced by Edward Caird's profound respect for John's Gospel.[22] But Temple himself declared that 'for as long as I can remember, I have had more love for John's Gospel than for any other book'.[23] The depth of his insight into this Gospel is amply attested by the fact that his *Readings in St John's Gospel* was still in print more than fifty years after it was written.

In his sacramental theology, Temple teaches the reality of matter and the respect that we ought to have for the material. Matter is not alien to us, as materialists who have claimed that the mind is a mere epiphenomenon may have believed. Matter is real, and when conjoined with spirit can effect spiritual consequences. But neither is matter unreal, as some idealists may have held. Temple took quite an objective view of sacramental action and subscribed to a doctrine of *ex opere operato*, not in any magical sense, but in the sense that because of the dignity of the material and its fitness to be a vehicle for the divine, the reality of the sacrament does not depend on the changing moods of those who celebrate it or even (though Temple seems less sure on this point) of those who receive it. But in fact there are many who engage in sacramental worship ready to testify that when their faith has been low, their religious experience minimal, or when they have been more sensible of God's absence than of his presence, regular sacramental participation has brought them to a revival of faith and a renewed sense of God. Temple's views lead to a theory of eucharistic presence called 'transvaluation', which avoids some of the difficulties of the traditional belief in transubstantiation, difficulties caused by the gradual erosion of the concept of substance. This theory of Temple's itself rests on his insistence on God's immanence in the world, a view which leads him to speak of a sacramental universe.

When we turn to Temple's social teaching, the transition is a smooth one, and we are moving within the ideas of a thinker who consciously sought to unify his vision of life. One who makes the doctrines of divine immanence and incarnation central, and believes that the very word of God has entered the material and historical sphere is bound to be concerned with the material and historical conditions of human life. Temple is quite explicit too about the importance of the sacramental for one's practical attitudes. He writes: 'It is in the sacramental view of the universe, both of its material and its spiritual characters, that there is given hope of making human both politics and economics, and of making effectual both faith and love.'[24] Of course, broadly the same motivation lay behind that whole tradition of Anglican social concern that found expression in the heroic labours of priests and sisters in slum Tractarian parishes in the nineteenth century, and in the Christian social thought of such men as Maurice Reckitt and Vigo Demant in the twentieth.

I have already mentioned how Temple from his early days was already engaged in activities aimed at humanizing and Christianizing the fabric of society. His short book, *Christianity and Social Order*, published in 1942 during wartime, has rightly become something of a classic and is much better known than his larger learned volumes on theology and philosophy. But the same theological principles of immanence and incarnation are at work. To someone reading Temple's book on social order sixty years after its publication, it may seem very mild and reformist, though it has also anticipated and caught up with the new concern over environmental issues. Is not a sense of the immanence of God a large part of the answer to such problems? It should not be forgotten that this book of Temple's had a considerable effect on the formation of post-war Britain. We find Temple writing: 'Land is not a mere "natural resource". The phrase "mother earth" stands for a deep truth about the relationship of man and nature.' Of course, such teaching follows directly from the theory of value he had propounded years before.

I wrote that Temple's teaching might strike us today as mild and reformist. This was not meant to be an adverse criticism. A few years ago, I myself published a little book called *The Concept of Peace*. One reviewer said of the book that it was a reformist document in a revolutionary situation, and no doubt he meant this statement as a criticism, but I think that the Christian is bound to be reformist rather than revolutionary. Temple himself had a doctrine of original sin, and he points out that anyone holding such a doctrine must be intensely realistic and 'conspicuously free from utopianism'.[25] Like Reinhold Niebuhr, he remains far from being superseded and offers us a more realistic and, I believe, more Christian socio-political doctrine than do many of the present practitioners of 'political theology'.[26]

Such then was the multifaceted yet unified Christian vision of this remarkable man. Some of us can still remember the high hopes that were entertained when he was appointed Archbishop of Canterbury in 1942. Alas, these hopes were never fulfilled. Ill health and the constraints of wartime prevented him from giving the leadership that had been expected, and he died only a little more than two years after his appointment. Moreover, the world by then was looking much bleaker than it had appeared when Temple was at the height of his powers. In 1942, he wrote in a letter: 'What we must completely get away from is the idea that the world as it now exists is a rational whole ... The world, as we see it, is strictly unintelligible.'[27] Was this statement a repudiation of his earlier beliefs? Certainly it was a repudiation of an optimism that had sometimes found expression in his writings. It was not a repudiation of the essence of his vision, but he had come to recognize that the way would be longer and more difficult than he had once supposed. The operative words are 'at this time' and 'as we see it'. The hope that all things will be gathered up in God remains. For us, the world is even more fragmented than it was for him, but this is all the more reason for not losing his vision that the world reveals a potentiality of a final wholeness which is its ultimate destiny.

4

Moltmann on the Suffering of God

Jürgen Moltmann (b. 1926) has established himself as one of the two or three leading Protestant theologians who succeeded the generation of Barth, Bultmann and others. He has not produced a full-scale dogmatic theology, but one could say that he has in fact produced two 'dogmatics in outline' the first of them being the trilogy consisting of *Theology of Hope*, *The Crucified God* and *The Church in the Power of the Spirit*, titles which already announce a trinitarian pattern, and then, in greater detail, *The Trinity and the Kingdom of God*, *God and Creation*, *The Way of Jesus Christ*, *The Spirit of Life*, *The Coming of God*. Among them, these books span a lifetime of theological work in which all the main themes of Christian doctrine are treated.

There are, I think, two features that give to Moltmann's theology its distinctive power. The first is that he takes the eschatological character of Christianity with complete seriousness. For a full century, we have been hearing that the New Testament is deeply imbued with eschatological and even apocalyptic beliefs. Weiss and Schweitzer, Barth and Bultmann and a host of others have all hammered home this point, though they have interpreted it in different ways and have assigned to it varying degrees of importance. But (with the exception of the early Barth) none of them took it seriously when faced with the constructive tasks of systematic theology. The heady ideas of primitive Christianity were in one way or another defused, demythologized or simply dismissed as offensive to modern minds. Moltmann, on the contrary, insists that eschatology is no merely accidental ingredient in Christianity, a dispensable relic of first-century mythology, but of the very essence. This bold recognition lands Moltmann into a number of intellectual difficulties, but it cannot be denied that it makes his theology exciting. His is no suave presentation of Christianity that has smoothed out all the intellectual problems, but in so doing has also deprived Christian faith of its vital appeal.

The second feature is Moltmann's deep concern with the contemporary world, especially with the widespread oppression, deprivation and inhumanity of the present time. He began his theological reflections when he was himself a prisoner of war, and perhaps that firsthand experience of the anomalies of a disordered world kindled his interest in the social and political implications of Christian faith. At any rate, Moltmann could never be counted among those whom Marx accused of seeking only to understand the world without seeking to change it. For Moltmann, theory and practice, theology and its socio-political working out, stand in the closest reciprocal relations. This also explains why his thought has been influential among theologians of the third world, though less so than Moltmann had hoped. Where social and political concern is united with a future-oriented eschatological theology, the result is necessarily dynamic, though not always coherent.

Let us turn our attention first to *Theology of Hope*, for that volume provides the foundation on which Moltmann's theology has been built. It was published at a time when Christianity was becoming increasingly problematical. Some theologians were already advocating a 'death of God' theology and our contemporary culture was being described as 'post-Christian'.[1] It seemed to many that we live in a world in which God no longer is, and Moltmann accepted the godlessness of our present world. But this was not an atheistic stance on his part. The startling difference between Moltmann and the death-of-God theologians was that whereas they taught that God has died and no longer is, Moltmann accounted for our present godlessness by asserting that God has not yet arrived. There is all the difference between a 'no longer' and a 'not yet'. When this 'not yet' is taken seriously, we see that it is incorrect to say that Moltmann in his early book was 'triumphalist' or offers us a *theologia gloriae*, if this last expression means that God already rules over all or that his kingdom has come on earth or is identical with the Church. That was never Moltmann's view, any more than was atheism, and the hope which he holds out is a vulnerable one, coming to us as hope in a time of darkness.

The idea that God is 'not yet' reigning in full control and that his purposes are still unfulfilled is in itself a departure from the idea of a fully transcendent and omnipotent God. For this reason, Moltmann claimed that the category of 'revelation' central for theologians of Barth's generation, should be replaced by the category of 'promise'. The categories in which Moltmann develops his theology are categories of the 'not yet': hope, resurrection, the renewal of all things. This has been seen as a theological counterpart to the philosophy of hope, elaborated by the neo-Marxist philosopher, Ernst Bloch.[2] Though this philosopher has been generally considered an atheist, it might be more accurate to think of him as a pantheist, for he attributed to the universe a latent potentiality for something like spiritual advance. In his early phase, Moltmann was influenced by Bloch, but gradually grew away from him.

But although Moltmann owes something to the philosophers, especially those in the tradition of Hegel and Marx, it is the Bible rather than philosophy that determines his thinking. Modern Old Testament scholarship, Moltmann claims, has shown the centrality of the notion of promise in God's dealings with the world. The promise–fulfilment scheme, he believes, pervades the whole Bible, New Testament as well as Old. To take eschatology seriously, therefore, is to come to terms with the role of promise in the Bible. Those theologians who made revelation central to their theologies neglected the eschatological character of the revelation. Moltmann does not deny revelation, but holds that it comes in the form of promise. He is severely critical of any understanding of revelation which thinks of it as a kind of 'epiphany', a word which Moltmann understands in a somewhat idiosyncratic way as a static, ever present, unchanging manifestation of God. He writes:

The difference does not lie already in the assertion of 'divine revelation' as such, but in the different ways of conceiving and speaking of the revelation and self-manifestation of the Deity. The decisively important question is obviously that of the context in which the talk of revelation arises. It is one thing to ask where and when does an epiphany of the divine, eternal, immutable and primordial take place in the realm of the human, temporal and transient; it is another to ask when and where does the God of the promise reveal his faithfulness, and in it himself and his presence. The one question asks about the presence of the eternal, the other about the future of what is promised.[3]

It is clear that Moltmann's preoccupation with the future renders him unsympathetic to the 'realized' eschatology that has been much in favour among many modern biblical scholars. He wants to go back to the futuristic expectations of the very earliest Christians. But he believes that here we do have a contact with the present-day world, for we are living in a time when there is intense preoccupation with the future[4] – technological planning, environmental concern, radical politics, to name three areas. He argues that these can only co-exist with hope. He can speak of the 'utopia of the beyond', though this is surely a dangerous expression. In some ways, Moltmann is a representative of that utopian stream in Christianity, in the wake of such figures as Joachim of Fiore and Thomas Münzer. Moltmann is certainly much more sophisticated. But I think he fails to make his case when he appeals to the various contemporary concerns with the future. These concerns are purely dependent on human resources, and would reject any notion that the 'promises of God' enter into their calculations. A secularist planner might admit that these earlier Christians were groping toward ideas of progress and the radical reconstruction of society, but would also say that they needed to be purged of mythological and religious associations. The Christian might reply that the contemporary secular efforts leave sin out of their thinking, and are in fact a desperate effort by human beings to pull themselves up by their own bootstraps.

Here we have to face one main difficulty that stands in the way of Moltmann's theology of hope. Do we not have here a putting back of the theological clock in the sense of a remythologizing of the Christian message? It is significant that Moltmann recognizes Bultmann as his greatest theological opponent. Moltmann's futuristic eschatology and Bultmann's demythologized eschatology are in head-on collision with each other. Whereas Bultmann demythologizes resurrection (whether it is the resurrection of Jesus or the general resurrection of the future), Moltmann holds that these are real events of history. Whereas Bultmann accepts the historical critical method, Moltmann tries to get away from what he calls 'positivist' history and demands a new conception of history that would be able to accommodate the event of resurrection.[5] Unfortunately he never succeeds in making this new conception clear.

I am not saying that to accuse Moltmann of remythologizing is to settle the debate in favour of Bultmann. The latter has his own difficulties. Perhaps he was too restrictive in his demythologizing; or perhaps he failed to recognize the power of narratives in expressing truths about God; or perhaps he was too little conscious of the nature and function of religious symbols. Even if these criticisms were established – and Moltmann does not establish them – there would still be the task of constructing a credible new conception of history. Moltmann's mind is indeed exercised by the question of what he would consider a theologically adequate conception of history, and likewise with the question of an acceptable conception of resurrection, but he has not produced these. One of his perceptive (but sympathetic) critics, Christopher Morse, has written: 'Even Moltmann's insistence that the nature of history is such that it cannot precisely be defined, and that it can only be understood in heuristic and logically equivocal modes of thought, cannot be taken as sufficient reasons for his conceptual vagueness.'[6]

Let us turn now to *The Crucified God*, the second volume of Moltmann's programmatic trilogy and in my opinion perhaps the finest theological book by a Protestant author to be published in the second half of the twentieth century. It not only develops further the ideas contained in *Theology of Hope*, but introduces modifications and corrections, introducing especially a darker, more tragic note. Moltmann specifically mentions early dialectical theology and existentialist philosophy as two influences which have left their mark on this second volume.[7] Although I have said above that *Theology of Hope* was not a *theologia gloriae*, there is nevertheless a *pathos* in the second volume that was not apparent in the earlier one, though it arises from the diminution of the divine transcendence through the teaching that God is 'not yet', but still on his way.

The focus shifts from resurrection to cross, but these two cannot be separated in Christianity, and Moltmann intends to keep them together. The greatest achievement of the second volume was to present a fully (or almost fully) Christianized understanding of God in his relation to the world. For too long, western theology continued to be dominated by a monarchical conception of God, derived from natural theology and from the Old Testament, but not subjected to the radical rethinking demanded if we take seriously 'the cross of the outcast and forsaken Christ' as 'the visible revelation of God's being for man in the reality of his world'.[8] Moltmann is determined to know God through the suffering Christ, and he offers a thoroughgoing critique of what he misleadingly calls 'theism' (*Theismus*), though in English we would call it rather 'deism', the doctrine of a distant God who leaves the world to its own devices. In classical theism, God does not suffer, he is impassible. This is a consequence of its teaching that although God affects the world, he is not affected by the world. In the panentheistic revision of classical theism, it is claimed that the world is indeed capable of affecting God, and even of causing him to suffer. After all, if we strip the Christian story to its barest form, that God's Son took upon him the sins of the world and suffered for them, can we suppose that the Father was immune from the suffering of the Son? Admittedly, the Father–Son relation is in this case metaphorical, but it is understood as so intimate that the conclusion that the Father is passible (susceptible to suffering), seems to be inevitable, even if to accept it brings us into conflict with classical Christian theology. To think of God as impassible would surely be to fall short of the God revealed in Jesus Christ, a God of love who participates in the sufferings of his creatures and is perhaps the greatest sufferer of all.

Among the philosophers, Arthur North Whitehead is the one whom we most readily associate with the idea of a suffering God. Though most contemporary panentheists have looked to Whitehead's philosophy for their inspiration, it is doubtful if he himself could be called a panentheist, for if we take that term in its basic sense of 'all things contained in God', this would not be true of Whitehead's own system. I do not think there is any direct influence of Whitehead on Moltmann, but the two are linked accidentally by Whitehead's famous description of God as 'the great Companion, the fellow-sufferer who understands'.[9]

In at least one place, Moltmann does explicitly apply the word 'panentheism' to his own theology.[10] But his use of this philosophical term does not contradict the point I made above, that his views are biblical and doctrinal rather than philosophical. If Moltmann is a panentheist, it is because of his attachment to the trinitarian understanding of God. God as Father is transcendent, but as the Son he is involved in the history of the world, the Word has become flesh, and as Spirit strives in and with the creation for the fulfilment of God's purposes. Thus Moltmann is a panentheist because of his interpretation of the doctrine of the Triune God. There are of course many theologians who would strongly deny that commitment to the doctrine of the Trinity must lead to panentheism.

In spite of its merits, it seems to me that Moltmann's *The Crucified God* has at least one major flaw or defect. I wrote above in a parenthesis that Moltmann's idea of God is 'almost fully Christianized'. That qualifying 'almost' takes note of an inconsistency. For most of the time, Moltmann is thinking of God in Christ. God the Father is in Christ, even on the cross, and it is in and through the crucified Christ that we learn about God. But, as a concession to the Calvinist tradition in which he stands, Moltmann feels that he has to make something of the idea that Christ is punished by God for the sins of mankind, forsaken and rejected, which must mean that the Father is elsewhere than in Christ. Here we seem to strike on an unexpended residuum of the monarchical ideal. The ghost of God the executioner is still lurking on the fringes.

But even with its faults, the book is a splendid piece of Christian theology. The distinctively Christian understanding of God which emerges and which I have briefly described, illustrates what Moltmann calls the trinitarian history of God, the appropriate Christian way of conceiving the God who enters into his creation and takes the creation and its sufferings into himself:

> The human God who encounters man in the crucified Christ thus involves man in a realistic divinization (*theiosis*). Therefore in communion with Christ it can truly be said that men and women live *in God and from God*, 'that they live, move and have their being in him' (Acts 17.28). For in the hidden mode of humiliation to the point of the cross, all being and all that annihilates has been taken up in God, and God begins to be all in all.[11]

For Moltmann, the doctrine of the Trinity is no mere liturgical formula or high-flown speculation but a necessary way of speaking about the God whom we have known in the crucified Christ. 'Through the Holy Spirit the history of Christ with God and of God with Christ becomes the history of God with us and hence our history with God.'[12] Yet at this point he does pay his tribute to Hegel, for he says 'that the trinitarian history of God . . . also brings us face to face with that insight into the dialectic of life for which we have to thank Hegel, the philosopher of the Trinity'.[13]

Perhaps in ending this chapter on Moltmann and the suffering God, it is worthwhile to repeat a warning that was mentioned earlier (see pp. ix–x above). The reduction of the stress on transcendence in speaking about God and the correspondingly increased stress on immanence must be dialectical. One cannot abandon transcendence, for only a God who is transcendent and infinite can take suffering into himself and not be overcome by it. We human beings can take quite a lot of suffering, but in the end may become embittered and destroyed. Only God can have the power to overcome suffering, and even to turn the evil into good, as surely happened with the cross of Christ. Fortunately, Moltmann and Whitehead too were proof against sentimentalism, but the danger in the Church today is that we forsake the transcendent God in order to replace him with a nice human God. A proper balance must be maintained. The history of the crucified Christ is, in a sense, the concrete manifestation of the conflict between the Christian God and the gods of the pre-Christian era – between, that is to say, the God of suffering but almighty love, and all the power gods created by human ideologies. Moltmann may possibly have made this as clear as any theologian has.

5

Mascall and Transcendental Thomism

Throughout history, theology and philosophy have usually been in conversation with each other. Sometimes the conversation has been friendly, and profitable to one or both of the participants, at other times it has taken the form of acute controversy, especially if one discipline tries to dominate the other, as when theologians talk of philosophy as the 'handmaid of theology' or when philosophers try to make theological ideas fit into their systems, as some idealists did. It is not difficult to think of instances from history of both forms of domination. But when the relation is a healthy one, the profit of the theologian is that the philosopher may be able to supply categories of thought and methods of investigation which are appropriate to the theological enterprise, and they may also be the means of communicating theological teachings in an understandable language, since philosophies usually reflect the moods and mental attitudes of the society which has produced them. So the relation to philosophy may be very valuable to the theologian, even indispensable, if theological teachings are to be heard in the wider world that lies beyond the confines of the Christian Church.

In this chapter, we shall be considering one case of the philosophy–theology relation from recent years – the place of Thomism in the theology of Eric Mascall (1905–1993). His relation to Thomism was, I think, a healthy one. Mascall had a deep respect for St Thomas Aquinas, and would never have considered that Thomism was a mere tool or even handmaid for the elaboration of his own theology. Equally, he did not feel that he had to conform his theology to fit in with Thomism. In one of his books he writes: 'I am not concerned to say what is Thomist, but what is true.'[1] He saw Thomas as one who might help him to find the truth, but not as a teacher who had to be slavishly followed in everything.

But why, one may ask, would a twentieth-century theologian turn to Thomism? It is true that Pope Leo XIII had recommended Roman Catholic theologians to a renewed study of St Thomas, but Mascall was an Anglican. Why should he have turned to Thomism? I have mentioned that sometimes theologians turn to philosophy in order to interpret Christianity in the language of the particular historical and cultural environment in which they are placed. Why had not Mascall selected as his philosophical partner one of the twentieth-century philosophers, such as a British empiricist or a continental existentialist, as so many other theologians of the century did? I suppose at some point he must have come to the conclusion that Thomism is in some sense the *philosophia perennis* and indeed Thomism has enjoyed a kind of rebirth in the twentieth century. Mascall says himself that although Thomism had its origins in the thirteenth century, he understood it from the point of view of a twentieth-century man.

I have not been able to discover just how it came about that Mascall first became interested in Thomism. His university studies were in the area of physics and mathematics, and his brilliant achievements in these fields won him the coveted Cambridge title of 'wrangler', and prove that he had a modern outlook. He seemed to take a rather dim view of the Anglican theological colleges, but he would have been unlikely to get much solid teaching in Thomism at any of them, for they, like the British universities, seem at that time to have adopted the advice of Hegel, and put on 'seven-league boots' in order to skip merrily over the medieval period as if there were nothing of importance to be learned there. So I presume that Mascall's Thomistic studies may have been pretty well pursued on his own. But however he got into Thomism, he certainly ended up among the world-class Thomistic scholars of his time. Perhaps only in France could one have found his equal in the field, and

Mascall was certainly an avid reader of French theology and philosophy.

He told me that when the new Blackfriars bilingual edition of the *Summa Theologiae* was being published in sixty volumes over a period of several years from 1961 onwards, he read and reviewed every single volume. He must have been one of very few equipped for such a Herculean task, and the fact that he was not only equipped but actually carried out the work is indeed the mark of a genuine master.

Thomism is part of that wider stream of Christian philosophy, often called 'scholasticism'. It began in the early Middle Ages, and was predominant during the whole of that period. It lost its dominant position at the time of the Renaissance and Reformation, but it still continued as one of the great philosophies of the West and has kept showing new bursts of life so that it deserves the title of the 'perennial philosophy'. The broad tradition, as I have mentioned, is often called 'scholasticism' or school-philosophy and the title is used almost as a term of abuse for a philosophy which in some of its episodes has immersed itself in highly abstract or even unreal problems, and has delighted in minute hair-splitting distinctions.

These criticisms may have been true of some forms of scholasticism, but they fail to do justice to the true character of this type of philosophy, best seen in the work of St Thomas himself. This is shown by the philosophy's capacity for renewal, something that has happened repeatedly. When an intellectual movement that has begun to flag renews itself, this often means a return to the sources where the movement gets a fresh vision of the original intentions. In the case of Eric Mascall, though he was a Thomist and kept well abreast of developments in Thomism, he was above all a student of Thomas himself, and had an amazingly wide knowledge of the texts that had been composed by the 'Angelic Doctor'. When we remember that Thomas died at the early age of forty-nine, it seems incredible that one man could have written so much, and with no padding or waste of words, but concentrated argument supported by constant appeals to Scripture and to other scholars: the *Summa*

Theologiae, still unfinished and running to two million words; the *Summa contra Gentiles*, another mighty work; a Commentary on Aristotle's Metaphysics (a mere half million words!), and many other scholarly works, to say nothing of his hymns. Thomas lived long before the computer-age, but he had a group of secretaries round him, and dictated his works to them. According to Anthony Kenny, who must have rivalled Mascall in his knowledge of the Thomist texts:

> When one reviews the sheer bulk of Thomas's output between 1269 and 1273, one can believe the testimony of his chief secretary that it was his habit, like a grand master at a chess tournament, to dictate to three or four secretaries simultaneously; one can almost believe the further testimony that he could dictate coherent prose while he slept.[2]

Even if one cannot quite believe this last item, one must stand utterly amazed at the mental capacity and agility of Thomas in his works. The story is told that when he was being considered for canonization, the usual question was raised as to whether it could be shown that he had performed two well-attested miracles. The Pope of that time simply said: 'There are as many miracles as there are articles in the *Summa*.' Someone like Eric Mascall, who had taken aboard and could find his way round all that vast field, excites something of the same admiration that we feel for St Thomas himself.

But to return to the historical sketch of scholasticism which we had barely begun, an important date to notice if one wants to name a date for its beginning was the year 529. In that year, the Christian Emperor Justinian closed the ancient Academy of Athens, where Plato and his successors had wrestled with the great problems of philosophy for something like 800 years. One may say that was the end of the old pagan philosophy, a noble centuries-long endeavour to solve the problems of the universe and of human life out of the resources of reason and experience alone. Much had been achieved, especially in the field of moral philosophy and even in the quest for the knowledge of God, but perhaps there was a growing realization that there are limits to what human reason can attain. The future of philosophy was for many years to be determined by another event which also occurred in 529, an event not directly connected with Justinian's closure of the Academy. I mean the founding by St Benedict of his famous monastery at Monte Cassino. For the next millennium or so, philosophy would flourish in the monasteries rather than in the academies, and the great philosophers would be drawn from the religious orders, the Franciscans, Benedictines, Dominicans and, later, the Jesuits, such men as St Anselm, St Thomas himself, St Bonaventura, to mention only some of the more outstanding of a great multitude. The new philosophy which evolved was consciously Christian, and it tried to bring together reason and faith. The old philosophy of the academies had relied on reason and human resources, the new philosophy continued to be rational and in its best exponents had great confidence in reason, but believed that the human mind needs revelation as well as reason, and that the philosopher needs contemplation as well as logic.

To some extent there was a conflict between reason and faith even within the scholastic tradition. Five years before 529, which I mentioned as a significant date, the scholar Boethius, sometimes regarded as the last great representative of the ancient classical world, had died. He was a Christian, but it is significant that his apparently most treasured writing, composed in prison, was entitled *The Consolation of Philosophy*. In him, perhaps reason counted for more than faith, and this would be true likewise of some of the medieval philosophers. On the other hand, in the later Middle Ages, some philosophers such as Duns Scotus tended to lay most of the stress on revelation. St Thomas in a remarkable way held reason and revelation together, and this, I think was scholasticism at its best. I would say that in Mascall too there was respect for reason and the objectivity of truth, shown in his championship of natural theology, but at the same time, as Brian Horne has shown, he saw the believing community as the milieu in which the truth comes alive.[3] To quote Mascall's own words:

The theologian is right in desiring objectivity, but objectivity is not to be achieved by pursuing it as an ultimate ideal, with frequent glances out of the corner of the eye for the approbation of the secular scholar. The theologian needs, of course, certain gifts of intellect and a technical training, but most of all, he needs that feel of truth, that 'knowledge by connaturality' which comes from living as a member of Christ in the Church, which is Christ's body.[4]

These words point us forward to the problem that will engage us in the third part of this book, but let me elaborate a little upon them here. When we look at his natural theology, we see both his closeness to Thomism and his independence even from St Thomas himself. Mascall accepts the worth of natural theology, but at the same time is very conscious of its limitations. Of the famous 'five ways' by which Thomas sought to demonstrate the reality of God, Mascall relies almost entirely on the third, the argument that the finite contingent beings which we know in our human experience could not exist at all unless there were some absolute Being not dependent on anything beyond itself, that is to say, self-subsistent Being. This, Thomas claims, is what we mean by God, but Mascall is careful to point out that in fact it falls short of what a Christian theologian means by the word 'God'. The argument may establish a transcendent ground for the physical universe, but it is concerned with the question of existence or being, not with the nature of the transcendent ground. The nature of God is treated in Thomas's fifth way, which is the argument from design. The presence of design (or what appears as such) in the universe has been cited as evidence for a transcendental Designer, and this has sometimes been regarded as the strongest argument in the arsenal of the natural theologian. But Mascall dismisses the argument from design quite brusquely: 'If the argument from design proves anything at all, it might well seem to prove that the designer, if there is one, is either malicious, quixotic or incompetent.'[5] He makes this judgement after considering the highly 'ingenious' life cycles of certain parasites which 'manage' to get from one host to another so as to cause disease and death among them. A good example is the malaria germ. Evidence for a designing beneficent God on such grounds is, to say the least, ambiguous. However, in a later writing, he uses more conciliatory language about theologians who use the argument from design, while restating his own preference for the third of the five ways, what is usually called the 'cosmological' argument. He quotes his own book, *Existence and Analogy*, where he had said that in the last resort Thomas has only one datum for an argument for the existence of God, namely, 'the existence of beings whose existence is not necessitated by their essences, that is, beings in which existence and essence are really distinct'.[6] He adds, 'I still think this is true.'[7] It is interesting to note that his preferred argument is not treated by Mascall as a purely logical argument, a mere syllogizing, but is linked with what he calls the 'capacity for contemplative wondering'.[8]

It is important to note this move in Mascall from essence to existence, for it is typical of transcendental Thomism in all its exponents. Thomism, in spite of the views of its founder, had drifted along with the whole scholastic tradition into a philosophy of fixed essences. The new Thomism that emerged from the 1920s onward was concerned with existence as alive and active. This is evident in the new understanding of 'transcendence'. It had been understood as a fixed unchanging mode of being far removed from the changing moments of history, but now it began to be applied to the human being. Man is a being in transcendence, whose destiny is to attain likeness to God, while God on his side is not a static essence but the very act and energy of existing. I shall return to this point shortly.

Whether scholasticism in its various forms leaned toward rationalism or toward dependence on revelation, it always had a place for God. But after the decline of scholasticism from Renaissance times, European philosophy became secularized and even atheistic. Descartes still made use of some scholastic arguments, and taught a theistic philosophy, yet he shifted the basis of philosophy so decisively that it was almost inevitably driven in the direction of atheism. For the basis of Descartes' philosophy was the human ego, rather than absolute or self-sufficient Being, that is to say, God. So already in Cartesianism there is concealed the atheistic humanism of the nineteenth century, the philosophy that found its extreme and most influential exposition in Nietzsche. If humanity is made the ground of all certainty and the foundation of being, as was the case in the famous dictum, 'I think, therefore I am', then man must eventually take the place of God and put his full trust into his own knowledge and skills, as has indeed happened in the technological age. Man has become, in Nietzsche's language, 'superman', the author and arbiter of his own destiny and likewise his only ground of hope.

It was in the very heyday of nineteenth-century atheism, when what remained of scholasticism had become a discredited survival from the past, that Pope Leo XIII issued in 1879 his encyclical *Aeterni Patris*, recalling Catholic philosophers and theologians to the study of scholasticism and especially to the study of St Thomas as the brightest star in the scholastic firmament. The adviser who was especially responsible for the encyclical was Désiré Joseph Mercier, who taught at Leuven (Louvain) and later won fame as Cardinal Mercier, the heroic Belgian primate who protected his people at the time of the Great War, and later (with Lord Halifax) organized the Malines conversations between Roman Catholics and Anglicans.

But of equal importance was Mercier's work in reviving Thomism. He encouraged the sciences, but believed that their findings need to be brought together in an inclusive philosophy, and he believed that Thomism had the resources to do this. 'Sound philosophy,' he claimed, 'sets out from analysis and ends in synthesis.'[9] Two points may be noted in Mercier's teaching, both with their roots in traditional Thomism and both of them prominent also in Eric Mascall's thinking. One was the belief that reason will confirm the truths of Christian faith, so that the Christian theologian does not need to forsake reason so as to depend on revelation alone. The other was a fear of subjectivism, which led him to set him face against the 'modernism' that was affecting the Roman Catholic Church at that time. Other pioneers of neo-Thomism, as it was called, were a colleague of Mercier at Leuven, Maurice de Wulf, whose *History of Medieval Thought* became a classic work in its field and did much to increase respect and understanding for the philosophy of the Middle Ages, and Peter Coffey, a professor at Maynooth, who was a very competent philosopher, though perhaps excessively devoted to neo-Thomism. But in the next generation neo-Thomism had come into its own, and produced at least two outstanding philosophers who would have an honoured place in any roll-call of the leading philosophers of any school in the first half of the twentieth century, namely Jacques Maritain (1884–1978) and Etienne Gilson (1882–1973).

Of these two major figures in modern Thomism, Mascall was closer to Gilson than to Maritain, and I say this because both of them insisted on the dynamic character of Thomism, which in the period of its decline had tended to become a philosophy of static essences. Gilson believed that Kant, rather than Descartes, marks the beginning of modern philosophy. Kant had declared metaphysics to be inadmissible and had directed philosophy into the confining sphere of positivism. Gilson believed, however, that the metaphysical problem is not one that can be evaded, and it was this belief that had led him to reach back beyond Kant to the Thomistic tradition, and especially to Thomas himself. For Gilson, the question of philosophy is the question of being. What does it mean to exist, and why does anything exist? 'To this supreme question,' says Gilson, 'the only conceivable answer is that each and every existential energy, each and every particular existing thing, depends for its existence on a pure Act of existence.'[10]

In that sentence we recognize, in spite of the difference of language, the third of the five ways of St Thomas, the one which Mascall had claimed as the heart of Thomas's whole argument about the reality of God. But Gilson's way of stating it lays stress on the active notion of existence, rather than the static notion of essence. 'True metaphysics,' he claimed, 'does not culminate in a concept, it does not even culminate in an essence, be it that of being itself. Its last word is not *ens* but *esse*, not "being" but "is".[11] Metaphysics ends with this last word, and it is then that it passes over into religion. The pure Act of existence to which metaphysics leads us is the same as the God who revealed his name to Moses as I AM or I AM WHO I AM, and the truths which lie beyond the reach of unaided reason are illuminated by the biblical and Christian revelation.

In Mascall, we find a passage very similar to the one just quoted from Gilson. Mascall wrote:

> Whether or not *QUI EST* (HE WHO IS) is an accurate translation of the Hebrew name of God revealed to Moses, there is no doubt that Thomas's radically existential interpretation of the phrase as signifying not a static perfection but the absolutely unlimited Act and Energy is thoroughly in line with Hebrew thought; and it is this that underlies his assertion that God is pure Act.[12]

He also says: 'To exist is not just to lie about the place exemplifying characteristics; it is to do something, to be exercising an activity, to be tending to an end.'[13] This very dynamic understanding of existence which he applies even to God might have led one to believe that Mascall would have been sympathetic to existentialism. In fact he was not, but the reason for this was his belief that existentialism is a kind of subjectivism. However, Mascall was familiar mainly with French existentialism, especially the variety expounded by Sartre, and if he had been better acquainted with the more original German version as found in Heidegger, he would probably have taken a more affirmative attitude, especially since Heidegger had been trained in scholastic philosophy and shows its influence in his writings.

However, the major transformation of Thomism in recent years, the emergence of what is called 'transcendental Thomism', was still to come, and Mascall was very much aware of and influenced by it. The credit for originating this transcendental Thomism is usually given to Joseph Maréchal (1878–1944), though some of the ideas are close to those we have noted in Gilson, who nevertheless was very critical of Maréchal. The latter is not well known in the English-speaking countries, but he had begun work on the reconstruction of Thomism as early as 1927 and continued to develop it in a very longwinded multi-volume work, entitled *Le Point de Départ de la Métaphysique*. Although Mascall was referring to a book on mysticism by Maréchal in *He Who Is* (1943), it was not until *The Openness of Being* (1971) that he engaged in a discussion of Maréchal's metaphysics. Two complete chapters of that book (Mascall's Gifford Lectures) are devoted to transcendental Thomism, and his judgements are both sympathetic and critical. He reviews in turn four of the chief representatives of this form of Thomism, beginning with Maréchal and continuing through Rahner and Coreth to Lonergan.

Like Gilson, Maréchal believed that it was Kant's critical philosophy and his negative view of metaphysics that marks the point of divergence between traditional Thomism and modern secular European philosophy. But, unlike Gilson, Maréchal had tried to come to terms with Kant. He believed that even in the presence of the phenomenal there is concealed a 'co-positing' or co-apprehension' of absolute Being, perhaps an echo of Thomas's own teaching that 'being' is the first idea to fall under our minds, though only implicitly. Mascall thinks that at this point Maréchal's argument is not clear, and I would agree with Mascall's judgement, though I believe myself that some of the confusion in transcendental Thomism generally has been due to the insufficient care in distinguishing between the terms 'transcendent' and 'transcendental'. In Kant himself and among his followers and critics, 'transcendent' refers to entities beyond space and time, the realities or supposed realities which were the province of metaphysics; 'transcendental', on the other hand, refers to that mode of knowledge which is concerned not with the objective world but with the conditions which govern and perhaps limit the range of human understanding when thought begins to think about thought itself. At any rate, Mascall shrewdly pointed out that the most consistent followers of Maréchal have been found not in France but in Germany.

Among the German representatives of transcendental Thomism,

pride of place belongs to Karl Rahner (1904–1984), the most
influential Roman Catholic theologian in the years both preceding and following Vatican II. Rahner, like Mascall, was primarily a theologian rather than a philosopher, but both men had
incorporated into their thinking important philosophical ideas.
Rahner's main philosophical work is *Spirit in the World* (1957).
The book is prefaced by a complete article from the *Summa
Theologiae* (1, 84, 7). The article treats the question, 'Can the
intellect actually know anything, through the intelligible species
which it possesses, without turning to the phantasms (sensuous
images)?' Though the article comes straight out of Thomas, it
also connects with Mascall, and through him with Kant and
modern philosophy in general. Thomas answers the question in
the negative, as far as embodied intellects are concerned, just as
Kant had said that concepts without intuitions are empty. But
Thomas admitted that nevertheless we can have some knowledge
of non-sensible things by reaching out beyond the sensible. The
idea of reaching out is of great importance in Rahner's interpretation of Thomas. He is not trying to interpret Thomas according
to the actual letter of the master's texts and says that he relies
more on the actual driving dynamism of Thomism (connaturality?) than of specific texts. So perhaps we should not enquire
too closely about how far Rahner's teaching is rooted in
Thomas's actual words. Rahner himself says:

> For scholastic readers, who are perhaps in danger of taking
> exception to some Kantian-sounding expressions in *Spirit in
> the World*, let it be said here explicitly that the concern of
> the book is not with the critique of knowledge but the meta-
> physics of knowledge ... in the sense of a thoroughgoing
> determination of knowing by being.[14]

Is this the essential/existential divide again?
   An idea which is fundamental to Rahner but only implicit in
Thomas is the understanding of the human subject as spirit in
process of transcendence, and by 'spirit' he says that he means
'a power which reaches out beyond the world and knows the

metaphysical'.[15] Spirit is itself 'transcendence' and the latter term is understood by Rahner somewhat differently from the way it was understood in the tradition. For Rahner, transcendence is an activity rather than a quality or state of being, the act of reaching out toward and even crossing the horizon, of going out beyond the point at which one is and crossing to the new. The human being is a reaching out toward God. This kind of transcendence is very close to what Heidegger calls 'existence'. Heidegger was in fact one of Rahner's teachers, and Rahner retained an abiding respect for him. One should notice also the specifically theological and Christian elements which enter into Rahner's philosophical speculations. The human being is interpreted in a Christian way, with Jesus Christ as the archetypal man, and this is the foundation of Rahner's well-known doctrine of the 'anonymous Christian'.

While Mascall is obviously close to Rahner in some matters, especially his dynamic interpretation of Thomism, he distances himself from Rahner's involvement with Heidegger, and we have already noted Mascall's distrust of existentialism, though this may have been in part due to a misunderstanding. I doubt if Mascall would have been happy with any anthropological approach to the problems of philosophy and theology, though one of his own books, *The Importance of Being Human*, has some fundamental similarities to what we find in Rahner and Heidegger. I am thinking here especially of Mascall's teaching about the openness of human nature.

In his extensive survey of transcendental Thomism in his Gifford Lectures (*The Openness of Being*) Mascall follows his treatment of Rahner with a brief mention of Emerich Coreth, another German adherent of the school. Coreth is the author of a large book which he entitled simply *Metaphysics*. Broadly speaking, Coreth's work parallels that of Rahner and shows the influence of Heidegger and existentialism. The basic element in the argument is, once again, that in the apprehension of finite being, the human mind 'intends' absolute being. What is distinctive in Coreth is the emphasis which he lays on the 'horizon' of knowledge. The human being is finite, but he has an infinite horizon, for his very finitude implies that there is an Infinite, so there is a sense in which the human spirit tends towards the Infinite. To quote: 'The virtual infinity of the human spirit is the infinity of the horizon within which our inquiry and knowing take place, and our knowledge of beings as beings occurs.'[16] There are clear echoes of Heidegger in this sentence, and a more distant echo of Schleiermacher, the so-called 'father' of modern theology, who defined religion as the 'sense and taste for the Infinite'.[17]

So we can understand that while Eric Mascall approved of Thomistic elements in Coreth, he would have been unhappy if he had appeared to be fraternizing with Heidegger and Schleiermacher.

But among the transcendental Thomists, the one to whom Mascall felt closest was Bernard Lonergan, a Canadian of British descent whose philosophical ideas were closer to the British tradition than that of the German writers we have been considering. In several of his works Mascall discusses Lonergan at some length, and regards him as an 'impressive contemporary figure whose work derives much of its inspiration from Maréchal but is free from the existentialist idiom in which most of Maréchal's disciples have felt it desirable to clothe their thought'.[18] I would be inclined to say myself that Lonergan perhaps stresses the human intellect more than other transcendentalist Thomists, and consequently sees the fundamental drive in human life as the desire to know. It is the mind rather than the heart that has the primacy in Lonergan, not indeed that the heart is left out, but he believes that we must understand and not rest in feeling or inner experience. He thought that the same view had been held by Thomas himself, and writes: 'For Augustine, our hearts are restless until they find rest in God. For Aquinas, not our hearts but our minds are restless till they rest in seeing him.'[19] It is this restless drive of the human mind that forms the main theme of Lonergan's principal work, a book of 800 pages, entitled *Insight*, in which he gives a simple explanation of what he means by 'transcendence'.

He writes: 'Transcendence means "going beyond" . . . In spite of the imposing name, transcendence is the elementary matter of raising further questions. It means a development in man's knowledge relative to a development in man's being.'[20] In the book Lonergan shows how the human mind proceeds from one level of thought to another, from common sense to science, from science to metaphysics, from metaphysics to theology and the knowledge of God.

Mascall's theology owes a great deal to the Thomistic tradition which gave an important place to divine immanence alongside divine transcendence. Of course there has always been a Thomist influence in Anglican theology. The first great theologian of the Church of England, Richard Hooker, resisted the attractions of the fashionable continental theologians of his day, and gave due weight to the thinkers of an earlier time, including St Thomas. More recently, William Temple turned to Thomas in working out his ideas about a Christian social order. Eric Mascall and Austen Farrer are further examples of modern Anglican theologians whose work has been enriched by Thomism and who in turn have themselves enriched the Thomist tradition. And, as things have turned out, there was nothing 'old fashioned' in their return to Thomas, for especially since the 1960s and the deliberations of Vatican II, the greatest names in Christian theology have largely been products of the Thomist revival. Those of us who belong to the Church of England can take pride that among them an honoured place belongs to Eric Mascall.

6

Berdyaev: A Russian (not very)
Orthodox Mystic

In the early chapters of this book, we have been studying various religious teachers, beginning with Jesus, who in their day have contributed to rethinking the concept of God in ways that would correct and supersede some of the existing caricatures that have been around both before and since.

Our next exemplar is the Russian philosopher, Nicolai Berdyaev (1887–1948). He has a distinctive place, for whereas some of those considered so far may have had mystical tendencies, Berdyaev was a mystic in the full sense. He stood in the Russian Orthodox tradition, but like most mystics, he believed that his direct experiences of God permitted him a degree of liberty with respect to the ecclesiastical dogmas concerning God, and this is why I have ventured to call him 'not very orthodox'. We find in him speculations about God which take us far beyond the more sober thinking of the philosophers and theologians who have so far come to our notice. In all or most of them, we have seen that the traditional emphasis on divine transcendence has been tempered by a renewed concern for divine immanence, but this tendency is carried further in Berdyaev. In his view, God must be *wholly* transcendent and *wholly* immanent. For the mystic, God as Creator must be at the opposite pole from the mystic himself, and so must be found in the furthest reach of experience. Yet as eluding human comprehension, but as immanent in everything, God must be discoverable in the every-day situations of life. He is paradoxically both furthest and nearest. Mystics are perhaps eventually bound to fall back on the teaching of Nicholas of Cusa, however paradoxical, that God is a *coincidentia oppositorum*, a coincidence of opposites, for Cusanus claimed that the language of the finite falls short of the Infinite and must lapse into apophatic silence. It must also be said that although Eastern Orthodox (especially Russian) influence is very deep in Berdyaev, there are some critics who might question whether his thought falls within the boundaries of Christian theology at all.

Berdyaev certainly was a Christian and a theist, a convert from Marxism and one who firmly believed that in embracing Christianity he had entered a faith far more liberating and enlightening than Marxism. Yet the God presented in his writings is at certain points clearly differentiated from the God as presented in the mainstream of Christian theology. We have seen, however, that in recent decades Christian theologians have been much divided among themselves in their understanding of God, and that a rethinking of the idea of God is a preoccupation of modern theology. So it may be the case that some of Berdyaev's teachings about God can find a place in the theological reconstruction that is going on, even if there are elements that seem to be irreconcilable with the Christian vision of God.

We begin by considering some of the sources from which Berdyaev drew his ideas, in addition to the Christian tradition. If we consider these sources in chronological order, we have to go back to the ancient world, in particular, to the various Gnostic sets that flourished in the early Christian centuries. Gnosticism represents a mood, to which parallels can be found in other cultures (for instance, in ancient China) when people became acutely aware of the evil in the world, and were no longer able to feel at home on earth. Such people are alienated from their environment, and may develop myths, which tell how the human race, as they believe, must have its origin elsewhere, and has somehow been led astray, perhaps by demonic forces, into this vale of tears. A Gnostic fragment expresses the mood thus:

Having once strayed into the labyrinth of evils
The wretched soul finds no way out.
She seeks to escape from the bitter chaos,
And knows not how she shall get through.[1]

Traces of this sense of alienation are indeed to be found in the New Testament, stemming from the apocalyptic elements in earliest Christianity. But Christianity firmly rejected Gnosticism, as incompatible with the biblical teaching that the world is the creation of God and therefore, as such, good. Berdyaev was too much of a Christian to be accepting of Gnosticism, but he did show a measure of sympathy toward it. He writes: 'One may disagree with Marcion, the Gnostics and the Manichees, but one cannot help respecting them for their being so painfully conscious of the reality of evil.'[2] He rejects as 'superficial' the attempt to account for evil as the misuse of human freedom and believes, as we shall see, that it has a deeper root in a prehuman, prehistorical event. Very significant is a remark which Berdyaev makes at the beginning of his autobiography: 'I know for certain that from the very beginning I was aware of being thrown into an alien realm.'[3] This sounds like a pure manifestation of the Gnostic mentality. I wrote above of Gnosticism as a 'mood', by which I meant that it is not a philosophy which has been logically excogitated, but springs from an existential or emotional awareness. In Berdyaev's case, he seems to have had from the beginning a sense of alienation from the world. As with some other philosophers, such as Kierkegaard, his deep personal feelings enter into and contribute to his thinking.

Next we come to medieval and Reformation influences on Berdyaev, especially two great mystics, one from each of these periods. I mean, Eckhart and Boehme. At least two ideas from Eckhart are important for Berdyaev. One is that of a God beyond God, or a God above God. Eckhart in turn derived this idea from the neo-Platonist philosophy as it had been introduced into Christianity by Dionysius, and is dramatically expressed by Eckhart as a kind of breakthrough to ultimate Reality. In the mystical experience, even our highest conceptions of God, as, let us say, the Holy Trinity, must be set aside if we are to come to the ineffable Reality. It is this final breakthrough that Eckhart had in mind when he wrote his famous but sometimes misunderstood words about 'man's last and highest parting, when for God's sake he takes leave of God'.[4] For Eckhart, this means not atheism, but a passing beyond even the Persons of the Trinity to the divine Essence, an undifferentiated unity in which all distinctions have disappeared. This is also the apophatic moment, when one cannot say what God is but only what he is not. This brings us to the second idea concerning God, which Berdyaev derives from Eckhart, the idea of the divine Nothing. Here, however, I would disagree with Berdyaev as to how this 'nothing' is to be understood. He thinks of the 'nothing' (and we shall see this more clearly in a moment when we come to Boehme) as a nothing or an emptiness outside of God. I prefer to read it, in accordance with the neo-Platonist tradition, as a nothing within God, or that God is himself a nothing. That is to say, he is not a being or an existent, but Being itself, and from the point of view which takes cognizance only of the beings, Being itself is nothing. In the words of St Thomas, who refers back to Dionysius (Denys): 'God himself is not an existent (*existens*), but above existence.'[5] Among theologians closer to our own time, a similar idea is found in Tillich. This again is not atheism, but the recognition that if there is a reality to be designated 'God', such a reality is of a different order from all beings (*entia*).

In turning from Eckhart to Boehme, we should, I believe, note a significant difference between these two mystics, though I think it was missed by Berdyaev, who assimilates Eckhart to Boehme. Just like Eckhart, Boehme seeks to pass beyond God or beneath God (using the imagery of depth rather than height or distance), and he discovers there the *Ungrund*, the abyss which has no bottom. But this abyss is not the essence of God and within God (as it is in Eckhart) but something other than God, outside of God, deeper than God and anterior to God. This abyss is a second principle alongside God. But if it is nothing, how can it be a second principle? The answer can only be that it is not an absolute nothing, there must be some potentiality in it. It is paradoxically a nothing which is also a something. In fact, Berdyaev tends to identify the nothing with freedom. I have written myself elsewhere that freedom is such an elusive concept and so difficult to define precisely because in a deep sense it is nothing at all.[6] It is the empty space that has not yet been filled or determined. Yet it is not enough to say that freedom is nothing at all. Freedom also implies desire, longing, creativity, the potentiality to fill the vacant space with a new reality. Berdyaev's abyss, like Boehme's, has a creative capacity. Indeed, it has this creative power in an altogether pre-eminent degree, for according to Berdyaev, the *Ungrund* creates even God! Berdyaev is not content to begin with the creation of the world, he reaches back to a theogony beyond the beginning of time. 'Out of the Divine Nothing . . . God the Creator is born. The creation of the world by God the Creator is a secondary act. From this point of view, it may be said that freedom is not the creation of God, it is part of the nothing out of which God created the world.'[7] I doubt if the passage just quoted is free of inconsistency and it does not clarify the difference between the abyss and God. Are these two different realities, or is the abyss simply the inaccessible depth of God, as might be claimed in the expression 'The Divine Nothing'? Is not God already hidden in the abyss, or else how could he be born from it? And if God and the abyss are ultimately one, how could it be argued that the mystery of evil arises from a freedom that is independent of God?

These questions will reappear later, but at this point we may briefly compare what Berdyaev says about the 'God beyond God' and what we find in Tillich,[8] the only western theologian of recent years who has explored this notion in an attempt to reconstruct traditional Christian theism. Both Berdyaev and Tillich make use of the Greek expression, *me on*, 'nothing' or, more literally, 'not anything that is'. The Greeks had another expression for 'nothing', *ouk on*, and experts on the language generally tell us that only the second of these two expressions means 'nothing' in the strictest sense, sheer nullity or negativity, while the first of the two expressions conveys the hint of an indeterminate potentiality. It does seem to me that by making this distinction, Tillich has been more successful than Berdyaev in bringing the 'God beyond God' formula into the discussion and integrating it into a Christian context and even into the wider context of the philosophy of religion, for it may point a way to a solution of the problem of how to reconcile the views of religions which insist on a personal God with those which conceive the ultimate reality in non-personal terms (an expression which includes the suprapersonal as well as the subpersonal).

A further medieval influence is to be detected in Berdyaev, that of Joachim of Fiore who combined mysticism with apocalyptic expectations. In particular, he taught that there are three ages in history – the age of the Father, the age of the Son and the age of the Holy Spirit. This scheme is taken over by Berdyaev, and intensifies the apocalyptic and eschatological aspects of his thinking.

Among Enlightenment philosophers, it is perhaps Kant who had most influence with Berdyaev. He accepts Kant's view that the human mind lacks the power and faculties for metaphysical investigation, but Berdyaev did not consider the ban to be an absolute one. 'Kant did not end all metaphysics, but only the metaphysics of the object.'[9] We should note that for Berdyaev 'objectification' is a word of disapproval. In our positivistic age, we tend to restrict the term 'knowledge' to those areas of knowledge that can be objectified. But we have knowledge also by other channels that afford a more direct access to what we know, such as our moods and emotions, our personal relations to others, mystical experience, to name three. I call them 'more direct' because they seem to be like our perceptions. Berdyaev says: 'The whole man, not just reason, constructs metaphysics.'[10] Here Berdyaev is moving toward the existentialist camp. Of course, Kant believed that through moral experience we break through the bounds of sense, but what Berdyaev had in mind was probably something more dramatic, something like a mystical or ecstatic breakthrough.

One further source of Berdyaev's thinking may be mentioned,

and that is the Russian tradition. Partly this came to him through Orthodox theologians, such as Bulgakov, who was for a long time his fellow exile in Paris. Berdyaev claimed that there is to be found in Russian Orthodoxy more freedom, more feeling of the brotherhood of man, more kindliness, more true humility and less love of power, than in the Christianity of the West.[11] But equally important were Russian literary influences, especially the writings of Dostoyevsky and Tolstoy.

Our brief survey of the principal influences that worked on Berdyaev has already given us a preliminary sketch of the idea of God that emerged in his own writings. We have before us the elements, so to speak, and have now to see how he brought them together in a (more or less) coherent structure. First we consider the dualistic (Gnostic?) traces in his thought. They are clearly very important for him, but they immediately raise difficulties both for the Christian theologian and for the philosopher of religion. For the theologian, the unity of God is a central part of the Judaeo-Christian tradition, and is not annulled even by the doctrine of the Trinity; for the philosopher of religion, logic seems to demand that, if there is indeed a God possessing the attributes usually assigned to him, there can be only one such. There cannot be two Infinites, two Almighties, and the like. To do justice to Berdyaev, we have to try to understand what it was that attracted him to dualism, even a qualified dualism. We have already noted (see p. 66 above) that from the beginning of his life, he had experienced some alienation from the world. But in addition to that, he believed that monism, the doctrine that there is only one ultimate reality, stifles all creativity and implies a universe which, even if it were perfect and not the imperfect universe which it actually is, would be utterly static and lifeless.

It would be the kind of world described by Parmenides (as Berdyaev understood him), a world in which all change and movement are illusory. The world demands a dynamic rather than a static interpretation. It seems to have been the dynamic element in Marxism that attracted Berdyaev to it in his pre-Christian days, though he abandoned Marxism because of its lack of spiritual content. Berdyaev himself tries to keep a place for dynamic creativity by making freedom rather than being the basis of his philosophy. In some cases he seems to ally himself with those German philosophers, for instance, Boehme, Schelling, Schopenhauer and, to some extent, Nietzsche, who exalted will, rather than reason, as the ultimate principle. Is there an irrational will in the universe, standing outside of the rational will of God? Again, what is meant by 'God's longing for his other self'?[12] Is God in some sense incomplete? Does he have the longing to incorporate into himself the Nothing from which, according to Berdyaev) he has been born?

This tangle of questions, beginning to verge on the fanciful, does not perhaps permit of any coherent answer. It brings us to the point where language falls silent, though it may still be pointing us toward regions on the very frontier of speculation. It suggests a cosmic struggle in which the forces of creativity are seeking to overcome the drag back into the nothing. Yet this nothing is itself to be understood in meontic terms, that is to say, not as pure negativity but as undifferentiated potentiality. And here, I think, we do come to a dilemma. To set up the nothing as an equiprimordial principle with God (a true dualism) may go far toward solving the problem of evil, but on the other hand it is a surrendering of theism and is incompatible with Christianity. But Berdyaev's thinking on these matters is not unambiguous. Sometimes he speaks as a dualist, and the abyss stands alongside God or even takes precedence. Yet when he calls the *Ungrund* the 'Divine Nothing' and says that it gives birth to God, has he not located it in God's own depths? The same ambiguity is to be found in some of Berdyaev's mentors, especially Boehme. In him, such terms as the 'nothing', 'freedom', the 'will', the 'incomprehensible', are virtually interchangeable, and seem sometimes to point to realities outside of God, sometimes to be attributes of the Father, the Source of everything.

The tortuousness of the language may be judged from the following quotation from Peter Erb's introduction to Boehme's major work, *The Way to Christ*: 'The Nothing is a single unified will willing Something. The will turns in upon itself, and within the will the Son is begotten, the discovery on the part of the Nothing of the Something within itself, which is itself the ground of the abyss.'[13] It would be easy to dismiss this language as nonsense. How, for example, could an abyss have a ground? But if we are willing to accept that there are many kinds of language, and among them is the language of the mystic, then one may read this to mean that the Father (the ultimate Source of the Trinity in Eastern Orthodoxy) is also the abyss, so that there is no second ontological principle alongside God, and that the reality of evil does not call for such a second principle, but arises from the incomprehensibility to finite minds of the counsels of God. These, as apophatic theologians have maintained for centuries, lie beyond the reach of human speech and conceptuality.

Berdyaev may seem to embrace a dualism more definite and more extreme than Boehme, but if we take seriously Berdyaev's talk of the Divine Nothing, then I think that his theism cannot finally be doubted. Yet, in view of the dynamic history of Christianity, one may certainly question whether Berdyaev was correct in thinking that the acceptance of only one ontological principle (and this is apparently what he means by 'monism') entails a Parmidean world-view in which change and creativity are impossible, or, at any rate, illusory. If we find evil in the world that God created (and we do find evils which the subtlest theodicies seem unable to explain away), is it not more likely that they arise out of the transcendent mystery of the divine Being itself, rather than from the intrusion of some alien ontological principle? As I suggested above, Tillich is more successful than Berdyaev in handling Boehme's legacy of the abyss and the meontic. Just as on the solar disc there are dark spots, and these are no less part of the sun than the bright expanses, it might also be the case that, if we had an adequate understanding, the dark areas in God – not outside of him – could be seen as not ultimately in conflict with his goodness.

In the course of this argument, I have mentioned Berdyaev's theism, though it might have been more accurate to have used the term 'panentheism', meaning all things in God. We must be perfectly clear, of course, that 'panentheism' is intended to be quite distinct from 'pantheism'. But neither is it the same as classical theism. Panentheism differs from classical theism in laying less emphasis on the transcendence of God over the world, and stresses rather his immanence. Again, panentheism claims that because of his own nature as creative and loving, not for any external reason, God needs the world and man, and even shares in their suffering. These points seem clear in Berdyaev's talk of God's seeking his other, and in his talk of the creation as an enterprise in which both God and man take part – the latter certainly as the junior and fallible partner. On this view, God needs man just as man needs God. This can be asserted without implying that there is some external Destiny, some God beyond God in the sense of a more ultimate reality. It is to be understood that the very nature and constitution of God is that he seeks an Other, in the first instance, a Son (see above, p. 70), and with that Son, the whole human race. This is surely in accordance with the biblical teaching that God is love, and with the later theological teaching that the Persons of the Trinity have their being in a perfect communion which, Berdyaev holds, is open also to men and women and any comparable creatures. (See the similar teaching of Moltmann in Chapter 4 above.)

Yet we have also to say about Berdyaev's teaching that there is a reciprocal need of man for God and of God for man, that this is a point at which his theology conflicts with the tradition. In classical Christian theism, God has no need for anything beyond himself, and while he can affect created beings, they can have no effect on him. This may well be a point at which classical theism needs to be challenged and rethought. But before pursuing the question further, we must get a fuller grasp of Berdyaev's conception of a human being. Obviously, in his thinking, the being of God and the being of man are closely intertwined. Humanity, he tells us, is not a mere product of natural evolution, but a spiritual being destined for God. Yet a human being is not purely spiritual. Berdyaev says, 'man is the child of God and the child of freedom, of nothing, *to me on* . . . Being was mixed with non-being.'[14] This talk of a mixture of Being and non-being brings a Gnostic or Manichaean element into the discourse. It belongs to a world of mythology, though that is not to deny that it may contain some genuine insight into the mystery of what it means to be human. Nowadays, however, we would get more illumination from such thinkers as Heidegger, Jaspers and Tillich, where the problem of human existence is seen as the conjunction of freedom and finitude, shorn of any speculations about a precosmic fall, when Being and non-being came to be tragically mixed.[15] It would be wrong, however, to attach too much importance to this passage in Berdyaev, or to conclude that he believed there is a fundamental dualism within the human being or in the cosmos generally. What is important, and what gives to the human race its distinctive status is the destiny of man to be the partner of God. Between man and God, there is (at least potentially) a fundamental relation.

Berdyaev thus rejects the view of Kierkegaard and the early Barth that between man and God there is an infinite qualitative difference, and that God is wholly other than man. From his (qualified) panentheistic viewpoint, Berdyaev is able to say that 'the one and only reason for belief in God is the existence of the divine element in man. The very idea of revelation is made meaningless if the one to whom God reveals himself is a creature of worthless insignificance who in no respect corresponds to the one who reveals himself.'[16] Even in his sinful condition, the human being retains something of the special relation to God, in whose image and likeness he was created. Berdyaev can go so far as to say: 'Beyond the finite, the Infinite is concealed, and it gives signs of its presence. The depth of my ego is steeped in infinity and eternity, and it is only a superficial layer of my ego which is illuminated by the mind, rationalized and recognized on the basis of the antithesis between subject and object. But out of the depth signs are given, whole worlds are there, and there is all our world and its destiny.'[17] This is what Berdyaev means by 'existential metaphysics' an ontology founded on the human experience of existing.

He mentions Heidegger as a guide in these matters, but

elsewhere he expresses the same view in terms of the human being as the microcosm, a view which goes back to ancient philosophy and was part of the neo-Platonist stock of ideas. Berdyaev writes: 'Man is not a fragmentary part of the world, but contains the whole riddle of the universe and the solution to it.'[18] This ancient idea is the understanding of the human being as the one who sums up in himself or herself the various levels of reality, material, biological, personal, and the relation to God, so that human being is seen as the most promising clue to the mystery of being. This existential metaphysic is contrasted with objective metaphysics, in which everything is turned into an object, 'cooled down', as Bergson sometimes says, that is to say, frozen and immobilized.

But even if the human being has been destined for partnership with God, must not the fact that he derives part of his being not from God but from the ambiguous nothing, imply that in the work of co-creation with God, the junior human partner will always be introducing faults into the divine–human enterprise? Sometimes Berdyaev can write very pessimistically about the future of humanity. To quote him again, 'man's historical experience has been one of steady failure, and there are no grounds for supposing that it will ever be anything else'.[19] But his pessimism is not the last word, for in the passage quoted, he is writing of the modern secularized man who has discarded God. Here we have to remember that in Berdyaev's view, the human being is destined to become the partner of God, even to be incorporated into the life of God. Again, this is an ancient idea, going back to the era of patristic theology, though with a continuous history ever since in the Eastern Orthodox tradition. It is the doctrine of *theosis* or *theopoiesis*, the divinization of man. The expression is not to be understood in a pantheistic sense, still less in the Promethean sense in which Nietzsche's *Übermensch* (*Superman*) usurps the place of God. It is a way of expressing the Christian belief that through Jesus Christ human life is freed from sin and established anew (though not absorbed) in the divine life. So at this point we have to consider more carefully than we have done so far those elements of

Christian theology (especially in its eastern expression) which have been incorporated into Berdyaev's scheme of thought. The remainder of our discussion of Berdyaev will therefore be chiefly taken up with theological questions.

First of all, we note that Berdyaev fully accepted the doctrine of the incarnation of the divine Logos in Jesus Christ. This was God's redemptive act in human history, the decisive moment in the *theosis* of the human race. But if a human being is derived partly from God and partly from the abyss (and this part of his heritage includes the freedom of the human being), how can we understand God's becoming man, for the abyss and freedom are independent of God? The difficulties in formulating a coherent theology of incarnation are not peculiar to Berdyaev, though they seem to have a special acuteness in his case. The Church has asserted that Christ is fully human and fully divine, and it is hard to see how Christ could be the Redeemer if, as the God-man, he did not combine these two descriptions.

But there are obvious problems, and they were soon recognized. Even in the New Testament some of the writers claimed for Christ a virgin birth or virginal conception, and this was presumably meant to affirm for him a status outside of sinful humanity. In the fourth century, there appeared the idea of *anhypostasia*, according to which Christ had no human hypostasis or personhood, for his hypostasis was said to be that of the divine Logos. But the virgin birth and the anhypostatic being of Jesus Christ seem alike to undermine his genuine humanity and encourage that docetic tendency which has haunted christology from the earliest times. Berdyaev quite probably accepted these doctrines as part of the Orthodox tradition, but he does not attempt to give a detailed theology of incarnation and takes refuge in the apophatic position that this is a mystery beyond the reach of human understanding. Yet he clearly states the purpose of incarnation to be the restoration to humanity of that divine image in which it was created. As to how this restoration and renewal is accomplished, Berdyaev does not posit any magical instant change, but holds that within the Church the bestowal of grace is bringing about a continuing *theosis*. We have noted already that Berdyaev believed that the history of humanity has been mainly a history of failure. He begins his book on history by asserting that in our own time, 'everything is tottering'.[20] Yet he is not finally a pessimist, and accepts the eschatological outlook of Christianity. He believes that if history is meaningful, it will have an end, but what this end will be is expressed only in metaphorical or even mythical terms. While the divine–human creativity prepares for the kingdom of God, this is not to be realized in a progressive, evolutionary manner. It will come about by a critical event, which Berdyaev calls, in terminology drawn from the New Testament, 'resurrection' or 'transfiguration'.

So what has Berdyaev contributed to the perpetually recurring problem of God? We have seen that some of his ideas would be hard to reconcile with the classical theism of mainline Christian theology. But perhaps this theology calls for revision and rethinking. Would a philosopher of religion be more sympathetic to Berdyaev's ideas than a theologian? Most of these ideas have been around for a long time, but Berdyaev has put them in a new context and in new relationships with one another. One of his interpreters, C. S. Calian, has possibly exaggerated in claiming that, in the twentieth century, Berdyaev is 'the Christian philosopher of freedom and creativity *par excellence*',[21] but his teachings are still worthy of careful study, especially if we take a sympathetic view of mysticism and allow a role for speculative philosophy.

Christianity without Incarnation?

1. Some Critical Questions

The sensational title of the book, *The Myth of God Incarnate*, published in 1977,[1] was unfortunate, for it was bound to provoke an emotive reaction, especially among large numbers of people who did not take the trouble to read the actual text. It may at once be agreed that the story of a divine being who descends to earth as a man is technically a myth and not a straightforward history, though one of the troubles of the book is that its writers waver between a critique of the *myth* of incarnation (the underlying story) and the *metaphysics* of incarnation (the conceptual expression of the idea in doctrinal statements), and some confusion arises from failure to distinguish the two kinds of language. The book is a serious discussion by a group of scholars[2] as to whether the idea of incarnation can still have in Christian faith the place given to it in the past. The authors are correct in saying that 'there is nothing new in the main theme of the book'. Many readers will in fact have the impression of *déja vu*.

At least since the time of Schleiermacher, systematic theologians have criticized the traditional christology on many grounds – the confusion of the terminology, the remoteness of the concepts from modern thought, the obscuring of the humanity of Christ, and so on. Michael Goulder, for instance, spends much time and ingenuity in trying to show that incarnation was an idea taken over from the Samaritans, and he seems to think this is enough to discredit it – surely an almost perfect example of the genetic fallacy. There is hardly any mention in the book as a whole of the constructive insights of such contemporary writers as Pannenberg, Rahner, Schoonenberg, Kasper, von Balthasar and others such as the English-speaking writers David Jenkins and John Knox. All of them are quite aware of the difficulties raised by the authors of *The Myth of God Incarnate*, but have not thought it necessary to reject the idea of incarnation and have tried to rethink it in a broader, more modern context of christological interpretation.

A defect of the book is the failure to use terms consistently and, more generally, to attend to the peculiarities of religious and theological language, especially its oblique and often paradoxical character. Leslie Houlden does in fact make a beginning toward a discussion of language, but his essay hardly goes far enough. The general failure to come to grips with the language problem may be illustrated from an essay by Frances Young. She writes: 'There are strong reasons for seeing the patristic development and interpretation of incarnational belief not as a gradual dawning of the truth inspired by the Holy Spirit but as a historically determined development which leads into the blind alleys of paradox, illogicalism and docetism.'[3] But when she comes to defend her own robust (if almost purely functional) faith in Christ, she tells us that we have to live with unresolved contradictions and even that 'religion is destroyed without mystery – without paradox'. What makes her paradoxes acceptable, rather than the patristic ones which she has dismissed as 'blind alleys'?

Incidentally, the talk about patristic thought being 'historically determined' expresses an attitude that is to be found elsewhere in the book, for instance, in Leslie Houlden's statement that 'we must accept our lot, bequeathed to us by the Enlightenment, and make the most of it'.[4] If our thinking at any given time is so strictly determined by the prevailing historical and cultural conditions that there is no room left for rational judgement, does not this imply a scepticism that is eventually self-destroying and takes away the possibility of rational discrimination and new departures of thought?

But to come back to the main theme, consistency in the use

of the key term 'myth' would seem to be important, but it is not until one is three quarters of the way through the book that the term is discussed in detail by Maurice Wiles, and, as he points out, it has already been freely used in the earlier chapters without any adequate discussion.[5] His own discussion is clarifying and helpful, even if it comes late, but it surely calls into question the looseness of usage that can be found in other parts of the book. The very first use of the term 'myth' occurs in the Preface, where we read: ' "Orthodoxy" is a myth, which can and often does inhibit the creative thinking which Christianity sorely needs today.'[6] What does the word 'myth' mean when the editor uses it in this sentence? Are we to take it in its technical sense, to mean that 'orthodoxy' is expressed in the form of mythological stories? If so, that statement is clearly false, for much 'orthodoxy' is conceptually expressed in dogmatic definitions. Or are we (which seems more likely) to take the word 'myth' in its popular sense as something merely false, so that the assertion ' "Orthodoxy" is a myth' means either ' "Orthodoxy" is a collection of falsehoods', or (less likely) 'It is false that there is an unchanging body of opinions called "orthodoxy" '? If the second or third interpretations are taken as correct, then in both cases the word 'myth' is being used in much the same sense as the word 'mirage' used two sentences earlier in the Preface, and it is surely inexcusable that in a serious work of theology the key term 'myth' is introduced for the first time in its loosest popular sense.

There are problems too in the use of the term 'incarnation'. One of the contributors wants to reject a 'literal incarnation doctrine', but it is not clear, given the oblique character of theological language, what a 'literal' incarnation could mean. Another contributor seems to come nearer to the mark when he says that 'literal' and 'metaphorical' are not distinguishable in the talk of incarnation, and that the doctrine 'is not a theory but a mystery'. It is an image rather than a concept. Still, it is an image that tries to express some things about Jesus Christ that may not be expressed or may not be so clearly expressed by other images, such as Messiah or Lord or Liberator or whatever. In using images to speak of Jesus Christ or of God, it is important not to apply the logic that would be appropriate in the case of clearly defined concepts. In using images, one normally needs a plurality of such images, one supplementing or correcting another, perhaps even one in apparent conflict with another.

I would think that at least three points are implied in any doctrine of incarnation, though I shall try to designate them here without employing mythological language or outmoded philosophical terminology: (a) the initiative is from God, not man; (b) God is deeply involved in his creation; (c) the centre of this initiative and involvement is Jesus Christ.

Obviously, some of these points are accepted by some of the contributors to the book, and to that extent I would say that they are assenting to at least part of what many Christians would understand as a genuine incarnation. These contributors might, as I would myself, seek to avoid some of the traditional language, but they might subscribe to the ideas which that language was trying to express. For example, Frances Young appears to accept (a) and Leslie Houlden (b). Don Cupitt would seem to have a problem with these two points, because he emphasizes so much the transcendence of God (or did so at the time he was writing his article) and has an iconoclastic horror of representing God by anything or anyone belonging to the created order. His critique of incarnation is in fact very telling if one reads it as the exaltation of a human being by his human admirers to the level of Deity, but it loses its force if one thinks of the movement as coming from the opposite direction, as Barth did in his teaching about the humanity of God. All the contributors would give some assent to (c), for even if they do not allow that Christ is God incarnate, they do acknowledge that he has an important place in the history of God's relation to mankind. Maurice Wiles, however, seems to lean toward the old idealist belief that Jesus is simply the historical exemplar of the timeless truth of the unity of God and man.[7]

In the preceding paragraph, I used the expression 'God incarnate', which is part of the title of the book being discussed but is a somewhat sloppy and inaccurate expression, and a further cause of trouble. From the New Testament onward, the teaching of the Church was not that God *in his completeness* was incarnate in Jesus Christ – to say that would indeed have been mythological – but that some aspects of God were incarnate. Along with the development of christological doctrine there went the development of trinitarian doctrine. There is one God, but he is a God in three Persons, and in Christ it is the Second Person, the Word or Son, who is incarnate, not the Father or the Holy Spirit. At the time of the Reformation, Lutheran and Calvinist theologians argued whether even the Logos or Word was *completely* incarnate in Christ. The earliest Christian converts were not asked whether they believed that Jesus Christ is God, but whether they believed that he is the Son of God, and it is this more subtle relationship, obviously metaphorical, that chiefly occupied the early christologists, though it is virtually ignored by the writers of *The Myth of God Incarnate*.

The contributors to the book are united in their dissatisfaction with traditional doctrines of incarnation, and they are not without some justification. But they have no common reconstruction of belief to offer. Inevitably, therefore, the impression produced is negative and reductionist. According to Maurice Wiles, the abandonment of the doctrine of incarnation 'would not involve the abandonment of all the religious claims associated with it'.[8] But we are entitled to ask, 'If not *all* the claims, then which ones?' Christian doctrines are so closely interrelated that if you take away one, several others tend to collapse. After incarnation is thrown out, is the doctrine of the Trinity bound to go? What kind of doctrine of atonement remains possible? Would the Eucharist be reduced to a simple memorial service? What a rewriting of creeds and liturgies, of prayer books and hymn books, even of Holy Scripture, would be demanded!

Finally, one has to ask whether such a reduced Christianity would move us either to acceptance or rejection. No doubt Christianity would survive as literature, but hardly as a living religious faith. It would be an anachronism to describe the positions taken up by the contributors to this book as Arian, deist or unitarian, but unquestionably there are affinities with these movements, and it is hardly likely that an 'updated' Christianity without incarnation will prove any more successful than these dead ends of the past.

A strange feature of the book is that it contains an Epilogue by Dennis Nineham, and this Epilogue seems to draw the carpet from under the feet of the other writers. Owing to pressure of other work, Nineham did not contribute a chapter to the main body of essays comprising the book, but he had taken part in the discussions now summarized in these essays and claims that he had frequently warned his associates that they were making claims for Jesus that go far beyond what the historical evidence allows.[9] They call Jesus 'the man for others', and by various other descriptions which would make him the exemplary man or the archetypal man, the man in whom the divine purpose in creating the human race was realized. This is what may be called a 'faith-image' of Jesus Christ as held by a believer, it is the 'preached Christ' and does not coincide with the 'historical Jesus' as uncovered by historical research – or, at least, cannot be shown to coincide. So how is it possible to make absolute claims for him, as seems to be done by incarnationists and non-incarnationists alike?

I think that perhaps Nineham is asking for the impossible. It is generally agreed that the Gospels do not provide enough material for a biography of Jesus. We have virtually no information about his early life, and what we know about the closing period (three years at the most) is mostly not in chronological order. But even if we had all the material that a modern biographer would require, would we be any nearer to finding a historical Jesus who would match the Christ of faith? Not much, for as Kierkegaard pointed out long ago, these are two different forms of discourse, proceeding with different presuppositions and different ends in view. How could they coincide? On the other hand, we might judge them to be inconsistent, if the historical information pointed to Jesus being some kind of fraud, incompatible with the idea of a man without sin.

But even a biography is not a mere chronology, is not simply a recital of the incidents in someone's career. It aims at somehow presenting an impression of the whole person as revealed in both life and death. This could not possibly be a complete catalogue of a lifetime's thoughts, words and deeds, some of them not understood or remembered by the subject of the biography, himself or herself. The biographer can only present, as honestly and accurately as he can, the character of the person as revealed in the available information. The New Testament is content to say of Jesus that he was 'sinless'. This cannot be an empirically verifiable assertion, especially in the case of Jesus, who recognized sins of thought as well as of word and deed, and such sins of thought must inevitably be private and not discoverable by a biographer. The Gospels of the New Testament are more like portraits produced by painters, who are not aiming to exhibit every detail of the subject's career but honestly and conscientiously seeking to show what kind of person he or she was, what total impression of character that person left behind. It is true that the acceptance of the picture demands an act of faith on the part of those who see it and accept it, whereas in the case of a historical presentation, proof might be demanded for every detail. In the case of the Gospel portraits they can be accepted only if we believe that the evangelists are reporting a credible impression of Jesus' character. Nineham himself admits the impossibility of satisfying the demands of strict historical scholarship on the subject of the moral perfection of Jesus. But he does seem to offer an important concession: 'As for the rise of the early Church,' he writes, 'Jesus must, of course, have been all that he needed to be to account for the rise of Christianity, and on any sober assessment, that certainly suffices to guarantee his basic historicity and his possession of many outstanding qualities.'[10]

In matters of faith, we cannot insist on absolute proofs, for then we would be claiming not faith but knowledge. Faith always takes some leap beyond what can be known with certainty, but a wise faith will be guided by probability. It will therefore (and perhaps this is all that Nineham wishes to say) be careful to avoid statements that are too dogmatic or that are claimed to be irreformable. The questions raised by Nineham raise deeper questions about how we can say anything about God at all, and we shall have to pursue these questions in a later part of this book (see below chapters 13–18).

2. *The Debate Continued*

Two years after the appearance of *The Myth of God Incarnate*, SCM Press put out a sequel, no doubt intended to renew the controversy. This sequel was entitled *Incarnation and Myth: The Debate Continued*, and the contributors were the original contributors to *The Myth of God Incarnate*, except Dennis Nineham, together with an equal number of defenders of the doctrine of incarnation, including Brian Hebblethwaite, Stephen Sykes, C. F. D. Moule, Nicholas Lash, John Rodwell, Graham Stanton, Lesslie Newbigin and also Basil Mitchell, as a kind of arbiter. The editor of this second volume was Michael Goulder, one of the original seven.

In this new book, Maurice Wiles wrote candidly: '*The Myth of God Incarnate* is an untidy book.'[11] That is perhaps one of the least of its defects, and it is not remedied by this new volume, which leaves us with a situation in which not only are the major issues unresolved, but it is not even clear what these issues are.

For instance, it remains unclear whether we are being urged to throw out the whole idea of incarnation, root and branch, as irredeemably mythological, or simply to rethink and reformulate whatever religious truth was trying to find expression, and, in particular, we are being urged to move away from over-literal ways of understanding the matter. I think the more negative position is taken by Don Cupitt, who says that 'attempts to prolong the life of incarnational theology are now too costly',[12] and perhaps also by Michael Goulder. On the other hand, Leslie Houlden, in a conciliatory essay, suggests that a wider frame of reference might find common ground between the authors of *The Myth of God Incarnate* and their opponents.[13] John Hick is ambiguous, for while he holds that the doctrine of incarnation is self-contradictory, he can write very sensitively about the

imaginative power of the incarnational motif and accords it the
status of a basic metaphor, though it is not clear whether such
a metaphor is given any cognitive value. Maurice Wiles writes
that 'when the view that Jesus is to be identified with God is
replaced by one in which he symbolizes and expresses God's
action towards the world, an appropriate reconstruction of
Christian belief will prove possible'.[14] But surely mainline Christian theologians have never claimed that Jesus is to be *identified*
with God. The relation has always been conceived more subtly
than that. Later in the book, Don Cupitt rules out identity as a
way of understanding the statement, 'Jesus is God' and says that
'no theologian would defend it'.[15] When Professor Wiles says
that 'Jesus symbolizes and expresses God's action towards the
world', is not this an important part of what has been traditionally meant by claiming that he is the Logos of God? That, as I
pointed out in Section (1) of this chapter, makes clear that
although the Second Person of the Trinity is said to have been
incarnate in Jesus Christ, this is not a claim that God in his
completeness was incarnate or that God and Jesus are identical.
Without seeking to prove that Dr Wiles is an 'anonymous incar-
nationist', I think that his view does fall within the broad boundaries which I suggested (see p. 81 above) as the basic structure
of an incarnational doctrine in contemporary terms. He seems
to acknowledge the possibility of such a reconciliation with the
tradition when he speaks of an 'appropriate reconstruction of
Christian belief'.

Dr Wiles is very cautious and tentative in considering the pros
and cons of the debate. On the question of logical coherence,
he says: 'More clarification on the purely logical issues seems
to be needed.'[16] On the question of the coinherence of incarnation with other Christian doctrines, he acknowledges: 'There
is much work for theologians to do here.'[17] On the evidence of
the New Testament and Christian origins, he goes even further:
'We have to accept that the evidence is likely to remain pretty
inconclusive.'[18] This modesty is most commendable, but it calls
more than ever in question the fanfare which heralded the publication of *The Myth of God Incarnate*, and the confident,

sometimes highly polemical deliverances of some of Dr Wiles' less judicious collaborators. Would not the attitude of a reasonable man in such an uncertain situation be that expressed by Dr Moule, who is quite open to the introduction of new language to express the significance of Jesus Christ, but warns that 'until it is discovered, merely to jettison incarnational language without replacing it seems to do less than justice to the phenomena'?[19]

To the untidiness (or confusion) arising from differences among the authors of *The Myth of God Incarnate*, one has to add the further untidiness which arises when they confront their opponents. It is significant that the sequel is subtitled a 'debate' rather than a conversation or dialogue, and the lines of communication must have been extremely strained at times. When one goes from reading Don Cupitt or Michael Goulder on the one side to Brian Hebblethwaite and Nicholas Lash on the other, one seems to have passed into a different world of discourse. The first two are empirically minded and concerned with facts, data, evidence, causes. The latter two are concerned mainly with meanings, values, with what is 'really real'. Not surprisingly, they accuse their empiricist adversaries of 'insensitivity', of using 'crude' tools, even of lack of seriousness, and sometimes not without justification. For instance, Cupitt's discussion of the logic of 'Jesus is God' is not merely pre-Wittgensteinian but superficial and even trivial. On the other side, Lash and Hebblethwaite are open to the complaint that they have not been sufficiently rigorous in the pursuit of intelligibility and coherence. I doubt, for instance, whether Nicholas Lash's concluding essay, though it has many interesting points, really throws much light on the mysteries of christology by employing the obscure ideas of George Steiner.

In a debate among persons having such different presuppositions, it is almost inevitable that there is some misrepresentation. Moule, Lash, Hebblethwaite and Sykes all complain that their views have been 'travestied' and 'caricatured' – and some of them make the complaint more than once. It is noticeable that the complaints all come from one side and it is understandable that the authors of *The Myth of God Incarnate*, since they think of themselves as crusaders against the 'traditional belief' are more likely to set up straw men for their attack. Don Cupitt in particular, though weak in logic, is skilled in rhetoric and polemic, and goes for the quick kill. But as Basil Mitchell points out in his summing up, there are no quick or decisive answers on the complex questions being debated. We are dealing not with isolated propositions, but with cumulative cases and inter-locking systems of thought that call for patient examination.

There is, I think, one essay in the book that stands out for its constructiveness and originality, and that is the contribution of John Rodwell of the University of Lancaster. Building on the philosophy of Karl Popper, he has many illuminating things to say about the nature of theological enquiry. This essay could well serve as the starting point for the next phase of christo-logical discussion – it might turn out to be the 'wider framework' for which Leslie Houlden has asked, and deliver us from the constraining parameters of *The Myth of God Incarnate*.

3. *Myth or Metaphor?*

In 1993 John Hick published another book, this one entitled *The Metaphor of God Incarnate*.[20] This time he was not editor but sole author. Asked to write a review-article on the book, I began by quoting some well-known lines of Shelley:

> Hail to thee, blithe spirit!
> Bird thou never wert,
> That from heaven, or near it,
> Pourest thy full heart
> In profuse strains of unpremeditated art.

This poem begins with metaphors, and in the following stanzas comes a whole series of metaphors and similes. The humble skylark is a 'blithe spirit' and it is 'pouring' its heart out in anthropomorphic fashion. There is also a touch of paradox, perhaps inseparable from any metaphor and an indication of the indirect nature of the language. The poet says the lark was never a bird! How ridiculous that would be if we took it literally. We all know that a lark is a bird and has never been anything else. Yet the language of the poem is powerful and moving, and tells us important things about a skylark that plain descriptive language could never do.

So when we hear that John Hick's latest book is entitled *The Metaphor of God Incarnate*, we need not be alarmed. Hick is simply making a point that has often been made before, namely, that when we want to talk about incarnation or any other topic involving God, we have to use metaphor, symbol, paradox, analogy and other indirect modes of speech. The language of theology is nearer to that of poetry than to that of the sciences. There is an old theological axiom from Augustine which says: *Deus comprehensus non est Deus* – 'A God whom you can grasp is not really God.'

The finite human mind does not have command of words and concepts that can comprehend the being of God. Tillich held that everything we say about God is symbolic, except when we say that God is Being itself. Yet even this may not be a literal statement. When we say, 'God exists', we are not using the word in its customary sense, as when we say that a rock or a giraffe exists. God is a mystery, and so are the ways of God, including incarnation. Hick is rightly suspicious of the appeal to mystery if it is made the excuse for sloppy or evasive thinking. We find him saying that 'we cannot defend a defective hypothesis by dubbing it a "divine mystery"'.[21] But later he tells us that 'the ultimate divine Reality . . . exceeds human conceptuality'.[22]

A moment's reflection on some of the New Testament's basic statements about Christ shows that, if taken literally, they are frankly nonsensical. If someone says that 'Jesus Christ is the Son of God' this is obviously metaphor. A literal understanding of sonship would include a biological relation, and since God as the Bible thinks of him is not a biological organism, he could not be involved in such a relation. But there is much more to sonship than biology, and those other connotations, for instance, that a son may be the agent of a father, throw light on the relation of Jesus Christ to his divine Father. Again, when

Paul says 'God was in Christ', this is nonsense if taken literally. How could the infinite God be contained in a finite human being? The word 'in' does not have its ordinary spatial sense. But if we get beyond crude literalism, we see that Paul is saying something very important and – I would say – quite credible, that in the encounter with Jesus Christ, men and women have been put in touch with God. A further example is, 'The Word became flesh'. It is impossible even to imagine what could be meant by a word literally becoming flesh. But these are or, in Paul's time, were figurative expressions. The Word is the self-expression of God, the flesh is human historical existence. The sentence means that in the human existence of Jesus Christ, God gave to the human race a new communication of himself.

We have already seen (p. 78) that John Hick was the editor of the earlier book, *The Myth of God Incarnate.* As he now admits, that was a polemical book, and he hopes that the present book will be less so. Certainly, the use of the word 'myth', largely because in the popular mind it connotes falsehood, made the earlier book inevitably polemical. Is the present book less likely to stir theological passions, as Hick seems to hope?

The substitution of 'metaphor' for 'myth' in the title is certainly less 'provocative', to use Hick's own word. But I find myself wondering again whether the expression 'God incarnate' is not a distorting oversimplification of what Christians have traditionally believed. The belief has been not that God in his entirety was incarnate in Jesus Christ, but that the Logos or Word, the Second Person of the Trinity, the outgoing or expressive mode of the divine Being, was incarnate. The complexity of the relation is not well expressed by Hick but is really caricatured when he uses (as he does more than once) the words, 'Jesus of Nazareth was God the Son leading a human life'.[23] The words suggest that Jesus was the personality or animating principle of a body which did not affect him, rather as in the heresy of Apollinarius, in which (so it was judged) the body of Jesus was simply a framework of flesh, blood, bone etc., not an integral part of the being of Jesus. This would have been a very 'loose' kind of incarnation that would make doubtful the genuine humanity of Christ. It is the kind of loose connection of body and soul that underlies, for instance, eastern beliefs in reincarnation, in which a person may 'dwell' in one body after another and still be the same person. It was with this in mind that I have sometimes said that it is a pity that the word 'incarnation' has become the standard term of theologians for the relation of the historical Jesus to the Father, stressing as it does the fleshly and bodily aspects of Jesus, rather than his whole personal being, better conveyed in the Greek word *enanthropoiesis*. It is possible that similar questions may have been in the minds of those Greek patristic writers (Athanasius and Cyril are examples) who insisted, though in a dualistic terminology, that Jesus had a human soul as well as a human body. But the complexity of these questions does make clear that even if someone rejects the ideas of *The Myth of God Incarnate*, this does not mean that he or she denies that christology calls for rethinking.

In spite of Hick's hope of avoiding sharp polemics, he is in fact very critical of quite a number of theologians and philosophers who have written on incarnation and related topics. Brian Hebblethwaite, Thomas Morris, Richard Swinburne and others are subjected to scrutiny and castigated with varying degrees of severity. But the nature of the criticism is a little surprising. If Hick's main contention is that incarnational language is inevitably metaphorical, this must be the case even with writers who were not fully aware of the metaphorical character of their statements. But Hick appears to treat the writers I have mentioned as 'literalists', and spends much time pointing out inconsistencies in what they have written. Often, however, these writers were aware of the problems, but believed that an element of paradox is unavoidable if one attempts to speak of God and the ways of God.

If language about incarnation, atonement and the like is of necessity metaphorical, then it should be criticized in ways that are appropriate to that kind of language, not in ways that are appropriate to scientific or philosophical hypotheses. Surely, one of the main dangers in the use of metaphors is to become fixed on one or more comparisons, instead of allowing them to be confronted and perhaps corrected by others. When a metaphor is given too much prominence, it may cease to illuminate and even become a distortion.

One of John Hick's earliest publications was a review of Donald Baillie's work on christology, *God Was in Christ* (1948), which has become a classic in its field. (Incidentally, Hick at that time was complaining that Baillie had not been sufficiently Chalcedonian in his treatment.) But the point I want to make is that Baillie in the book gave a very helpful illustration of what might be called 'metaphor criticism' and the nature of paradox. Suppose, he said, you have two maps of the world, one in Mercator's projection, the other on an equal areas projection. On the former, the northern landmasses, such as Greenland, are very much distended, while tropical areas are very much compressed. In the second, the relative areas are fairly accurately represented, but the shapes of the continents are now grossly distorted. There is no way of avoiding these misleading results, because one is trying to show a spherical surface on a flat sheet of paper. We don't throw out one of the maps and use the other exclusively. The best we can do is to set these representations side by side and allow them to correct one another. This is the kind of thing that F. W. Dillistone did in his book, *The Christian Understanding of Atonement* (1968), where he considers a variety of 'parables' and 'analogues' for atonement, and that John McIntyre did in *The Shape of Christology* (1966),[24] where he considers some basic types of christology, such as the 'two natures' model and the 'psychological' model.

The famous Chalcedonian model might seem to be an exception in the sense that it employs a technical vocabulary which might seem to invite us to take its statements literally. Hick's own attitude to Chalcedon is somewhat ambiguous. At one point he suggests that the formula sets before us a mystery rather than a clear and distinct idea, and he goes so far as to say that it is not a divine mystery but one created by a group of human beings.[25] Certainly, the formula is a human creation, but was it not evoked by a divine mystery?

Having been in the main critical of Hick in this chapter, I

should like to end by expressing agreement with him on an important point. He has become justly celebrated for promoting relations of respect among the great religions of the world. This has been very much one of my own concerns for nearly forty years,[26] and I agree with Hick that the Christian doctrine of incarnation should be understood and taught in such a way that it does not stand in the way of such a *rapprochement* or suggest that there can be no genuine knowledge of God apart from the revelation in Jesus Christ.

8

The Legacy of Bultmann

More than twenty-five years have passed since the death of Rudolf Bultmann. For most of his long and productive life (he was born in 1884 and died in 1976) he had a major influence on Christian theology. Many of his theological contemporaries regarded him as a radical of the extreme type, but whether friendly or hostile to his views, many of those competent to judge consider him to have been the foremost New Testament scholar of the twentieth century. It may be still too early to make so definite a claim, but enough time has passed for us to be able to make some tentative assessment. What is the legacy of Bultmann likely to be? How deeply have his often controversial views had an impact on the continuing development of Christian theology?

To attempt even a provisional answer to such questions, we may begin by recalling that Bultmann's work fell into two main parts, different but related. The first of these areas was historical investigation. The whole field of Christian origins – the life of Jesus, the beginnings of the Church, the composition of the New Testament, the background of these events in the contemporary Judaism and Hellenism – were subjected to a critical examination that was both extensive and detailed. Simply as a historian of Christian origins, Bultmann rivalled in the scope of his knowledge that great scholar of the preceding generation, Adolf Harnack. But Bultmann was much more than a historian. He did not think of Christianity as simply a phenomenon for historical research. At its core, he believed, is a *kerygma* or proclamation originating from God and having something to say to our times just as much as it had in the first century of our era. Here the aptest comparison with Bultmann would be with his Swiss contemporary, Barth. Although these two would increasingly drift apart, in their formative years they were quite close. Both thought of themselves as rebels against the Protestant liberal theology of the late nineteenth and early twentieth centuries. So we have to consider Bultmann not only as a historian but equally as a theologian who was seeking to interpret and commend the New Testament message to men and women of the twentieth century. Even in his lifetime, his work in historical research came to be overshadowed by his work in hermeneutics, that is to say, the problem of how to interpret the New Testament in an age very different from that in which it was written. In what follows, we shall consider first the historical legacy of Bultmann, and then his views on hermeneutics, especially his controversial theory of demythologizing.

I think that the first time I heard the name of Rudolf Bultmann must have been when I was just beginning to take a serious interest in theological matters, some time in the late 1930s. Bultmann had been in his early theological thought attracted by the ideas of the so-called 'history of religions school', a movement headed by such scholars as Bousset and Reitzenstein. Those who belonged to this school saw Christianity not as a unique revelation, but as part of the general history of religion. They were therefore greatly interested in parallels between Christianity and other religions flourishing at the time when it arose. In the early years of the twentieth century, there was particular interest in a tiny sect called the Mandaeans, and Bultmann, among others, was drawn to the belief that these Mandaeans might have had a considerable influence on the early Christians. The Mandaeans still survive in northern Iraq.[1] They revere the figure of John the Baptist, and themselves practise a form of baptism. On the other hand, they appear to have been always hostile to Christianity. Bultmann frequently quotes parallels between the New Testament and Mandaean literature in his

book, *The History of the Synoptic Tradition*, originally published in 1925, and mentions a theory of Reitzenstein (later
abandoned) that one of the Mandaean texts comes from a source
older than Q.[2] I doubt if any reputable scholar nowadays believes that Mandaeism can throw any significant light on Christian origins, for it seems to be later in coming into existence than
was formerly thought. The fact that Bultmann once toyed with
such ideas has been largely forgotten.

However, although the Mandaeans dropped out of sight in
Bultmann's writings (there is scarcely a mention of them in his
important book, *Christianity in Its Contemporary Setting*, first
published in 1949), he then shifted his sights to a broader target,
and claimed that Gnosticism, of which Mandaeism may claim
to be a variant form, has had important influence in the shaping
of Christianity, especially as expounded by Paul and John. For
a long time it had been thought that Gnosticism was primarily
a Christian heresy, in which the teachings of the New Testament
had been distorted. In opposition to that view, Bultmann
claimed that 'further research has made it abundantly clear that
[Gnosticism] was really a religious movement of pre-Christian
origin'.[3] Unfortunately for Bultmann's theory, there has been a
great deal of further research since he wrote the words quoted
here, and the indications are that Gnosticism is in the main a
post-Christian phenomenon. It may be misleading to say simply
that 'Gnosticism is an acute hellenization of the Gospel', as
Harnack did, for there were gnosticizing tendencies in both
pagan and Jewish thought before the time of Christ, but the
current consensus among New Testament scholars (if there is a
consensus) would seem to be that whatever borrowing took
place between Christianity and Gnosticism was mainly by the
latter from the former, and not the other way round, as
Bultmann asserted.

Although there were many varieties of Gnosticism, there were
some recurrent themes. There was a sharp dualism between
matter and spirit, and this is symbolized in many related dual-
isms – darkness and light, falsehood and truth, ignorance and
knowledge, and so on. Since matter is evil, it could not have

been created by the good God, and must therefore have been the work of demons, or else of an inferior God, sometimes identified with the God of the Jews. The true God is said to be unknown, but he is believed to be engaged in the saving work of rescuing spirit from the matter into which it has fallen, or light from the darkness which threatens to quench it. The human race is essentially spiritual, but has become imprisoned in the material world. Some people, the true Gnostics, 'remember' their spiritual origin, and seek to escape from the clutch of matter by, for instance, ascetic practices. A spiritual Redeemer, who is identified with Jesus in those forms of the Gnostic mythology considered as deviant sects of Christianity, may be sent by God to teach human beings who they really are, that is, to teach them the true *gnosis* or knowledge of themselves.

Bultmann has at least a measure of success in relating these Gnostic themes to some characteristic features of the Gospel of John. Jesus is the light that comes into the world. 'The light shines in the darkness, and the darkness has not overcome it' (John 1.5, 9). Although the noun *gnosis*, 'knowledge', does not occur, references to 'knowing' in its verbal forms are far more common in this Gospel than in the others. Some commentators have claimed to see a docetic tendency in the Johannine presentation of Jesus, who comes from heaven and is never a fully human being (so E. Käsemann and J. A. T. Robinson). But against these evidences must be placed the strong counter-evidence that John denies that the material world is evil and cannot be the creation of a good God. It has, like everything else, been created by God through his Word (John 1.3).

Even if Bultmann has some success in his efforts to find Gnostic parallels in John, he seems to have had virtually no success with Paul. I shall consider only one instance, Bultmann's linkage of the 'body of Christ' in Paul with the Gnostic myth of the 'last statue'. This somewhat obscure parallel is most clearly to be seen in Ephesians. Though Bultmann does not accept that Ephesians is a letter of Paul, he does believe that it comes from a Pauline community and reports Paul's teaching. In Ephesians, we meet the idea that the body of Christ is being built up through the incorporation of believers into the body (see especially Eph. 4.12, 15–16). This imagery is compared by Bultmann with that of a Gnostic myth, in which the spirits rescued from their involvement in matter are being built up into the statue of the Primal Man.[4] The connection here seems quite tenuous, and when one considers also that the myth of the last statue appears to be quite a bit later than Ephesians, then Bultmann's suggestion has little to commend it. In fact, I think we may well decide that his whole attempt to build the case for an important Gnostic influence in parts of the New Testament has been, to say the least, much exaggerated.

The point is not without its importance. If Bultmann had shown that Gnostic ideas had been to any large extent imported into the New Testament, especially into the influential writings of Paul and John, that could hardly have failed to weaken our trust in the New Testament witness, and might have suggested that the New Testament writings are little more than specimens of Hellenistic religiosity. But at this point we are already catching sight of the problems which Bultmann would later raise in his theology of demythologizing.

Up to this point, our enquiry into Bultmann's position as a historian of Christian origins has been disappointing, and his concern with Gnosticism has turned out to be something of a red herring. His work depended on his belief that Gnosticism was a pre-Christian movement, but this presupposition has been much weakened. We now know much more about Gnosticism than it was possible for Bultmann to know when he was writing the material we have just been considering. Much of what scholars knew about Gnosticism in Bultmann's time had been gathered from early Christian writers, such as Irenaeus, for whom Gnosticism was a heresy, a distortion of Christianity. These writers were uniformly hostile to Gnosticism, and only a very scanty amount of original Gnostic material was available. All that changed dramatically just about the time when Bultmann was writing his book, *Primitive Christianity in Its Contemporary Setting*. In 1945 a whole library of original Gnostic texts was discovered at Nag Hammadi in Egypt. They were published slowly over the following decades.[5] If Bultmann had had access to them at an earlier point in his career, he might have written very differently on Gnosticism. But we can only speculate about that. It is important, however, that we do not judge Bultmann's historical work as a whole by his treatment of Gnosticism and Christianity. It attracted a good deal of attention at the time but was not the main contribution but rather a sideline to his historical researches into early Christianity.

The main part of his historical work was a continuation of the application of modern scientific principles of historical research to Christian origins and the formation of the New Testament. Much of the ground had already been opened up since the time of the Enlightenment, and Bultmann was simply extending and radicalizing the work of predecessors. Already in the eighteenth century some critics had begun dismissing miracles and the supernatural generally as unhistorical, and in 1835 David Friedrich Strauss, in his epoch-making book, *The Life of Jesus Critically Examined*, had carefully sifted the Gospel material, and eliminated large parts of it as unhistorical. Strauss argued (and in this he is closely followed by Bultmann) that a major difference between the modern mentality and that which prevailed in the time of Jesus is that whereas the latter allowed for direct divine intervention into the texture of events in the world, the modern mind sees the events of this world as meshed together in an immanent interactive system. This cannot accommodate the supernatural events of which we read in the Gospels – miracles, demonic activities, angelic visitations, voices from heaven and so on. Bultmann may have had Strauss's principles in mind when he wrote, 'We cannot use electric light and radio, and, in the event of illness, avail ourselves of modern medical and clinical means, and at the same time believe in the New Testament world of spirits and wonders.'[6] At least, we cannot if we desire to think consistently and if we wish to commend Christianity to a world shaped by the scientific mentality. Of course, the rejection of what they believed to be mythology and legend was only part of the destructive criticism of the New Testament record by both Strauss and Bultmann and many others. Even where the supernatural does not come into the story, that story is vulnerable to other criteria accepted by modern historians. For a record to be credible, it must be roughly contemporary with the events which it describes, or be based on sources which are roughly contemporary. For a long time, it was believed that the Gospels are the work of eyewitnesses or at least based on the reports of eyewitnesses. Even before Strauss's time, there were doubts about these matters, and these came to a crisis just about the time when he published his *Life of Jesus*.

The crisis took the form of the 'synoptic problem'. It had been supposed that Matthew's Gospel was the first to be written, and that therefore it was the work of an actual companion of Jesus who had gone about with him during his ministry. Strauss himself believed this at the time when he wrote his *Life of Jesus Critically Examined*, but another German scholar, Karl Lachmann, brought forward a theory that made Mark's Gospel the oldest that we possess, and held that Matthew and Luke had derived much of their material from Mark. Now Mark was not one of the Twelve, though an early tradition tells that he derived his material from Peter. But whatever the precise facts may have been, the direct link with the life of Jesus had been put in serious question. Lachmann's theory in various revised forms has gradually come to be accepted by the majority of New Testament scholars, and inevitably this has shaken the authority of the Gospels as *historical* documents, though they may very well have authority of a different kind. If indeed Mark is the oldest of our Gospels, and a prime source for Matthew and Luke, then the basic story that all three of them tell comes not from an eyewitness, one of the Twelve, but, at the very most, from the interpretation of an eyewitness by someone editing his memoirs and writing thirty years or possibly more after the events recorded by Mark and perhaps a further twenty or more years in the cases of Matthew and Luke. Thus modern historians, Bultmann foremost among them, tend to be highly critical of the historical credentials of the synoptic gospels.

What then about John's Gospel? It has been recognized from

patristic times that this Gospel stands apart from the others, and is more concerned with the spiritual significance of Jesus Christ than with a historical record of his life.[7] This is not the place to go into details, but most scholars date John's Gospel toward the end of the first century, which is late enough to cast serious doubts on its historical reliability. But we should note that in all these matters there is disagreement among the experts, and that some scholars still maintain that Matthew's Gospel is indeed the oldest, while others have claimed that John has preserved important early material.[8] But our concern here is limited to Bultmann, and he belongs to the radical wing of New Testament historical scholarship.

Bultmann was one of several scholars who developed a special form of New Testament criticism, known as 'form criticism'.[9] We must take note of this, since it introduces a further factor weakening our confidence in the historical trustworthiness of the Gospels. To put it very briefly, form criticism begins from a fact that can be noted by any reader of the synoptic gospels, namely, that the narrative is made up of short paragraphs, each of which has a unity in itself. The entire narrative embracing these paragraphs has been compared to a string of beads. The explanation of this structure is (so the advocates of the theory contend) to be sought in the period of several decades between the ministry of Jesus and the writing of the Gospels. During that time, the events of Jesus' life and his teachings must have been preserved through oral transmission. There may have been some incipient attempts to produce a written record, but nothing of importance is known about this until Mark's Gospel was written and has survived as the earliest of the writings that we call Gospels. The oral tradition did not provide a full narrative of Jesus' deeds and sayings from the beginning to the end of his ministry, but a collection of those brief paragraphs which could be used in preaching or teaching. Each paragraph contained a saying or group of sayings, or narrated an incident such as a healing miracle, and the form critics have tried to classify them into types – healings, conflict stories, items of teaching and so on. When these units were (to go back to the metaphor of the beads) 'strung together', there was little or no regard to chronological order, for it was no longer remembered what the exact order of events had been. Furthermore, it is quite possible that some sayings current in the Church as part of its teaching were ascribed to Jesus, though they had not originally come from him. So anything like a biography of Jesus, tracing his ministry and showing the development of his teaching, seems to be beyond our reach.[10]

Is anything that might be called 'factual history' left when Bultmann's wide-ranging critique of the traditional material is all put together? One often hears quoted some words from his early book on Jesus: 'I do indeed think that we can now know almost nothing concerning the life and personality of Jesus, since the early sources show no interest in either, are moreover fragmentary and often legendary; and other sources about Jesus do not exist.'[11]

At first sight, this sentence seems to express an almost total scepticism. But if by Jesus' life is meant a connected narrative of the events of his life, then we see that Bultmann is correct if these events have come down to us in a more or less arbitrary order determined by the editing activities of Mark and other evangelists. Of course, the order is not entirely arbitrary, for the baptism by John comes at the beginning, the passion and resurrection at the end. But it remains true that there is not the material in the synoptic gospels for what might qualify as a biography.

What is to be said about Bultmann's further claim that we know almost nothing of Jesus' personality? Bultmann himself explains the claim by saying that we know virtually nothing about Jesus' development and inner thoughts. The formative years of Jesus' life are passed over in the Gospels, and wholly hidden from us. Perhaps Bultmann thinks that, with Jesus as with other figures of the past, not his personality but his achievements are what matter. But the two are clearly connected, as Nineham pointed out, when he said that the founding of the Christian Church demands an outstanding person at the beginning (see above, p. 84). In the same context, it is pointed out that the character of a person may be expressed and conveyed better in a 'portrait' than in a temporal narration of events.

But more needs to be said on these topics. In contrast to the scepticism we find in the statement that we can now know almost nothing of the life and personality of Jesus, which might suggest that Bultmann would be sympathetic to those who have alleged that Jesus never did have a historical existence but is simply a creation of mythology, we find him emphatically declaring: 'The doubt whether Jesus existed is unfounded and not worth refutation.'[12] More affirmatively still, he declares that form critics 'do not dispute the view that the Church had its origin in the works of Jesus, and has preserved many of his sayings in its literary creations'.[13]

Bultmann's arguments that we know virtually nothing of Jesus' history and personality take a different turn when they are extended beyond the synoptic evangelists to the Gospel of John, as he treats it in the volume of his *Theology of the New Testament* devoted to the Johannine writings. Here his fascination with Gnosticism re-emerges. 'It turns out in the end that Jesus as the Revealer reveals nothing except that he is the Revealer.' A little further on, Bultmann shows the Gnostic orientation of his thought, lying behind his remark: 'In the Gnostic myth, whose language John uses as his means of expression, it suffices that the revelation consists of nothing more than the bare fact that a revelation has been given, that is to say, that the Revealer has come and gone, has descended and been exalted again.' Bultmann also writes, 'John in his Gospel presents only the fact (*das Dass*) without describing its content (*das Was*).'[14]

Can one make sense of this? Anyone who reveals is a revealer, but this is just a fact of language and is not itself a revelation. If he or she has revealed nothing, then no revelation has taken place and the person concerned is not a revealer after all. If one wanted to be charitable to Bultmann, one might say that the Revealer is in person himself the revelation, but this would imply that we know enough about the Revealer's history and person to be able to read a message through the deeds and personality of that person. I think that Donald Baillie had already pinned down Bultmann's error at this point. The fact that Jesus existed, even that he was crucified, would be meaningless, certainly nothing to be proclaimed as a gospel, unless we knew quite a lot about the person who had so lived and died. Many people were crucified or otherwise done to death by Pontius Pilate and other tyrants. The bare fact that such things happened did not transform the victims into Revealers of God, though their deaths did reveal the depths of human sin.[15]

Fortunately, Bultmann, like most human beings, was not quite consistent in his utterances. In a late article (1962) he offered a summary content for Jesus' life:

> With a bit of caution, we may say the following concerning Jesus' activity. Characteristic for him are (1) exorcisms, (2) breach of the sabbath commandment, (3) the abandonment of ritual purifications, (4) polemic against Jewish legalism, (5) fellowship with outcasts, such as publicans and harlots, (6) sympathy for women and children; it can also be seen (7) that Jesus was not an ascetic like John the Baptist, but gladly ate, and drank a glass of wine. Perhaps it could be added that (8) he called disciples, and gathered about him a small company of followers, both men and women.[16]

Is this minimal – and, I would say, somewhat arbitrary – characterization of the Jesus of history enough to meet the demands of Baillie and others who believe that there must be some historical content belonging to the name of Jesus before he can have the soteriological significance that Bultmann seems to grant to the mere 'that he was'? I doubt very much that it can, even allowing for the moment that historical evidences can support the requirements of faith. Bultmann seems to take the view that they could not, even if they were available. Here we may note a difference between Strauss and Bultmann. Both of them went far to destroying the historical content of the New Testament. Strauss, following the Hegelian philosophy, took the view that to deny the historical component in the Gospels did not mean the end of faith, for it is the unity of the divine and the human in general that is attested, and this is a belief unshaken by particular events of history. But Strauss found this compromise too burdensome, and lapsed into a kind of agnosticism. Bultmann, like Strauss, believed that the virtual loss of a historical element does not mean the loss of faith – indeed, when people asked him how he could remain a Christian after having swept away so much of the tradition, he took a kind of religious satisfaction as a good Lutheran in the fact that he had not tried to gain salvation by works (in this case, historical research) and committed himself to the Reformation principle, 'By faith alone!' (*sola fide*). How he tried to reconstitute faith in Jesus Christ in the face of the many objections and criticisms to which it is subjected in recent times, not least by Bultmann himself, will occupy us in the remainder of this chapter, but we are already coming up against the stubborn problem that will occupy us more fully in the chapters comprising the final third of this book. 'By faith alone' is not an answer acceptable to the writer of this book nor should it be to Christians willing to think about their faith and to face the difficulties which confront it.

When Strauss had completed his destruction of the historical veracity of the Gospels, he sought to reassure his readers in a 'Concluding Dissertation' that the destruction of the history did not mean the end of faith. In place of an individual (Jesus Christ) he was offering an idea: 'Humanity is the union of two natures, God become man, the infinite manifesting itself in the finite and the finite spirit remembering its infinitude . . . This is the absolute sense of christology.'[17] The language here can hardly fail to strike us as an echo of Gnosticism, even if Strauss did not intend it in this way. But his reassurance must have seemed somewhat hollow to himself, for he eventually relinquished Christianity. Bultmann too, we have seen, assures us that the findings of historical research do not take away the possibility of faith, but his prescription is very different from that of Strauss. The latter offered his readers an *idea*, but Bultmann was altogether more practical and ethical, and claims to offer a possibility of *existence*. It is through existential interpretation that the New Testament can be meaningful and even challenging for those persons of the modern age who are unable to accept its witness in the way in which it has been traditionally understood.

How then are we to understand this demand of Bultmann for existential interpretation (also called 'demythologizing') of the New Testament? The first condition demanded in Bultmann's existential hermeneutic is that in elucidating a text, one must ask the 'right questions'. We never approach a text without some presuppositions, and these will determine the kind of questions which we ask, and therefore to some extent the kind of answers that we receive. In Bultmann's view, the questions we address to a book such as the New Testament are questions arising out of our own existence. What is this text saying to me as I make my own particular choices and decisions in the world? The historical researcher asks about what happened in Jesus' ministry. The speculative philosopher of religion asks about the ideas and theories underlying the text. Both lines of enquiry have their own legitimacy, but the New Testament is not primarily a history book or a book of metaphysical doctrine, but in its primary intention a *kerygma*, the proclamation of a way of life, a proclamation which impinges on us as responsible agents in a world where we have the task of becoming persons in the fullest ways that are open to us. A further important point in Bultmann's hermeneutic is that if we are to pursue this hermeneutic in an intelligent and systematic way, we must bring to it the best understanding we can find of the structures of human existence. This explains the close connection between Bultmann's theology and existentialist philosophy, especially the early philosophy of Martin Heidegger.[18]

I have mentioned that existential interpretation is also called 'demythologizing'. There is a slight difference of meaning between the two terms. When one speaks of existential interpretation, though the method of interpreting is the same, the reference is broader than when one speaks of demythologizing. We talk of demythologizing when we are dealing with a mythical or legendary event, such as walking on water, which is not to be understood literally but as a powerful symbol of the precariousness of our human existence. But if we are talking of a

well-attested event in the history of Jesus, let us say, his crucifixion, this was no mythical experience, and it is better to talk
of existential interpretation. An example from Bultmann himself
is his claim that 'to believe in the cross of Jesus is to make that
cross one's own'.[19]

A good illustration of Bultmann's demythologizing is to be
seen in his treatment of the eschatological mythology which
pervaded Christian thought in its earliest period. In the myth,
the present age would be superseded and there would be a new
heaven and a new earth. The event was conceived on a cosmic
scale. But, according to Bultmann, 'mythical eschatology is
finished, basically by the fact that the return of Christ did not
take place immediately, as the New Testament expected, and
that world-history continues and, as every schoolboy knows,
will continue'.[20] But if these mythical pictures are demythologized, they regain (so Bultmann believed) their force, and can
make us believe again in the seriousness of human existence and
the need for a present response, for every one of us is living in
the face of his or her inevitable end, namely, the universal human
phenomenon of death.

In the case just quoted, Bultmann's hermeneutic is partially
successful, but only partially, for although it makes sense of the
idea of an approaching end as an inescapable feature of the
human condition, it does so by individualizing and impover-
ishing what the New Testament had in mind. The old eschatology may have been a mythological event, but it was also a
cosmic event, with significant for the whole human race, even,
for the whole creation. Has a wider hope been abandoned by
Bultmann's reading of the texts? I think that not only in his
treatment of eschatology but in his work as a whole Bultmann,
in spite of his erudition and sophistication, sometimes appears
as a rather old-fashioned evangelical preacher, concerned with
individual decision and individual salvation, and not obviously
aware of the need for a social dimension.

To the question about individualism one may add another,
concerning a possible subjectivism. This objection is less clear,
since Bultmann believed, like the existentialists, that the human

mode of being is being-in-the-world, and he believes also in God. But when we probe these matters in his writings, we find that subjective elements are given a great deal of weight. For instance, he often speaks of faith as 'a new self-understanding'. We can appreciate his fear of objectivizing, but it is hard to be sure that his talk of God and of the grounds of faith have a reality outside of or beyond our ideas. He is right in recognizing that faith always has a subjective component, but surely it must be faith in someone, some thing, not a faith for faith's sake, if one may so speak. His fear of objectifying, of turning the divine into an objective phenomenon at our disposal, seems to be carried too far in his emphasis on the subjective. He denies that God is himself a myth, claiming that when we speak of God's act, for instance, this is not mythical but analogical language.[21] But his fear of objectifying language leaves this remark unclear.

Similar questions arise when we ask about his treatment of Jesus Christ. Does he have a christology? He is strongly resistant to any supposedly objectifying doctrine of the person of Christ and his own teaching is soteriological and blatantly individualist. 'How far is a pronouncement about him also a pronouncement about me? Does he help me because he is God's Son, or is he God's Son because he helps me?'[22] Bultmann argues that when we use language implying the divinity of Christ, we are not speaking of his nature or of a property that belongs essentially to him, but are simply expressing how we feel about him in the 'moment of encounter', as the apostle Thomas did when he said to Jesus, 'My Lord and my God!' (John 20.28).

Christology, however, is not just the knee-jerk response of a believer to a deeply moving encounter. It may indeed include such an encounter, but it must also reflect deeply on the encounter and its possible causes. Here again we see that an old-fashioned Lutheranism is as much an influence with Bultmann as existentialism. For the early thinking of both Luther and Melanchthon, the traditional teaching about the person of Christ was dismissed as a 'scholastic' encumbrance. Melanchthon wrote and is quoted with approval by Bultmann: 'The mysteries of the Godhead are not so much to be investigated as adored. It is useless to labour long on the high doctrines of God, his unity and trinity, the mystery of creation, the mode of incarnation . . . To know Christ is to know his benefits, not to contemplate his natures or the modes of his incarnation.'[23]

But frankly that just will not do. When the question concerns recognizing someone as having ultimate authority, then some reason must be advanced to show why this status is accorded to that person. Certainly, we would not expect a theologian of Bultmann's acumen to justify the claims made for Jesus Christ as resting on faith alone, even if that was enough for Lutherans of a former time. But when we look closely at what he says, he has quite a 'high' christology, even if it is not the traditional one of Nicaea and Chalcedon. He writes: 'The formula "Christ is God" is false in every sense in which God can be understood as an entity, whether it is understood as an Arian or a Nicene, an orthodox or a liberal sense. It is correct if God is understood in the sense of God's acting.'[24] Christ is understood as God only in the event when the word of Christ is understood as the word of God. In spite of sharing most of Strauss's sceptical findings about Jesus, Bultmann does not follow him into agnosticism, but has, as I have argued, quite a high christology. He believes that in the word of Christ we hear (at least on occasions) the word of God. I do not think he ever explains this very clearly, and perhaps he thinks this could not be done without falling into the 'objectivization' which he dreads. At any rate, he believes that one can go along with much of the scepticism of modern New Testament scholarship without abandoning Christian faith. Whether he is right about this will be reconsidered (see p. 213) when we have tackled the question of whether there are ways of knowing religious truths that can survive the criticisms that have been directed against the his torical and supernatural elements in the tradition concerning Jesus Christ. Bultmann's own legacy needs to be carefully and critically sifted.

DuBose on Christ, Humanity and Evolution

The next witness to be called in our investigation into the stubborn theological questions which relate to the person of Jesus Christ is one whose name has never become as well known as it should have done in Britain or even in his native America. William Porcher DuBose (1839–1918) has been described by Norman Pittenger as 'the only important theologian that the Episcopal Church in the United States has produced', and one of my own predecessors in the Lady Margaret Chair of Divinity at Oxford, William Sanday, said that 'the American Church should make much of DuBose'. The theology of DuBose followed the threefold pattern which has characterized Anglicanism since Reformation times, that is to say, it has its foundations in Scripture, tradition and reason.

That Scripture supplies the foundation for DuBose's thought is obvious. No memoir of him omits to mention that he carried his Greek New Testament with him while serving with the Confederate Forces, and his attachment to the New Testament had a major role both in his teaching at the University of the South, where he came in 1871, and in his writings. His most famous book was *The Soteriology of the New Testament* (1892), yet this book might be just as well classified as a work in systematic theology as in New Testament studies.

But although the Bible had a basic place in his thought, DuBose was no biblicist or fundamentalist. Like most Anglican theologians, he had a special regard for the councils and fathers of the Church, among whom the Bible unfolded into a continuing tradition, living and growing. The process continues, and the theologian of our own time cannot be content simply to recall the teaching of the Bible or to repeat the creeds and formulas of the first few centuries. The work of interpretation and reflection must go on. This work need not be reductionist; it need not water down Christian teaching to make it more easily acceptable in a sceptical age. Contemporary theologians are not being asked to say anything *less* than their predecessors, but they may well have to say it differently in the light of all the intellectual changes that separate the modern world from the ancient world.

Probably the greatest intellectual event that took place during DuBose's lifetime was the publication in 1859 of Charles Darwin's *Origin of Species*, setting forth the biological theory of evolution. The idea of evolution had, of course, been canvassed before, but now it was propounded with a precision and wealth of detailed evidence that placed it on a new footing and demanded that it be studied with respect and attention. We all know something of the intellectual shock which Darwin's theory caused in the nineteenth century, especially in theological circles. To many, it seemed like a deadly challenge to the Bible, and to such fundamental Christian beliefs as the existence of God and the creation of the world by God. Even today, in the United States of America, the debate rumbles on, and so-called 'creationists', who hold that belief in a Creator God is incompatible with evolution, argue that 'creationism' is an alternative explanation of origins and deserves to be taught as a distinct and different theory, over against 'evolutionism'. I think that if these self-styled defenders of what they take to be Christian truth had read the writings of DuBose issued around the turn of the nineteenth and twentieth centuries, they might never have fallen into controversy and error. DuBose accepted evolution because, as he said, 'that is the current science, and because the general fact or truth of evolution [apart from details of the laws of its working] can scarcely now be questioned'.[1] The arguments and explanations by which he incorporates the idea of evolution into his theology, especially in his book, *The Reason of Life* (1911) seem to me to be masterly and still for the most part convincing, almost a century later, and we shall be considering some of them later in this chapter.

I should say right away that when DuBose speaks of evolution, he does not have in mind a technical scientific theory – indeed, he expressly admits that he is no expert on the biological evidences which enter into the theory. By 'evolution' he understands a much broader, even metaphysical type of theory. On this view the whole universe is seen as unfolding itself so as to fulfil its rich potentialities. DuBose refers specifically to the work of the American philosopher John Fiske as one who had expounded the theory of evolution in broad philosophical terms. To be sure, he does not fully embrace Fiske's teaching, for he is too wise to identify himself or Christian doctrine with any secular philosophy, though clearly he has sympathy with Fiske's thought. But the latter was too naturalistic, too optimistic, too humanistic, to be fully acceptable to DuBose, and perhaps Fiske also saw the American way of life as the culmination of evolution, rather than Jesus Christ and Christian faith. DuBose's own explication of evolution is carried out in the form of a kind of dialogue with the Prologue to John's Gospel.

But before we turn to that, let us note one further point in his general comments on evolution. DuBose is on his guard against any kind of naturalistic or materialistic reductionism, that is to say, the procedure of trying to explain the higher in terms of the lower, the view that perhaps found its extreme expression in the assertion that the universe, including the human race, has arisen 'out of a chance collocation of atoms'. For DuBose, the ultimate agency is God, and he goes so far as to maintain that

> the evolution of the highest earthly life from the lowest, and through progressive forms or stages of itself, does not involve its evolution from or out of other forms than its own. The straight upward trunk and summit of the tree has not passed through or come out of any of the lower branches; so that the life that has at last culminated in rational, free and, ultimately, divine humanity, has not come about through any of the

deflections or ramifications of life into other or lower animals than men.[2]

There is a sense in which this claim by DuBose may be true; there is no switching of species, and a human being is not as some popular misconceptions of evolution have supposed, a highly talented monkey. But if one is taking the idea of evolution seriously, then surely one has to admit that the course of development which led to the human phenomenon must have passed through various subhuman forms of life.

There are still today unsolved problems about the mechanism of evolution, and DuBose seems to be going too far in what he claims for the line that leads to *Homo sapiens*. Actually, we find him on the very next page modifying his views somewhat. He acknowledges that neither reason nor life as we know it in the human being springs to birth fully developed and equipped, like Pallas Athena in ancient Greek mythology. He agrees that both in the race and in the individual a period of development is needed before the distinctively human emerges as such. Perhaps DuBose's fault here (which may also be seen in Teilhard de Chardin) is to assume that evolution proceeds in a much more direct way than it actually does. This in turn arises from a desire to interpret it in teleological terms and to exclude or minimize the elements of chance and the random gropings for a way forward which seem to be evidenced by the fossil record. More recent interpreters of evolution, such as A. R. Peacocke, make it clear that one can accept a considerable amount of chance and randomness in the actual mechanism and yet at the same time believe in an overwhelming creative divine activity.

DuBose, however, is justified in looking to the end product, which on our planet at this period in its history, is the human race, in order to read the character of the evolutionary process that has led to it. This evolutionary process has come out of darkness, so to speak. Yet concealed in that darkness there must have been the potency or potentiality for all that has subsequently emerged. Already our language is beginning to suggest that of the Prologue to John's Gospel, which DuBose uses extensively and fruitfully. The light that lights every human being shines in the darkness, and the darkness does not overcome it. The light is life, come to self-consciousness, life attaining to reason and personal being. This is the potentiality that has been in the process from the beginning, that must have been present even in the darkness from which the process mysteriously emerged. And that is to say that God himself was hidden in the darkness, for in Johannine language, God is both light and life. These remarks show us how DuBose, like many theologians of recent times (I mean the last hundred years or thereabouts) gives a central place to the human being in his theological reconstruction. Though he does not use the word 'microcosmos', DuBose holds the view that a human person is the universe in miniature and therefore a clue to the history of the cosmos. The notion of man as microcosmos has a long history in European thought. Humanity is not just a product of evolution but becomes an agent of evolution. Humanity begins to shape evolution. In DuBose's words: 'All rational, moral, spiritual creation is creation by and through ourselves. God does nothing in a self that is not also the doing of the self.'[3] Human beings have an inward drive that moves them onward and upward toward a goal which is nothing other than God, from whom they have originally come. This is the idea of human self-transcendence, found in many writers of the late twentieth century, including existentialists, transcendental Thomists, and even neo-Marxists. DuBose was himself using this language of human transcendence early in the twentieth century. He wrote:

We transcend ourselves originally in the acts or functions of self-knowing and self-determining, but, even more, in the human life-process of exercising these functions, we find that the one essential principle of self-becoming is self-transcending; we must be for ever going without ourselves and beyond ourselves in order to find ourselves. In other words, in order to live truly human lives, we must always be living away beyond ourselves. We are for ever and ever beings of the future; when a man ceases to live outside of and beyond himself, he has ceased to live. And there is no end or limit to this futurity or to our becoming. There is no goal but God.[4]

I think there can be no doubt that DuBose saw the relation of God and man in the work of salvation as one of co-working or 'synergism', to use the technical theological term. In other words, he rejects the Protestant principle of *sola gratia*, if this is taken to mean that the human being is entirely passive in relation to God. There is not only a descent of God to humanity, but a striving upward of humanity to God. 'Even God,' he says, 'cannot save us, or be our obedience and righteousness, without us.'[5] The incarnation itself, he suggests, is as much to be understood as the human drive toward God as the divine coming to humanity: 'The fact is, the whole truth of Jesus Christ is just as much *man* realizing and fulfilling himself in God as *God* realizing and revealing himself in man.'[6] Yet perhaps DuBose thought he was going too far at this point, becoming too Pelagian or diminishing the idea of a true incarnation or of a unique relation of Jesus to the Father, for elsewhere we find him saying: 'The Virgin Mary represents the highest reach, the focussing upward, as it were, of the world's susceptibility to God.' The meaning of this seems to be that the striving toward God which has characterized the human race since the beginning and which found its purest expression in the history of Israel, came to its climax in the Blessed Virgin, and that was the moment, the *kairos*, so to speak, when humanity had become ready to perceive the presence of God, the time (long preparing) when the Logos became incarnate in the womb of the Virgin, and there was realized in Jesus Christ the hypostatic union of humanity and divinity, if I may lapse into the traditional theological language.

Christ is the God-man, yet he realizes the divine presence in the world precisely by being human in the complete sense; not a hybrid figure, half man and half God, but a completely human being who has attained full humanity and has therefore realized the divine image and likeness accommodated to the finite level. On the one hand, our own human constitution, our conscience or practical reason, recognizes the fulfilment of humanity in Christ. In DuBose's words: 'We recognize by the instinct of a true humanity that [Christ] is the very truth of humanity.'[7] And it is this true humanity which is also his divinity. So we find DuBose also saying: 'There is no divinity visible in Jesus Christ beside or outside of his divinely perfect humanity.'[8]

The reasoning behind this has been used as a form of christology from New Testament times until the present day. It begins from the idea that humanity was created in the image of God, that is to say, it had the potentiality for manifesting and realizing the divine on the level of the finite. But the first Adam missed this potentiality and fell away into sin. Christ is the second Adam who realizes what the first Adam let slip from his grasp. This Adam type of christology, though couched in the language of the ancient myth, is readily intelligible and is prominent in DuBose, who expounds it in an important section of his book, *The Gospel according to St Paul*, a section dealing with the apostle's teaching about the first and last Adam in Romans. The teaching is developed in both the anthropology and christology of Irenaeus, and it is significant that DuBose quotes from this father: *longam expositionem hominis in se recapitulat*, which he translates, or rather paraphrases, in the words: 'The destiny of man, from its conception in the mind or reason of God to its fulfilment in the life of God, is contained and revealed in the story of Jesus Christ.'[9] At the beginning of modern theology, we find Schleiermacher declaring that Jesus Christ is the completion of the creation of humanity. In more recent times, similar ideas have been powerfully expressed by Karl Rahner. Beginning from the idea of human self-transcendence, Rahner sees this process brought to fulfilment in Jesus Christ, and, in words very similar to those used by DuBose, claims that it is precisely by being human in the fullest sense (which we never attain) that Christ is God's insertion into the world. Such christological teaching, incidentally, is not to be dismissed as 'adoptionist', as I shall show later. It is clear that the ideas of God at work in the cosmos, and then in human beings which the cosmos has brought forth in the course of evolution in a synergism, suggest a strongly immanent conception of deity. In this connection, DuBose introduces one of the very few technical terms required by his theology – the word 'encosmic'. God is a power within the world, so DuBose can write:

> There is a deity within the world which is God and yet not God; which, as God, cannot be thwarted or defeated, and yet which, unlike God, is constantly thwarted and defeated, is resisted, grieved, quenched in ourselves, blasphemed and contradicted in the world without us. It is [God] because as the mind or the will or the honour of God, it is inseparable from himself and therefore [it is he], but it is not [*the* God] because that which is immanent in, and therefore wholly contained by, the incomplete and imperfect, cannot be God who is complete and perfect.[10]

Here DuBose seems to be striving after a truly dialectic concept of God, as at once wholly immanent in the cosmos (encosmic) and yet at the same time transcendent of the cosmos. The distinction between 'God' and '*the* God' seems to be an allusion to the opening verse of John's Gospel, but the whole passage recalls Romans chapter 8, in which the Spirit of God is striving in the world, travailing to bring forth the children of God, sharing in and sustaining their struggle. Yet this is no mere World-Soul, but the Spirit *of God*, the ultimate creative Power on whom the cosmos depends for its existence. One could also compare DuBose's thought here with the notion we meet in some mystical or quasi-mystical writers of a God beyond God. DuBose can also say that the world is God's 'utterance', understood in the French sense as God's *outrance* or 'excess', his going out from himself into the finite world of his creation. In this we seem to have a suggestion of the neo-Platonist doctrine of emanation, or of its modern equivalent, in the Hegelian idea that absolute Spirit 'others' itself in the finite. It would be an error to see in this teaching any tendency toward pantheism. It is, I believe, a genuinely dialectical concept of God and of God's relation to the world, a concept in which immanence and transcendence are each given adequate expression, as they are also in the Christian doctrine of the Trinity. DuBose himself claims that 'there is a real and divine truth in the principle and fact of immanence, but it is only half, and the lower half, of truth'.[11] The upward drive of the cosmos toward God culminating in the self-transcendence of humanity is possible only if we presuppose a prior act of God, in his transcendence, going out in utterance or *outrance* into the world.

This last point enables us to go back and look again at the accusation that the christology of DuBose and others such as Schleiermacher and even Rahner is a form of adoptionism because it begins in the world with the human Jesus. By slightly paraphrasing what DuBose says about God's relation to the world, we can say likewise that the christology 'from below' (to use the current way of speaking) is only half the truth of christology, and needs to be completed by the incarnational christology 'from above', as does indeed happen in the New Testament itself, when we move from such early preaching as Peter's declaration that God has made the crucified Jesus 'both Lord and Christ' (Acts 2.36) to John's fully (or apparently fully) incarnational claim that 'the Word became flesh' (John 1.14). But there is in fact no rivalry here. If the so-called adoptionist view is a half-truth that needs to be completed and corrected by the incarnational understanding of christology, it is true also that the so-called christology from above could be a half-truth verging on the docetic heresy if it did not acknowledge the movement of humanity in Christ toward God the Father.

The most obvious characteristic of DuBose's theology considered in its more speculative or philosophical aspects is its thoroughgoing dynamism. Everything, even God, is active, moving, effecting. For this reason, contemporary process philosophers and theologians have claimed DuBose as one of themselves, or at least as a forerunner. Though there may be some validity in this claim, it should not be pressed too strongly. The process thinkers of recent times have based themselves on Whitehead, whose philosophy in turn was derived from the conception of the universe put forward by early twentieth-century physicists. DuBose's cosmology owes more to biology, especially to Darwin's theory of evolution, but the important difference is that the dynamism of DuBose centres in anthropology rather than in cosmology, in an understanding of personal being rather than living or physical being. DuBose has a richer and more penetrating understanding of the human person than can be found in Whitehead or his followers. In this respect, he stands nearer to existentialist than to process thinkers.

If we ask who was the philosopher who had the most profound influence on DuBose, the answer may be surprising, but I should think there is no doubt that the answer is: Aristotle. For DuBose, as for many medieval thinkers, Aristotle is simply *the* philosopher, the representative of human reason and wisdom so far as it reaches without divine revelation, though I wonder if any human thought is entirely independent of revelation. DuBose's last important writing was *From Aristotle to Christ*, which was published after the death of the author. The book deals with the transition from ethics to religion, from the highest human wisdom to the wisdom that comes from divine revelation.

Among the works of Aristotle, DuBose prized especially *The Nicomachean Ethics*. Clearly, Aristotle's conception of God as the 'Unmoved Mover', though it made a strong appeal to earlier Christian theologians, would not have commended itself to DuBose, with his much more dynamic conception of a God who goes out of himself into the finite and who works encosmically as an immanent formative force in the universe. Such ideas are to be gathered rather from Aristotle's teaching about human nature and ethics. The essential points are already expressed in the first ten pages of *The Soteriology of the New Testament*, where we find no fewer than three important mentions of Aristotle. The first tells us that 'man is by nature spirited only in the sense in which Aristotle would admit that he is [by nature] moral'.[12] Man is by nature moral only in the sense that he has the capacity for becoming spiritual or moral. This is explained three pages later, when it is claimed that to know the nature of anything, we must see it in the light of its end, that is to say, we must know not only what it actually is, but all that it can

become. DuBose quotes Aristotle and then translates or paraphrases as follows: 'What a thing is when its becoming has been
completed, that we call the *nature* of the thing, as, for instance,
of man.' Two pages further on, DuBose says:

> Aristotle, in discussing the *summum bonum*, the supreme
> good and final end of man, insists very much that it shall be
> . . . something human, something attainable for man and not
> beyond human reach. Any theory of human salvation and
> destination must present to us an ideal of man and man's
> condition not yet indeed realized, but realizable. Still, what
> we are in search of – although it must be an attainable ideal
> – is as yet an ideal. In Aristotle himself, the definition of a
> thing is not 'what it is', its actual, 'but what it were to be it',
> its ideal. *Man* is to be defined not by what he is but by what
> he would be if he fulfilled his conception, if he were all that
> it were to be a man.[13]

These points just mentioned supply the conceptual and philosophical basis for DuBose's anthropology and christology, and
also illustrate his tendency toward the ideas of later existentialists.

Another figure who had an influence in shaping the more
philosophical aspects of DuBose's thought was the German
theologian Isaak August Dorner, who was active during a large
part of DuBose's career. It is known that DuBose closely studied
Dorner's classic work on the history of the doctrine of the person
of Christ, translated into English in five large volumes during
the 1860s. Dorner's own *Systematic Theology* also appeared in
English at a later date. There was a strong Hegelian element in
those writings, especially in the treatment of the idea of incarnation. The incarnation of God in Jesus Christ was no instantaneous happening confined to the person of the individual Jesus
of Nazareth, but a long historical process, which continued to
be a process in Jesus' own personal biography. Incarnation is
not to be dated from Jesus' birth or conception. During his life,
his being was more and more taken into the being of God and
the complete hypostatic union took place only at the end of

Jesus' earthly life, when he resigned himself wholly to the Father in the death of the cross.

I do not think that DuBose went quite as far as Dorner in these matters, but his immersion in Dorner's work must have strengthened his own determination to understand the relation of Jesus to the Father in dynamic and dialectical terms. It may also have been the Hegelian idea that God becomes or will become incarnate in all humanity, not just in Jesus Christ, that encouraged DuBose to declare that 'the Church is as truly Christ as the body of flesh in which he was visibly present on earth, and its baptisms are as really his births into individual human beings as his birth of a Virgin was a real birth into humanity'.[14] This talk of Christ or even God being born into the self of the believer is obviously a very strong assertion of identity. It may possibly be an echo of some forms of mysticism, for very similar language was used by Meister Eckhart. Does this mean then that finally there is no distinction between the relation of Christ to the Father and the relation of Christian believers, perhaps ideally of all human beings, to the Father? Sometimes the language of DuBose suggests that this is the case. However, he also makes a distinction between the hypostatic union of the Father with Christ, and the mystical union with the Father of those who are related with him in or through Christ. Certainly, DuBose believed that the relation of the Church to the historical Jesus is so close that in him humanity itself has been reconstituted in a filial relation to God.

But to discuss who influenced whom is rarely fruitful. I suspect that if DuBose had not made a careful study of Aristotle, and, still more, if he had never read Dorner, he would still have conceived pretty much the same theology that he in fact produced. For ideas of development, dialectic, personal growth and so on belong to the general categories of human thinking, and it so happens that the career of DuBose fell at a time when these ideas were very much in the air. If it is not so very important to ask what thinkers influenced DuBose, it is even less important to ask who were influenced by him. His successors, whether process theologians, existentialists, or transcendental Thomists, have probably learned less from his writings than they ought to have done, but they have shared much from the same stock of ideas. But I think that very few of them, and perhaps none in the United States, have handled these ideas with the balance and illumination that we find in DuBose.

The Cosmic Christ

On the very morning that I began to write this chapter, I read in my newspaper an item reporting that a group of scientists, using data from the Hubble Telescope, had found reasons to believe that some of the galaxies are not simply moving apart from one another, as had been assumed to be the case in an expanding universe, but were, in the expression used by these investigators, 'drifting irregularly'.[1] This was an ordinary news item and would presumably be read by millions of ordinary people. I mention it (though whether it has turned out to be of any importance, I do not know) just to illustrate how far, even among those who would not claim any knowledge of cosmology, ordinary people have nevertheless absorbed some general idea of the modern conception of the universe. I use it to illustrate how far the commonly accepted ideas of the universe in our time have moved from those that prevailed in New Testament times. In the New Testament, we read, for instance, of a future scenario in which a gigantic dragon, with a sweep of its mighty tail, drew down 'a third of the stars of heaven, and cast them on the earth' (Rev. 12.4). That first-century view of the universe and our twenty-first-century view are, if one may say so, light-years apart. Presumably Jesus of Nazareth shared the first-century view (see Mark 13.25). How then can we talk of the 'cosmic Christ'? Are not Christ and the cosmos so utterly remote from one another that nothing is to be gained by trying to connect them? Indeed, the only result would surely be to increase the suspicion that Christ and the New Testament can have nothing to say to the world as we understand it today.

A relation can be established or re-established between Christ and cosmos only if we can acknowledge a truly immense development in the understanding of both Christ and cosmos during the past two millennia. If we think of Jesus of Nazareth as no more than a simple Galilean, 'a first-century Palestinian peasant', as he has been contemptuously called, then perhaps we can go no further. But if he was indeed more than that, if, for instance, in some sense God or even the cosmos came to expression and spoke in and though this man, so that in him we confront not just Jesus of Nazareth but the eternal Word, then we see that it may not be simply absurd to make the connection between Christ and cosmos. But to reach that transformed idea of Jesus Christ, we have to follow the entire development of Christian belief about Jesus Christ from the days when a few fishermen attached themselves to an obscure rabbi from Nazareth to the days when the Church arrived at its full faith in Jesus as the Christ, the development of that branch of theology which we call christology or the doctrine of the person of Christ; and we must acknowledge that the development of the understanding of Christ is just as immense as the development in our understanding of the cosmos from the first century until today.

But how are such enormous developments of understanding possible – developments in which the final stage seems so far from the beginning that we have to ask whether this really is development or something purely fabricated with no real attachment to what is now claimed as its origin? To that, I think, it has to be replied that in both theology and the natural sciences, each generation has to stand on the shoulders of the preceding one. However startling or revolutionary are the changes that come about, there is a thread of continuity that links the new with the old. Sometimes we recognize errors in what has been transmitted, and we discard them, but what we receive is usually greater than what we reject.

In one of his early writings, Karl Rahner argued that the human race has always been, so to speak, 'on the look-out' for revelation. For as long as there have been distinctively human beings in the world, they have had a sense of mystery. They have been watching or listening for any word or event that might shed light on the question of where they have come from or what might be the meaning or purpose, if any, of their lives. In Rahner's words, 'the positive openness for a revelation which God may possibly give, is part of the essential constitution of man'.[2] Originally these wonderings may have been confined to practical questions of human living, but at an early time in many cultures the sky and the celestial bodies became a kind of focus for these wonderings. Perhaps the vastness of the sky awakened the idea of the infinite and entered into relation with the human wondering about human existence itself and the direction it should follow. In the famous words of Immanuel Kant: 'Two things fill the mind with ever-increasing wonder and awe, the oftener and the more intensely we meditate on them: the starry heaven above me and the moral law within me.'[3] It is of course the intellectual element in religion that engages in and develops such wonderings, and religion has other strands besides the intellectual one. Nevertheless, it is in its intellectual wonderings that religion may find itself in contact with the sciences, and not least with cosmological speculations.

One of the things that impress the student of christology is the astonishing rapidity with which advanced understandings of the person of Jesus Christ developed. Our oldest record is found in the letters of Paul, written within a generation of the crucifixion. In his early letters, Paul sets forth his understanding of Jesus Christ in a fairly low key – Jesus Christ is the new Adam, the person who has realized God's original purpose for mankind. In Adam, that purpose had been thwarted by sin and the whole race was infected. That situation had been reversed by the righteousness of Christ, and this also had significance for the whole race. But within a few years, Paul's thought had developed to the point where Jesus Christ was being placed on a level with God himself and was given a share in the divine name: 'God has highly exalted him and bestowed on him the name which is above every name, that at the name of Jesus every knee should bow, in heaven and on earth and under the earth, and every tongue confess that Jesus Christ is Lord, to the glory of God the Father' (Phil. 2.9–11).

It is doubtful if Paul himself ever used explicitly cosmic language about Jesus Christ, though it might be claimed that his words in Philippians, as just quoted, constitute an implicit recognition of the cosmic status of Christ. It is, however, in the letters to the Ephesians and Colossians that we find the clear New Testament basis for relating Christ to the cosmos. Many scholars nowadays do not believe that Paul was the writer of Ephesians, and some take the view that he may have written only parts of Colossians. It would be interesting to know the facts of the matter, but from the theological point of view, the question is not important. Both of these documents are included in the New Testament canon, they both have Pauline features, and they appear to have been written in the early 60s shortly before the death of Paul. So we are dealing here with material that is in the Pauline tradition and that originated within a generation of the crucifixion.

Let us consider first the letter to the Colossians, which certainly shows continuity with Paul's thought. Of Christ, it is said that 'he is the image (*eikon*) of the invisible God, the first-born of all creation' (Col. 1.15). The claim that Christ is the image or icon of the invisible God is no more than another way of saying what in earlier letters of Paul is expressed by saying that he is the new Adam, for Adam, according to the creation stories in Genesis, was made in the divine image and likeness. But Adam fell into sin, and as a consequence the divine image was not realized in him, but was marred and disfigured. The creation was renewed in the new Adam, so that in Christ the image of God shines out in its purity, and the purpose of God in creating the human race has been realized. There now exists on the finite level a human being, Jesus, who, so far as the finite can express the infinite, presents an icon or visible manifestation of the invisible God. Jesus was therefore also said to be 'the first-born of all creation'. This does not mean that Jesus was there at the beginning (for the question of pre-existence, see below, pp. 134–9). It was Adam (however we may understand that name) who was temporally at the beginning of human history. But prior even to the first historical human beings (whom we may designate by the shorthand expression, Adam) there was the conception of humanity, to be defined not in terms of what it actually was but rather in terms of what it had the possibility of becoming (see above, pp. 119–20) – that is to say, a perfect humanity, made in God's own image and likeness. Before anything can be made or any deed done, there must be an idea in the mind of the Maker or Doer. This is a truth that we owe to Plato and that seems to be still valid. Jesus Christ is the first-born of creation in the sense of being the goal of creation. The goal was already inscribed in the beginning, or, shall we say, encoded in the first form of the creation as its highest possibility. This is, of course, a tremendous claim to make, but I think that Christianity has been making it at least in an implicit way since apostolic times. Is it too great a claim? We shall come back to the question.

Meanwhile, let us continue to examine what the letter to the Colossians has to say. 'In him, all things were created, in heaven and on earth, visible and invisible, whether thrones or dominions or principalities or authorities, all things were created through him and for him. He is before all things and in him all things hold together' (Col. 1.16–17). Here the claim becomes even more astonishing. Jesus Christ is not only the first-born of creation but the agent of creation, though it is an agency that is here very precisely nuanced through the use of prepositions – in whom, through whom and for whom. These prepositions suggest a creator who is not entirely external to what is created, but one who is both prior to the creation and participating in it, transcendent and immanent. But even if we allow that the mode of creating envisaged in these verses is not an arbitrary act of will on the part of some Power standing outside, is not the entire claim, however qualified, the expression of a Christian megalomania which has overshot itself? It is like the claim expressed by Pascal: 'Jesus Christ is the goal of everything and the centre toward which everything tends. He who knows him, knows the reason for everything.'[4] I freely confess that I have been myself trained so much to avoid dogmatism, that a claim like this frightens me and I feel an instinct to draw back. But when one thinks out the meaning of Christian faith, is one already committed to such a claim? If Jesus Christ is taken to be the icon or image of God, and at the same time he is characterized above all by self-giving love, then must not the confession that God is love (1 John 4.16) be at the heart of Christian doctrine, and the love of God as we have learned it in Jesus Christ is no less than the ontological principle through which all things hold together?

Returning to the text of Colossians, we come to another stupendous cosmic claim: 'For in [Jesus Christ] all the fullness of God was pleased to dwell, and through him to reconcile to himself all things, whether on earth or in heaven, making peace by the blood of his cross' (Col. 1.20–21). Here we may want to question the expression, 'all the fullness of God'. We have to remember that this is very early Christian discourse, coming from before the time of the doctrine of the Trinity had been clearly formulated. It is not to be supposed that the fullness of divine Being could dwell in a finite person, and in fact trinitarian theology does not demand that we should suppose so. The Word or Logos was incarnate in Jesus Christ, not the Father.

Much of the teaching in the letter to the Ephesians resembles what we have found in Colossians, though perhaps there is a stronger emphasis on reconciliation and the bridging of human rivalries in Christ. 'Before the foundation of the world' (Eph. 1.4) God had destined his elect, drawn from both Jews and Gentiles, to be his children in Jesus Christ. In him, the mystery has been revealed; it is God's purpose 'to unite all things in him, things in heaven and things on earth' (Eph. 1.10). These words may remind us of Rahner's belief that in the history of humanity, especially of Israel, there has been the expectancy of a revelation of God, and this has now come in Christ. God has 'raised him from the dead and made him to sit at his right hand in the heavenly places, far above all rule and authority and power and dominion, and above every name that is named, not only in this age but in that which is to come; and he has put all things under his feet and has made him the head over all things for the Church, which is his body, the fullness of him who fills all in all' (Eph. 1.20–23). This statement does indeed give to the Church more prominence than is accorded to it in Colossians, though it can be interpreted also as meaning that finally the Church, the cosmos and the body of Christ will all be one and the same.

There is a later passage in Ephesians which seems to have cosmological references. The writer quotes Psalm 68: 'When he ascended on high, [Christ] led a host of captives, and he gave gifts to men' (Eph. 4.8). Taking the words to refer to Christ, the writer of the epistle comments: 'In saying, "He ascended," what does it mean but that he had also descended into the lower parts of the earth? He who descended is also he who ascended far above all the heavens, that he might fill all things' (Eph. 4.9–10). The language here seems to suggest a cosmic journey from the highest heaven to the depths of the underworld and back again. This language of a journey is mythological, but it may illuminate the Greek expression, *pantokrator*, designating Christ as the one who has all authority, combined in Ephesians with the notion of omnipresence.

So within a period of not much more than thirty years, the Jesus who had died on a cross had been exalted in the mind of the Church into a universal ruler alongside God himself. The swiftness with which this happened testifies to the tremendous impression which Jesus had made in the minds of those who had been won to the new faith. The Christ-event was itself an explosive creative event. The initial impact issued in a stream of happening that is still going on. In this respect, Christianity exhibits a remarkable parallel to that cosmic event of possibly fifteen billion years ago, the birth of the creation so far as we know it. Stephen Hawking writes: 'Within only a few hours of the "big bang", the production of helium and other elements would have stopped. And after that, for the next million years or so, the universe would just have continued expanding, without anything much happening.'[5] In both Christianity and the world-process, the beginnings were dense and heavy with consequences that only unfolded over a long stretch of time.

In the second century, Irenaeus may have been the first to introduce the notion of development or even of evolution into the understanding of the rise of Christianity. Human beings cannot come into existence in an instant, as if ready-made. The very notion of a human personality demands experience, history and growth. So Irenaeus did not believe that Adam and Eve could have been created, already adults; they must have begun like children, who had to *grow* into maturity. To say they were made in the image and likeness of God did not mean that they already possessed those characteristics in their completeness. They had them as potentialities which had to be realized, and that needed time. 'Created things must be inferior to him who created them ... They come short of the perfect. Man could not receive this perfection, being yet an infant.'[6] The life of the human being is (or ought to be) the progression from the potency of the image to the realization of the likeness. The close relation or analogy between God and the perfected human being is expressed in the words: 'The glory of God is a living man, and the life of man consists in beholding God.'[7]

In the century after Irenaeus, the great Alexandrian theologian, Origen, made further contributions to the understanding of the cosmic aspects of Christ's person and work. In discussing the teaching of the letter to the Ephesians, I quoted the verse which declares that it is God's purpose 'to unite all thing in [Christ]'. The Greek verb here translated, following the Revised Standard Version, as 'to unite', is *anakephalaioun*, perhaps more commonly translated as 'to recapitulate' or 'to sum up'. Origen picks up this verb and sees the world-process as a cosmic redemption, in which whatever has gone wrong in the universe is being restored to its pristine perfection in Christ, that is to say, in what was the conception and intention of God. Again this may seem a very grandiose understanding of Jesus Christ, but he does not seem to have understood it as making an exclusive claim, for he tells us: '[God's] rays were not enclosed in this man alone ... or the Light which is the divine Logos, which causes these rays, existed nowhere else.'[8]

Some echoes of cosmic christology were heard in the theology of Schleiermacher at the beginning of the modern period, but broadly speaking Allan Galloway was correct in saying that 'after the great patristic period, the idea of cosmic redemption never again featured significantly in official Christian theology'.[9] But even as Professor Galloway was writing these words in about 1951, there was being made in what may be called 'unofficial' theology a major new contribution to the theme of Christ and the cosmos. I refer, of course, to the work of the Jesuit, Pierre Teilhard de Chardin, who was forbidden to publish during his lifetime, but whose writings appeared from 1959 onwards and achieved enormous popularity. Many of the old ideas reappear in these writings, but now combined with modern cosmology, understood on evolutionary lines,[10] and expressed in a new terminology which introduces such words as 'biosphere', 'hominization', 'christogenesis' and so on. I was teaching theology at the University of Glasgow at the time when *The Phenomenon of Man* was published, and well remember the sensation which it caused, especially among many of the scientists.

This book and others which followed it were undoubtedly brilliant achievements, but a fault which we already noticed in discussing DuBose (see above, p. 113) was that it made it appear too easy to move from the phenomena to a theistic interpretation. Rightly or wrongly, one got the impression that there had been in the course of evolution a fairly steady and direct progression from the earliest stages of the universe on to the emergence of the human race and then on to the birth and career of Jesus as the paradigm of the human race and even as the goal and summation of the whole process. The Vatican itself warned at one point against an uncritical acceptance of Teilhard's teaching. Teilhard's vision also received adverse criticism from some scientists, especially biologists.

But even scientists opposed to a theistic interpretation of the cosmos seemed no longer confident in holding that the cosmos had come about by sheer chance, if only on the ground that, on current estimates, the universe has not been in existence long enough for that to have happened. Richard Dawkins, for instance, entitled one of his books *The Blind Watchmaker*, an expression which obviously rejects the view of Paley that the universe was designed and created by some infinitely wise and powerful Craftsman, on analogy with the way in which a watchmaker would make a watch. But Dawkins does not think that pure chance is the answer to the problem. It would seem that the watchmaker is not totally blind, and indeed Dawkins does say that a little sight is better than none at all. There would seem to be too much evidence of tentative groping in evolution to make it easy to believe that an all-wise all-powerful Being is directing the process, but one need not leap from that to the view that chance alone is at work. Maybe even God cannot foresee everything and has to experiment. But in any case, if we were on the right lines in the earlier parts of this chapter, we have not been thinking of God as a Being outside the process, but also as immanent within it, so that the analogy of the watchmaker is one that we have already rejected, though on theological rather than scientific grounds.

Another theological objection that has been brought against Teilhard is that he was too optimistic. Sin does not play any large part in his scheme, and the idea of a fallen cosmos, found in some theologians, is not a Teilhardian emphasis. Jesus Christ, in his view, is not so much cosmic Redeemer as cosmic Consummator. This contrast is not new in theology, and perhaps varies from generation to generation, as the universe and its history looks sometimes more, sometimes less, hospitable to human life and hopes. Still, when these and similar criticisms are taken into account, we must acknowledge that with Teilhard de Chardin the idea of the cosmic Christ has made a powerful comeback. It would have been even more powerful if he had been allowed to publish his theories in his lifetime and so have been able to receive the benefits of criticism and been spurred to further reflection.

Reduced to its barest outlines, the theology of the cosmic Christ seems to be expressible in three propositions:

1. The universe, so far as it is accessible to human understanding, is a divine creation and has a purpose.
2. That purpose is, in the words of Keats, to be 'a vale of

soul-making', in which we can trace the advance from inanimate matter to life and then to mind and personal being, instantiated on this planet by the human race.

3. Within this race has appeared Jesus Christ who, on the finite level, represents for us the mind of the Creator.

That is a truly staggering claim. One shrinks from making it, even in the name of faith. As we have seen, Christianity itself in its doctrine of the triune God, or in its recognition that not all of God's rays are enclosed in this one man or even in the social reality, the 'Christ-event' as it is sometimes called, of which this one man was the centre and inspiration, puts limits to the claim. The cosmos is so vast in both space and time that we must constantly be aware of our own ignorance and limitations. We may, I think, believe in an incarnation of God in Jesus Christ, but if we try to spell this out too precisely, we overstep the limits of faith and end up in a position no better than that of the fundamentalist who accepts as literal truth the mythological idea that in Christ God was walking the earth in the form of a man. But can we say that in Jesus Christ there dwells not the fullness but the essence of God, that essence being love? And can we say, without overstepping our inescapably human point of view, that if God has revealed himself in other Christs or will reveal himself at other times and in other parts of this vast universe, it will be the same essence, the same eternal Logos, though in forms unimaginable by us?

The Pre-existence of Jesus Christ

In the middle section of this book on 'stubborn questions', theological questions that refuse to go away, we have been concerned with incarnation. The idea is central in Christianity, and this or similar ideas are to be found in other religions, yet we have seen that it raises many problems. In the preceding chapters of the section, I have in the main been defending what I take to be the central meaning of incarnation from its detractors, while at the same time admitting that many of the traditional ways of stating the doctrine have used language which is sometimes mythological, sometimes involved in the now obsolete terminologies of philosophies that are no longer current coin. Out of respect for tradition and to preserve the sense of continuity with Christian origins, that language can still be used in the liturgy, but for teaching purposes it needs interpretation, simplification and modernization, such as the three-point formula which I suggested above (see p. 81) as encompassing the essence of Christian incarnational theology. But I contested the views of those who either wanted to get rid of incarnationalism altogether, or proposed reductionist interpretations which seemed to leave out points of value in the traditional doctrine. In this chapter, I want to turn my attention to a different group, those who feel that I have made too many concessions to the advocates of innovation and revision. Some writers, mostly Roman Catholic, take the view that my own treatment of incarnation has itself been reductionist, and, in particular, that I have failed to give recognition to the pre-existence of Jesus Christ.

I have always, of course, insisted on the full humanity of Jesus

Christ. Equally, however, I insist that he is distinctive, though this distinctiveness is not of such a kind as would demand supernatural powers beyond human capacity. If Jesus had such properties, they would make him of a different species from ourselves, and therefore he could be neither a Redeemer nor an Exemplar for the human race but an alien being, and the idea of a genuine incarnation would be destroyed. Jesus has his distinctiveness not because of *additional* properties or powers, but, and this is the scriptural teaching, because of a *lack* of something which other human beings have in common. Jesus, it is claimed, is 'one who in every respect has been tempted as we are, yet without sin' (Heb. 4.15). According to this statement, Jesus did not have additional properties, but since what he lacked was something negative, the sin that separates from God and mars a true humanity, his distinguishing mark is simply a full humanity, a humanity which is indeed the icon or image in which God intended to create the human race.

I would gladly consent to the following words: 'Jesus is a man as we all are, and he is therefore accessible and knowable to us as a man, with no special capacities or potentialities, with no admixture of a quality alien to us, with no supernatural endowment such as must make him a totally different being from us. He is man in such a way that he can be the natural brother of any other man.'[1] These words were not written by someone who denied that Christ is also God nor by someone giving a reductionist account of incarnation, but by Karl Barth, and surely no one among theologians of recent decades has exalted Christ more than Barth. So much is this the case that sometimes one wonders if Barth held consistently to his strong affirmation of the humanity of Christ! Yet in this he is simply holding to the Chalcedonian formula, which accords to Christ a fully human nature as well as a divine nature, and forbids any mixing or confusion of the two. Though he uses a different language from that of Barth, another theologian of recent times, Karl Rahner, comes to a very similar conclusion: 'Only someone who forgets that the essence of man is to be unbounded ... can suppose that it is impossible for there to be a man who, precisely by being man in the fullest sense (which we never attain) is God's existence into the world.'[2]

We can now come back to the theme of Christ's pre-existence and ask whether this can be understood in a way which is not reductionist but at the same time does not contradict the belief in the full, genuine humanity of Jesus Christ. It must be acknowledged that a belief in pre-existence does tend to lead in the direction of docetic and even mythological ideas of the person of Jesus Christ, by ascribing to him additional properties of a supernatural sort which in fact infringe his human status and in truth destroy the core of belief in incarnation. My conviction is that there is no inherent contradiction between acknowledging the full humanity of Christ and at the same time believing as the Church claimed, in opposition to Arius, that 'there never was a time when he was not', though here we just lack the language, because we are talking about a 'time' when we are trying to say something about a state of affairs 'before' time was created. This tortuous sentence itself indicates how difficult any discussion of pre-existence is bound to become. My principal critic in the pre-existence debate has been the Irish Catholic theologian, Dr Niall Coll, in his book *Christ in Eternity and Time*.[3] Occasionally, he seems to suggest that I have simply rejected the pre-existence of Christ.[4] But he has been a careful reader of my writings, and knows that my endeavour has been to find more satisfying ways of expressing whatever is of value in the idea.

My first attempt to deal with the problem was back in 1966. At that time, a young Scottish pastor, John Harvey, whose work in a rundown area of Glasgow I much admired, had attacked the idea of pre-existence in *The Expository Times*. In a thoughtful article on the Christ-hymn of Paul's letter to the Philippians (Phil. 2.5–11), Mr Harvey criticized some of the popular 'kenotic' theories of christology that were influential at that time. According to these kenoticists, Paul was teaching that the Logos or second Person of the Trinity had surrendered some of his divine prerogatives to undergo a *kenosis* or 'emptying', so that he might manifest the life of God on the human level. This was one of the main scriptural passages (not the only one, of course) which was cited as evidence that before the incarnation Christ had lived with the Father in heaven. Hence the affirmation of the Nicene Creed: 'He came down from heaven, and was made man.' Mr Harvey thought that modern man 'no longer accepts such ideas as pre-existence' and that we have on the whole stopped thinking ontologically, and are starting to think functionally and existentially.[5] If pre-existence is understood mythologically in terms of an apocalyptic Son of Man who comes down to earth from another realm, or even if these ideas are refined into more metaphysical terms, then Mr Harvey was surely right in thinking that pre-existence has become a stumbling block to belief, rather than an explanation. But in my reply, I claimed that the idea of pre-existence has a value that goes far beyond its mythological associations, and that it would be wrong to reject pre-existence in favour of a thoroughgoing adoptionism. So my first grappling with pre-existence was a defence of the idea, not a rejection.

The idea of pre-existence is one of the ways in which the New Testament writers tried to bring to expression their belief that the initiative in the Christ-event lay with God; or, to put the point in a slightly different way, that the event is understood on a more fundamental level when we see it as God's coming among human beings rather than as a man's exaltation to Godhood. As Paul expressed it in one of his letters, 'All this is from God' (2 Cor. 5.19). When Justin the Martyr was asked by his critics in the middle of the second century whether the Christian doctrine of incarnation meant that God had manifested himself in the world only 150 years earlier, he replied by appealing to the already traditional doctrine of the Word or Logos; 'Christ,' he claimed, 'is the first-born of God' and 'is the Logos of whom every race of men were partakers.'[6]

But how are we to think of this Logos? Though God is said to be One and simple, yet as soon as we begin to think about him, we must make some distinctions. In Christian faith, we distinguish between God the Father, the ultimate source of all being, whom we might call 'primordial Being', and God the Son or Logos, whom we may call 'expressive Being', God as he comes forth from his hidden ultimacy; for God, as Christians believe, is not some static monolith, but the God who creates a world and its history, coming forth from himself and pouring out being upon the creatures. Creation is already a self-giving, a self-emptying and self-spending on the part of God. The early Christian writers associated the Word (and so Christ) with creation as well as incarnation. When in the course of time the expressive Being of God becomes manifest in the human life of Christ who utterly empties himself in love, we may see that the creation itself has been recapitulated and the mystery of God has been revealed. We look back from Christ to the beginning and confess that 'all this is from God', and in saying this we are confessing at least part of what was intended by the doctrine of Christ's pre-existence.

What do I mean by saying 'at least part' of what was meant by pre-existence? I mean that there is still more to be said, for if Jesus Christ is indeed true God and true man, our concentration on Logos doctrine can lead to a docetic emphasis and needs to be supplemented by asking about his humanity. It is interesting to note that whereas Justin speaks of Christ as the 'first-born of God', Paul speaks of him as the 'first-born of creation' (Col. 1.16). If there was a genuine incarnation in Jesus of Nazareth, this seems to imply that in him we can see not only the creative expressive Logos that has been active since the beginning, but also the truly human and responsible obedience of one who was creaturely and susceptible to temptations such as beset all human existence.

But what would it mean to talk of the pre-existence of the man, Jesus of Nazareth? Here, I think, we again get help from Karl Barth, and especially from his rethinking of the doctrine of election. Barth's teaching was that from the beginning of all God's works and ways his creation would not be just, let us say, a work of art, but a creation including personal finite beings who could live in communion with God and even become his co-workers, because on the finite level they were made in his own image and likeness. On this earth (and we need not concern ourselves over what may be true elsewhere in the universe) these finite personal beings would be men and women. This would be no mass production, for each man and woman would have special talents and special circumstances, bringing with them that individual's election or vocation to a special way in which he or she would carry out God's purpose. Jesus Christ was such a human being, from the very beginning he pre-existed in the mind and purpose of God. Dr Coll seems to think that this would be something not having the reality of a 'personal' pre-existence, but could there be any pre-existence more real? To be elected to be both Redeemer and Exemplar (see above, p. 135) of the whole human race, to have one's being within the Being and purpose of the Father is surely reality in the highest degree, but it is at the same time the reality of an entire human being, even his human body. Jesus Christ was, so to speak, 'on his way' during all those unimaginable ages of evolution, and then of the history of Israel, and then of the life-story of the Blessed Virgin; all that time before his eventual birth, is finally gathered up in Christ.

Dr Coll is also troubled about whether the ideas presented above do not altogether obliterate any difference between Christ and the whole human race. I do not think that they do. Christ is indeed human, but there still remains that 'more' in Jesus Christ, a more which is also a less. He is like us in all respects except that he lacks sin, that is to say, he remains consistently in the closest union with God the Father. But although men and women still remain alienated from God, we are pointed toward the hope of a final universalism, in which through Christ the whole human creation will share with him the divine likeness.

Christology from Above or from Below?

Jesus Christ is at the centre of Christian faith, and it stands or falls with him. But how are we to think of him today? The theological world is itself divided on the question, and the ancient creeds are being called in question by many modern theologians. What is Christ's meaning for us, two thousand years after he lived and taught and died in Palestine?

The mainline churches still maintain the creeds and conciliar statements that have come down to us from the early centuries.[1] These defined the meaning of Jesus Christ for the Christians of those days. But although they still constitute the official standards of belief for the churches, and although they may be regularly recited in worship, do they actually convey much to the worshippers when we say or hear them, or do they adequately express what in our hearts we really believe about Jesus Christ or want to say about him? All formulations, ancient and modern alike, inevitably belong to the times that produced them, not only in language but in the conceptuality expressed in it. The Council of Chalcedon in 451 produced a statement about Jesus Christ that was intended to settle the controversies over his person that had been going on in the Church virtually since New Testament times, and the fact that the Chalcedonian definition retains, even today, a normative status for millions of Christians shows that the Council had a remarkable degree of success. Yet for most people in our time, if they have not been well instructed in patristic theology (and very few of them have been so instructed) Chalcedon is more likely to put them off than to enlighten them. It was Chalcedon that Karl Rahner had in mind when he wrote: 'The clearest formulations, the most sanctified statements, the classic condensations of the centuries-long work of the Church in prayer, reflection and struggle concerning God's mysteries, all these derive their life from the fact that they are not the end but the beginning, not the goal but the means, truths which open the way to the ever greater truth.'[2] Chalcedon was an important milestone in the Church's progress toward a deeper understanding of Jesus Christ, but it left plenty of scope for further reflection.

I do not want, however, to seem now to be criticizing Chalcedon, after having in the chapters preceding this one defended the traditional christology against what I considered to be exaggerated and unjustified attacks. It remains an ecumenical document of the highest importance, uniting the churches in both space and time. In words of Aloys Grillmeier, '[In Chalcedon] as in almost no other formula from the early councils, all the important centres of Church life and all the trends of the theology of that time, Rome, Alexandria, Constantinople and Antioch, have contributed toward the framing of a common expression of faith'.[3] The underlying philosophy which found expression in such words as 'nature', 'substance', 'person', 'subsistence', represents a way of understanding that is no longer current, but we have to be careful that any new formula we may devise is one that does not leave out whatever was essential or judged to be essential in Chalcedon.

The Chalcedonian definition is often called the 'two-natures' doctrine, and although that is only a partial description, it does draw attention to an important feature of the definition. We might today have difficulties with this concept of 'nature'. In our time, some philosophers would deny that there is a universal 'human nature', while others would question whether it is legitimate to talk of a 'divine nature'. Yet the doctrine of the two natures was saying in its own way something that the Christian religion seems bound to say in some way or other, namely, that if Christ is indeed mediator between God and men, then he must somehow be – and here I find myself reverting almost unconsciously to some other language of the Council of Chalcedon – 'consubstantial' with God on the one side and with the human race on the other. The word 'consubstantial' here translates that notorious Greek word, *homoousios*, which might also be translated 'of the same being'. Here we begin to enter the tangled thickets of language which seemed to thrive at the ancient councils, and that have made their pronouncements virtually unintelligible to modern minds. We have to ask, for instance, whether to confess the double consubstantiality in Jesus Christ is the same as confessing that there concur in his person two complete natures, one divine and one human. This at once raises the question about the relation between the terms 'being' (*ousia*) and 'nature' (*physis*). Are these terms synonymous, and, if not, how do they differ? And how do they relate to the one 'subsistence' (*hypostasis*) of Jesus Christ, also called his one 'person' (*prosopon*)?[4] Lurking in the background is the more radical question raised by, among others, Bultmann, Schleiermacher and Luther whether such questions demand a correct answer from the person who asks whether salvation or a right relation to God is offered in Jesus Christ. (This issue is considered in the chapter on Bultmann, see above, pp. 108–9.)

Perhaps the awkward questions raised about Chalcedon in the last paragraph can be satisfactorily answered and, as I have already said, I am not embarking on a destructive criticism of Chalcedon. It has served the Church well and deserves our deepest respect. But it simply does not speak to the world of our time.

My point, however, is that any new formulations which we may attempt in our time must not say less than the Chalcedonian fathers attempted to say, that is, they must seek to say that Jesus Christ is one with God the Father and yet is also one with us human beings. That is the paradox at the heart of Christianity. To abandon it would mean the collapse of Christian faith. There is no more urgent task for contemporary theologians than to struggle with this paradox, to try to express it in terms more readily accessible to people of our time, to show that it is not sheer contradiction. If someone asks us today, 'What do you think of Jesus Christ?', can we give an answer that will make sense to a modern person, and yet will claim for Jesus what the Church has traditionally claimed for him?

The claim is so overwhelming and the paradox of the God-man is so acute that from the very beginning it has been difficult to maintain, and one side or the other has been abandoned. In the early centuries, there were many people impressed by the figure of Jesus who had little difficulty in believing that he must be a divine being, but who could not accept that he was truly human. Those who believed in this way were called 'docetists' for they held that Jesus only seemed like a man but was in fact a purely supernatural being from another sphere of existence. They failed to recognize that Jesus Christ could not be a genuine mediator unless he was fully and truly a human being – 'complete in humanity', 'truly human', 'consubstantial with us', to quote the reiterated phrases of Chalcedon. At the other end of the spectrum were those who recognized Jesus Christ as a profound teacher and as an outstandingly holy man, but denied that he should be accorded any divine status. But such a view is also destructive of Jesus' mediatorial position. Christian faith cannot relinquish its belief – some might say, its impossible belief – that somehow Jesus Christ bridges the gap between the divine and the human, and is 'at home' on both sides of the divide.

In the secular time in which we live, belief in God has declined, but there are probably many people who still respect Jesus Christ both for his moral teaching and for the inspiring example of his life and death, though there are others who regard him as a figure belonging only to the past, and having nothing to contribute to the modern world. But, within the Christian Church, the situation is different. Many of its members still think in docetic terms, especially so-called fundamentalists, even though the Church has condemned docetism for centuries. These fundamentalists think they honour Christ by stressing his divine otherness, though by doing so, they unintentionally break his solidarity with the human race.

This is the difficult situation in which the Church of today has to speak of Jesus Christ. It would be hard to find any modern creed that comes near to reproducing the evenhandedness and comprehensiveness of Chalcedon. We have the perhaps impossible task of speaking of the God-man without lapsing into docetism on the one side or falling into a reductionism on the other.

In seeking to re-express the teaching about the person of Jesus Christ, the first decision to be made is where to begin. There are two points of entry, and contemporary theologians are divided between them. In popular parlance (though its use can be found as far back as the third century) the choice is between 'christology from above' and 'christology from below'. The way from above begins from the divine side and is reflected in the official creeds. The Nicene Creed, for instance, speaks of Jesus Christ as 'the only Son of God' and tells how 'he came down from heaven' and became incarnate as a human being. In course of time, this christology from above, entrenched in the recognized creeds of the Church, became the dominant way of understanding christology. In this chapter, however, I shall be defending the christology from below, as the form most likely to be understood in a secular age like ours. Jesus Christ was indisputably not a mythical but a fully human and historical figure. As we are ourselves human beings and therefore have some knowledge of human nature, whereas the divine nature always remains a mystery, it seems only common sense that in thinking about the one whom we call the God-man, we should begin from that aspect of his being which is closest to us. I believe also that historically this is the way by which the first Christians entered into a faithful relation to Jesus Christ and that the approach to christology from the human side is the one that fits best with the idea of incarnation, God meeting us where we are.

One has to remember also (and this is often forgotten) that although thinking about Jesus Christ may begin from the human side, it does not necessarily end with a purely humanistic account of him, nor should we be intimidated by someone who tells us that the approach to christology from the human side is bound to end in adoptionism, as if that could settle the argument. There are various forms of adoptionism, and the word is often no more than a term of censure.

In any case, it is simply a matter of fact that at the present time responsible theologians in several traditions have decided that a new emphasis must be placed on the humanity of Jesus Christ, and that any theological account of his person must begin from that point and resist any temptation to compromise it. If Jesus Christ is the mediator or High Priest between God and man, then, whatever else may be true of him, he is human and in solidarity with the whole human race. 'For,' as the writer to the Hebrews tells us, 'we have not a High Priest who is unable to sympathize with our weaknesses, but one who in every respect has been tempted as we are, yet without sin' (Heb. 4.15).

This method in christology is no innovation. It could, in fact, be argued that it is the oldest of all. The early disciples had known Jesus as a man from Nazareth, before they thought of him as the Christ and long before they came to believe that he had an even more exalted status. Thus Peter, who had been the first to recognize Jesus as the Christ, declared in the course of his Pentecost sermon: 'This Jesus, whom you crucified, God has made both lord and Christ' (Acts 2.36). I used to tell my students that Peter was fortunate to be elected Bishop of Rome in the first century, for at a later time he would have risked being accused of adoptionism. It is a very similar christology that we meet in Paul. He elaborates it in terms of the first Adam and the new Adam or last Adam. The first Adam had indeed been created together with his spouse in the image of God, but very soon, it appears, that image was marred by sin and made virtually unrecognizable. The new Adam, by contrast, fulfils God's programme for mankind by showing forth in its fullness the divine image in which the first human couple had been created. This was virtually a new creation, the emergence of a new humanity, though this new humanity was the realization of the project that had been a potentiality from the beginning. (See Rom. 5.12–19 and 1 Cor. 15.42–50.)

But someone may object, 'Is this really an adequate account of Paul's christology?' There are other passages in his letters, perhaps especially the Christ-hymn (Phil. 2.5–11) which seem to speak clearly of a pre-existent divine figure who, at a particular time, lays aside his divine prerogatives and comes down to earth as a man. Must we not, on the basis of this and some other passages, ascribe to Paul the full classical christology of the creeds – a christology which is not from below but from above, since it begins from the pre-existent Son or Word, who for a time becomes man and lives on earth, and then returns to the heavenly places? This objection depends on questions of exegesis. While many scholars have thought that Paul did teach a doctrine of the pre-existence of the Christ, an increasing number nowadays believe that no such interpretation is demanded, at least, not in the sense of a personal pre-existence. Among them is James Dunn. He sees the Christ-hymn as of a piece with the Adam christology. Paul is telling a single story, with two foci. One focus is the figure of Adam, the hypothetical or mythological founder of the race, who was made in the image of God, but who, through sin, failed to fulfil God's purpose for him and so brought evil on all his descendants. The other focus is Jesus Christ, the historical founder of the new covenant who faced the same choices as Adam ('tempted in all things like as we are') but who did not sin, and who brought the image (*eikon*) of God to manifestation in human history.[5] The story is the one so beautifully told in Cardinal Newman's great hymn:

> O loving wisdom of our God!
>   When all was sin and shame,
> A second Adam to the fight
>   And to the rescue came.
>
> O wisest love! that flesh and blood
>   Which did in Adam fail,
> Should strive afresh against the foe,
>   Should strive, and should prevail.

The story takes place in the realm of 'flesh and blood', that is to say, in the human realm, in history. The principal figures in the story are the first Adam, the supposed progenitor of the human race, and the new Adam, Jesus Christ, the founder of a new and redeemed humanity. This christology of Paul therefore certainly begins from the human side, but, as I said earlier in the chapter, it is not necessarily confined to the human sphere. Perhaps in a historical sense it could be described as a kind of adoptionism, but an adoptionism free from the objectionable features found in later developments. In both Paul and Newman we have clear statements that the ultimate agent behind these human dramas is God and I believe we could extend the same interpretation to Peter's sermon in Acts. 'All this is from God who through Christ reconciled us to himself', writes Paul, while Newman sees at work 'God's loving wisdom' or the same thing seen from a different viewpoint, his 'wisest love'. Reaching back to Peter, we find him attributing the events of Jesus' life to 'the definite plan and foreknowledge of God'.

So this early christology, although beginning from below, is already recognizing that in a sense 'all this is from God', and is therefore pointing forward to the 'christology from above', stated clearly in the prologue to John's Gospel: 'In the beginning was the Word and the Word was with God . . . and the Word became flesh' (John 1.1 and 14). That later type of christology turns the first story around, and begins from God or the Word of God rather than from the humanity of Jesus. The later incarnational christology is more profound and was destined to be the type of christology that became dominant in the creeds. But this does not mean that the earlier christology was invalidated or rendered obsolete. Karl Rahner puts the question: 'Is the [early] christology which comes from below, with the human experience of Jesus, merely primitive? Or has it something special to say to us, which classical christology does not say with the same clarity?'[6] Of course, I need hardly say that Rahner is not commending any kind of adoptionism suggesting that there is a kind of automatic evolution toward christhood in the sense of a natural upward striving that leaves God out of account.

I think, however, that it may be claimed that an adequate christology must find room for both the approach from below and that from above. The centuries-long dominance of the approach from above has led to a persistent drift toward docetism, and in a secular age like ours, that simply means that Jesus Christ appears increasingly irrelevant. Thence comes about the current concern of theologians to restore a proper sense of Christ's humanity.

The old Adamic christology continued to appear in the period between the New Testament and the Council of Nicaea, though as one option among several. It was powerfully expressed in the second century by Irenaeus and much enriched by his teaching, which anticipated the modern view that human nature is not a static essence but open to growth and development, both in individuals and in the race. Irenaeus taught that Adam and Eve, though 'made in the image and likeness of God', did not have that perfection at the moment of their creation. They began like children who have to grow to maturity. The image of God in them was a potentiality which might or might not be brought to realization. In Irenaeus' own words:

> Now, it was necessary that man should be in the first instance created; and, having been created, should receive growth; and having received growth, should be strengthened; and, having been strengthened, should abound; and, having abounded, should recover from the disease of sin; and, having recovered, should be glorified; and being glorified, should see his Lord.[7]

The first attempt to create men and women in the image and likeness of God was frustrated through sin. But 'in the last times, not by the will of the flesh, nor by the will of man, but by the good pleasure of the Father, his hands formed a living man, in order that Adam might be [re]created after the image and likeness of God'.[8] As in the christology of Paul the Apostle, this Irenaean christology is completed by the recognition of the divine agency at work – it is the union of the Word with 'man living and perfect, receptive of the perfect Father'.

The most striking and controversial exposition of christology from below in the preconciliar period came from Paul of Samosata, Bishop of Antioch in the middle years of the third century. Emil Brunner, a conservative theologian of the twentieth century, showed his contempt for modern theology by describing Paul of Samosata as 'the first Ritschlian, or, in a more general way, as the first modern theologian'.[9] I should perhaps say that I do not share Brunner's hostility either to this early Bishop of Antioch or to modern theologians. Although the bishop's views were condemned in 268, like many other heretics or supposed heretics, he is probably due for at least a measure of rehabilitation in the more tolerant atmosphere of our times. However, he is still commonly regarded as the arch-exponent of the adoptionist heresy, but this may be an unfair judgement.

Actually, one cannot be quite sure of what Paul of Samosata taught, since we have only fragmentary information, but I would think that while he certainly taught a christology from below, he modified it in such ways that it could be incorporated into a more inclusive christology. According to the scanty information we have about his trial,[10] it seems likely that Paul did not believe in a personal pre-existence of Jesus Christ, but we have seen reason to doubt whether Paul the Apostle believed in such a pre-existence either (see above, p. 146). But Paul of Samosata, though affirming that Jesus Christ was a human being like us, recognized that he had a special relation to the Word or Logos. He claimed that the Logos came to Christ 'from above' (*anothen*) while his humanity was 'from here' (*enteuthen*). He denied that the Logos took the place of a human soul or mind in Christ, and he could hardly be faulted for this denial, for in the next century the Church would condemn Apollinarius precisely for affirming what Paul had denied. It may have been this denial on the part of Paul that led to the accusation that he held that Christ's relation to the Logos was one of love or friendship rather than ontological, a relation of being. But here we seem to be entering very debatable territory. Is a union in love not an ontological relation? I think that it is, but the meanings of the words used in this discussion need to be very carefully scrutinized. More problematic is Paul's apparent unitarianism, for even if we accept that there was a union between the Word and Jesus Christ, Paul seems to have separated the Word from the Father. But I think we must say that our knowledge of Paul of Samosata is so uncertain that the most charitable course would be to accept that his views were a legitimate theolegoumenon, especially when we remember that they come from ante-Nicene times.

After the time of the ecumenical councils, the christology from above was dominant among the great majority of Christians down to modern times. Schleiermacher, often regarded as the first modern theologian, was critical of the Chalcedonian definition, believing that its language was incoherent. He reverted to the older christology from below, and understood christhood as the unfolding of a true humanity. 'In Jesus,' he wrote, 'the creation of human nature has been perfected.'[11] He could also write: 'As certainly as Christ was a man, there must reside in human nature the possibility of taking up the divine into itself, just as did happen in Christ.'[12] This comes pretty close to a pure adoptionism. The language about human nature 'taking up the divine into itself' suggests that humanity can rise to divinity by its own power, whereas the traditional language has talked rather of 'taking of the manhood into God' (Athanasian creed). Schleiermacher's christology is certainly humanistic, but even he draws back from a pure humanism which would in any case invalidate his concept of christhood or God-manhood. So we find him claiming that in Jesus Christ there is a new implanting of the God-consciousness, though such an idea is not easily integrated into his christology as a whole.

Since Schleiermacher's time, there have been many attempts to construct a theology from below. I mention only some recent examples. Wolfhart Pannenberg declares that 'where the statement that Jesus is God would contradict his real humanity, one would probably rather surrender the confession of his divinity than doubt that he was a man'. He agrees that all christology points toward a doctrine of incarnation, but it is the conclusion of the argument, and if the idea is brought in too early, it introduces a mythological flavour.[13] Among Anglican theologians, David Jenkins[14] and John Robinson[15] have both made the human Jesus central in their christologies. The Eastern Orthodox theologian John Meyendorff is an enthusiast for Chalcedon, but he does not think that this conflicts with an anthropological approach. He finds such approaches already foreshadowed in Byzantine christology, and claims that 'human nature, at the contact of God, does not disappear; on the contrary, it becomes fully human'.[16] But the most convincing of all the contemporary examples of christology from below is that of Karl Rahner. His way into the subject is by an anthropology derived from transcendental Thomism, according to which a human being is characterized by self-transcendence toward God. Jesus Christ is the human being in whom transcendence has reached the point at which in his humanity the image and likeness of God are manifested. So Rahner can say: 'Christology is at once the end and the beginning of anthropology.'[17] Or, to go back to Paul the Apostle: 'He is the image (*eikon*) of the invisible God' (Col. 1.15).

I am not saying that the christology from below is the only possible way forward in our time, but it does have some advantages, not the least of which is intelligibility, and it certainly does not deserve to be dismissed as adoptionism.

13

Development of Doctrine

When I was teaching theology in the United States in the 1960s, I often felt bewildered by the sheer multiplicity of options that were competing for allegiance in the theological world of those days. As well as the mainstreams of theological opinion. Barthian, Tillichian, etc., new fashions were appearing, and one heard of the 'death of God', of the 'secular city' and its allurements, of 'black theology' and of other new theologies claiming to be on the cutting edge. How could one judge among the competing claims?

Perhaps that particular decade was more than usually unsettled. There have been many such times in the past history of theology, and very likely there will be more ahead of us. The belief that there exists a 'faith which was once for all delivered to the saints' (Jude 3) seems very questionable when we look back over the history of Christian doctrine. Current New Testament scholarship stresses the diversity of views already circulating in the first century, in contrast to the biblical theology of even fifty years ago when the unity of the whole Bible, not just the New Testament, was a popular theme. But today, no up-to-date dictionary of theology would omit an article on 'Development of Doctrine'.

It is true that the place of tradition has always been recognized, but whereas today the word 'tradition' is understood as the *activity* of passing on doctrines and practices with some possible modifications, it was formerly considered to be the *freezing* of an unchanging 'deposit', carefully preserved from each generation to the next. Now the fact of change is recognized, except among so-called 'fundamentalists', whether biblical, doctrinal or liturgical. So the question about change remains with us, and we have to make judgements about these changes. Development is not just something that occasionally happens in theology, it belongs to all theology even if it is sometimes more obvious than at other times. Because it belongs to all theology, it has become itself a topic for theological study.

Obviously, the factors entering into this development are numerous and complex. I wrote a moment ago that development does not just happen, and by that I meant that it is not just a fate originating outside theology and then determining its course. Yet that is only partially true. To some extent, theological development is influenced by the historical and cultural conditions in the midst of which theological study is pursued. Perhaps the theologian could make a strenuous effort to empty his or her mind of the presuppositions of the particular society or epoch in which reflection was taking place, but it is doubtful how far such presuppositionless thinking can be achieved. To a large extent, even though we may reject some elements in the prevalently received cultural outlook, we cannot escape its influence. In the modern world, we are for the most part bound to see and understand things as post-Enlightenment men and women, and this inevitably conflicts with the way in which people saw and understood similar events in New Testament, patristic, medieval or Reformation times. So to the extent that Christian doctrines incorporate presuppositions derived from those earlier times, we find that our minds are inhospitable to them. Many years ago, Rudolf Bultmann wrote:

It is impossible to use electric light and the radio, and to avail ourselves of modern medical and surgical discoveries, and at the same time to believe in the New Testament world of demons and spirits. We may think we can manage it in our own lives, but to expect others to do so is to make the Christian faith unintelligible and unacceptable to the modern world.[1]

D. F. Strauss wrote something similar a century earlier. When such a situation arises, either we have to give up Christian faith or its doctrines have to be developed in new ways to take account of the new knowledge.

Everyone knows that in the past two or three centuries great multitudes of people in the western world have in fact given up Christian faith as irreconcilable with the presuppositions of the scientific age. But it is also the case that many people have continued to be Christians. They have believed that there is something precious and irreplaceable in Christianity, and they have sought ways of re-expressing their beliefs in the post-Enlightenment age. They cannot 'prove' the truth of these beliefs with the kind of evidence used to support a scientific hypothesis, but it is amazing how far scientific and religious beliefs can be shown to be compatible. Whether or not one can say that there are religious or other non-scientific ways of knowing, e.g., mysticism, many people continue to believe despite the absence of 'proofs' for, as I said, they believe that something very precious is at stake here. Development is not just forced on theology by cultural changes or scientific advance. It does not just happen. It is something that arises out of theology itself as a theological task. Great ideas and great movements of the human spirit have a life and creativity of their own, so that they grow and develop in the course of history. If the theologian and the ordinary Christian believer are right in holding that with Jesus Christ a new revelation came to the human race, that is to say, a novel, profound and revolutionary understanding of God and of the highest values open to mankind, then they accept as an imperative the need to rethink the meaning of Christianity in relation to the world in which they live. Christian faith has within itself a dynamic which is always in search of new and more adequate ways of expression, not only in theology, but in morals, in society, in spirituality and so on. I am writing myself as a Christian theologian, but do not for a moment deny that comparable movements of the spirit are found outside of Christianity, as indeed was made clear in the very first chapter of this book on the 'parallel lives' of Jesus and Socrates (see above, pp. 1–12).

A word which has been used quite often by New Testament scholars in recent years and which helps to express what I mean is 'trajectory'. Of course, the biblical scholars use it in a more technical sense than I do, but it does supply a useful metaphor for what I am trying to say. The metaphor comes from artillery. When a shell is fired from a gun, it follows a certain path. This path depends on a great many factors – the weight, shape and velocity of the projectile as it leaves the gun, the pull of gravity and the effects of air resistance, the atmospheric conditions prevailing at the time, and so on.

If anyone feels that the comparison of Christian doctrine with an explosive shell is inappropriate, one could equally well express the idea by comparing with a golf ball driven from the tee. The path described by that ball being driven through the air will be determined partly by the skill of the player, who will have to calculate (though tacitly, one might almost say, instinctively) how much force must be put into the stroke, and how much elevation has to be imparted to the ball in order to counteract the force of gravity so as to cause the ball to travel as closely as possible to the green. But allowance has to be made also for factors not originating with the player, such as the wind blowing across the fairway and the humidity or dryness of the atmosphere. All in all, this simplified description indicates a highly complicated situation. If one tries to move from the physical image of the shell or golf ball to the subtler notion of a doctrine or theory moving through historical time, it is obvious that the factors involved are even harder to identify.

It may be worth quoting some words of the New Testament scholar Patrick Henry on this model of trajectories. While acknowledging that 'any application of models from one realm of discourse to another presents problems as well as new opportunities, and missiles and space ships moving through their trajectories are not the same thing as ideas and persons moving through history', he nevertheless sees the importance of the comparison in the suggestion that 'ideological tendencies and psychological states have a kind of independent life which can be plotted along historical graphs'.[2] The point is that ideas – or, at least, some ideas – have a kind of inherent dynamic. Scholars have spent much time and effort in trying to discover where ideas have come from, but the trajectory model suggests that one has to be concerned also with where these ideas are going.

There are, of course, different ways in which one might interpret these trajectories, for we have noted that many complex factors enter into them. I have stressed that development of doctrine does not just happen at haphazard, but sometimes it does seem to be the case that impersonal and even accidental factors do operate, for instance, the idea may be deflected from its original direction by some sudden political event. But such an event would rarely be a complete explanation. The dynamic creativity of the idea itself, to say nothing of the intelligent contribution of those who are seeking to propagate it, may ensure that the idea survives and even flourishes in a new form in the new milieu where it has arrived. Perhaps this sounds too idealistic, but there may be some truth in the ancient saying, *Magna est veritas, et praevalebit* (3 Esdras, 4.41, Vulgate) – 'Great is truth, and it will prevail.' The widespread occurrence of so-called 'heresy' in the Christian Church is evidence that truth does not always prevail and that Christian doctrine is not immune from corruption and always 'develops' rather than decays. On the other hand, the intellectual or spiritual strength of an idea or teaching is surely a factor in determining whether it is going to survive in spite of political or cultural hostilities. I suppose a Marxist historian, if he stuck closely to Marxist orthodoxy, would claim that Christian doctrines belong only to the superstructure of history, and are finally determined by economic factors which are supposed to lie more deeply. There are many positivist historians who would think along similar lines. But if the human being himself or herself is not simply a natural phenomenon wholly determined by material forces, then such reductionist accounts of human history are not adequate. I am not, of course, denying that they have the merit of drawing attention to important phenomena that do shape human destiny and that were often overlooked in a more idealistic era when the course of events was in too facile a fashion interpreted as the action of God or the self-realization of the human spirit.

The remarks made in the last couple of paragraphs show us just how important are our presuppositions when we consider such a topic as the development of doctrine. That development is itself one aspect of the history of the Christian Church, and I doubt if ecclesiastical history (or any kind of history) can be studied apart from some presuppositions, which cannot be dismissed out of hand as mere prejudices. We have in fact in earlier chapters acknowledged that people in our own time are deeply influenced in their thinking by the Enlightenment, though we have denied that it is not impossible to break free of it in some cases. I think we are now at a sufficient distance from the Enlightenment to be able to think critically about it. Is this not shown by the rise in recent years of 'postmodernism', no doubt itself open to damaging criticisms but not without some justification when contrasted with 'modernism'? It would be a betrayal of whatever was of value in the Enlightenment if we were to accept slavishly and uncritically everything it has bequeathed to us. If its challenge, as Kant put it, was 'Dare to know!' then we must be prepared to become enlightened about the Enlightenment itself, and where necessary to criticize some of its presuppositions.

Let me say a little more about this subject of ecclesiastical history, of which development of doctrine is a part. Is it possible to write ecclesiastical history without some prejudices, either for or against Christianity? Would a positivist, or even more a Marxist understanding of history be free of prejudice or in any sense truly scientific? Some years ago, when I was thinking about these matters, I asked a friend, a distinguished ecclesiastical historian, whether ecclesiastical history differs in any significant respects from general history. The scholar in question had in fact been professor of general history in a famous university before he took up teaching in the special field of ecclesiastical history. He answered my question in very moderate terms. He saw a great deal of common ground between the work of the two types of historian. Both have to ascertain as accurately as possible what we call the 'facts' of the matter (*wie es eigentlich geschehen*, 'how it really happened', in Ranke's famous phrase). 'Getting the facts right' is still what the popular mind regards as the chief task of the historian, there are ways of doing this which are recognized by all kinds of historians, and the rules governing historical method have to be respected if the work of the historian concerned is to have integrity. The facts have to be established as honestly and accurately as possible, but the work of the historian is still only beginning, for now questions arise about the causation, interrelation and interpretation of the facts.

Let me give an illustration of what I have in mind. About ten years ago, I was lecturing in Chicago, and my host kindly told me that on a certain evening he had arranged for me to have some relaxation in the form of an evening at the opera. He mentioned (or, rather, I thought he mentioned) that the work to be performed was Verdi's *Otello*, with Sir George Solti conducting. On the day of the performance, I discovered that the work in question was *Attila*, a rarely performed work of Verdi composed nearly forty years before *Otello*. A famous incident in the career of Attila is featured in the opera. About the year 452, Attila and his army of Huns came down from northern Italy and threatened Rome itself. Something, however, occurred and changed the action of Attila and his host. Instead of attacking Rome, they turned about and went off elsewhere. Rome had been saved. But what had actually happened? Three explanations were offered.

The traditional and popularly believed explanation was that Peter and Paul, the patrons of the city martyred there under Nero about 400 years earlier, appeared in the sky and scared off the besiegers. This scene was vividly presented on the stage, with the aid of modern theatrical effects. A second explanation was that the Pope of that time (Leo the Great of Chalcedonian fame) went out of the city gate to entreat with Attila and to reason with him about the merits of Nicene Christianity. This scene too was depicted by the broad-minded librettist. I was just sinking into what Coleridge called 'that willing suspension of disbelief for the moment', when a glance at the programme notes acquainted me with a third explanation. According to the author of these notes (perhaps a radical New Testament scholar with Marxist leanings?) the 'real' explanation of Attila's retreat from Rome was that there was an acute shortage of supplies for the army and that simultaneously there had erupted an outbreak of plague.

So how does one 'explain' Attila's departure? Let us go back to my friend the ecclesiastical historian, for we heard only the beginning of his reply to the question of how or whether an ecclesiastical historian might differ from a general historian. He would be at one with his secular colleague in rejecting the story of supernatural guardians coming from the skies to the defence of the city, as being inadmissible by the rules of what can be accepted as historical evidence. But equally he would have rejected the idea that one must look for the 'real' cause in some material circumstances, though such a circumstance as a threat to supplies may have been a contributory cause. He would have attached most importance to the conversation or negotiation between Attila and Leo. As he expressed it to me, he claimed that the ecclesiastical historian in seeking the motivation behind historical happenings allows a weight to such influences as faith, spiritual aspiration, religious belief – a weight which many secular historians would not allow at all.

One might think that this particular argument had been settled many years ago in the work of Max Weber. In opposition to the Marxist view that our beliefs, including our religious beliefs or even especially them, are determined by economic factors, Weber produced a vast array of evidence to prove that the modern European capitalist system was the product of developments in the understanding of Christian doctrine at the time of the Reformation. Weber, like my ecclesiastical historian, did not make the rash claim that the changes in belief wrought by Protestantism constituted the *only* cause for certain subsequent events. The complex web of history contains many threads, perhaps far more than historians identify. But especially if we are thinking of the history of thought and belief, we must recognize the role of intellectual, moral and spiritual factors, and need not seek them principally in, let us say, the political considerations that pressed on Constantine or on the German princes who supported Luther.

What point have we now reached in our enquiry into the development of doctrine? We have acknowledged that such development does take place, but we have tried to avoid one-sidedness. There have been too many lapses and ambiguities for us to believe in any facile way in a direct guidance by the Holy Spirit into an ever-deepening truth, as perhaps some fundamentalists do. We might be able to agree that as we meditate on events and sayings derived from the Christ-event itself through preaching or Scripture or liturgical action, we find these making an increasingly significant impression upon us as they unfold themselves in the life of the worshipping community. Such meditation may also bring with it new language for the better communication of new meanings.

Christianity or any similar movement which possesses a body of teaching is bound to become diversified in the course of its history, yet there are limits to what it can become without losing its identity. Christianity cannot become just anything. Discussing the development of doctrine in the early Church, Maurice Wiles writes: 'The idea of radical discontinuity in doctrine is not strictly conceivable.'[3] But how does one judge continuity and how much continuity must there be? Let us come back to the vexed question of christology for a concrete example.

Karl Rahner was bold enough to write: 'We have not only the right but the duty to look at [the Chalcedonian formula] as end *and* as beginning.'[4] The formula solved some of the problems that were vexing the Church in the fifth century and in that sense was an end, but history was going to continue and theological reflection was going to continue and a time was bound to come when Chalcedon would no longer be clearly saying what the Church then and presumably the Church now wants to say about Jesus Christ as the centre of its faith and of its knowledge of God. I believe we do not want to say *less* about Jesus Christ than the Chalcedonian fathers said – we do not want to be reductionist – but for many of our contemporaries, perhaps even for ourselves, the old language and its underlying conceptuality offers stumbling blocks to understanding and interpretation.

Let me now set beside it a statement from Maurice Wiles, published two years after *The Myth of God Incarnate* and suggested as 'an acceptable alternative' to incarnational christology. The statement runs as follows:

> [Jesus] was not just one who had taught about God; he was not just one who had lived a life of perfect human response to God. He had lived a life that embodied God's character and action in the world. As prophets in the past had expressed the word of God that had come to them not only in speech but in symbolic action, so in a far more comprehensive way did Jesus. The impact not merely of his teaching but of his whole person communicated the presence and the power of God with an unprecedented sense of directness and finality.[5]

This does seem to me to be an adequate statement of the Church's faith in Christ, and I would personally find it acceptable as saying all that was of importance in the Chalcedonian formula, or all that is implied in the notion of an incarnation. The last sentence in particular is almost like an echo or an exposition of the famous Johannine verse: 'And the Word was made flesh and dwelt among us' (John 1.14).

I do not think there is any major difference between what Wiles affirms about Jesus Christ and what I would affirm myself (see above, p. 81). I would, however, want to retain some of the ancient formulas, to emphasize the continuity of the Church of the past with that of the present. In particular, the Niceno-Constantinapolitan Creed is the most ecumenical document that we have, and when we recite it in the liturgy, it links together great masses of the faithful through space and time. But if the ancient creeds are used on liturgical occasions, it is desirable that their meaning is to be expounded in up-to-date formulations.

Although we have noted that development of doctrine has

always been going on in the Church, we have also seen that it has attracted special attention in modern times. The credit for bringing the problem of development to attention is usually given to Cardinal Newman. He had been thinking about the problem for several years before he published *An Essay on the Development of Christian Doctrine*.[6] This book was first published in 1845, the year of Newman's conversion from Anglicanism to Roman Catholicism, and the thinking behind it was not simply that of an academic theologian but very much the existential concern of a man struggling with the difficulties that stand in the way of faith. He had begun the book while still a priest of the Church of England, but it was published only after his conversion, and the definitive edition did not appear until 1878, by which time the book itself had undergone considerable development. I want only to make some brief comments on the seven 'notes' (he originally called them 'tests') by which developments are to be assessed. Newman offered these proposals quite modestly, saying they are not all of equal value and the list is not exhaustive. I have chosen four, that seem to me to be useful still.[7]

Newman's first note is 'preservation of type'. He explains this by means of a biological analogy. A doctrinal development is (to use his own word) 'genuine' if we can discern an underlying type in various manifestations. A butterfly, for example, preserves the type of its species, even if it begins as an egg and at a later stage of its development is a caterpillar and then a chrysalis, still very unlike a butterfly in its mature form. Newman gives as an ecclesiastical illustration, an institution rather than a doctrine, namely, priesthood. Christian priests have looked and acted differently at different times in history, but there is a persistent type recognizable in Chaucer's medieval parson, and again in Goldsmith's eighteenth-century vicar of 400 years later.[8]

Newman's third note is the 'power of assimilation'. New knowledge, even if it may seem at first sight to be damaging to Christian doctrine, may turn out to be amenable to assimilation. The example is not Newman's, but I would cite the biological theory of evolution as a good illustration. In an earlier chapter, we have seen how DuBose took evolution into his theology (see above, pp. 111–2), thereby adding new significance and wonder to the doctrine of creation. To many people, evolution seemed like the refutation of Christianity.[9]

'Logical sequence' is Newman's fourth note, and in spite of his use of the word 'logical', Newman seems to be thinking not of straightforward deduction of new truths from others already held but rather of a slow growth of knowledge based on meditation on a few basic ideas that seem to possess a certain dynamic which, once it has been glimpsed, impresses itself more and more on the believer. One may think, for instance, of the growth over three or four centuries of the doctrine of the triune God. This was not logical deduction as it would be understood by a scientist or philosopher, and I do not think either that it could be explained as making explicit what was already understood implicitly. It was a deepening rather than an extension of knowledge. I quote an illustration from Newman, who leaves a measure of vagueness over the question of just what mental processes are involved. He writes: 'Justin or Irenaeus might be without any digested ideas of purgatory or original sin, yet have an intense feeling, which they had not defined or located, both of the fault of our first nature and the responsibilities of our nature regenerate.'[10]

The seventh and last of Newman's notes is 'chronic vigour'. This appears to be a pragmatic mode of judging. False developments, Newman believed, have a transitory character, whereas the genuine development shows vigorous and continued growth. But this may well be too optimistic a view. It looks as if Newman may have too lightly accepted the *magna est veritas* principle. Arianism continued to flourish around the Mediterranean basin for a long time after it had been disowned by the Church, while Nestorianism survived for a long time in China. But how long is a 'long time' in the history of Christianity, and what would count as chronic 'vigour'?

The Oxford Movement and Theology

What are the theological implications of the Oxford Movement? I suspect that some people might think that it had no theological implications at all. They would see it primarily as a movement which affected liturgy, spirituality and many of the outward manifestations of the Church, but had little significance for theology. But they would be wrong and would be reinforcing the divide which can easily develop between the intellectual and the spiritual contributions to theology.

Certainly, the founders of the Oxford Movement were not innovators, but believed that they were laying hold on a heritage that was rightly theirs, but that had become obscured in the English Church. That was the heritage of classical Anglicanism. Even before the Oxford Movement had emerged, John Keble had edited the works of Richard Hooker, who, together with John Jewel and other sixteenth-century theologians, had instituted a way of theologizing, not so much in terms of content as in their way of going about the theological task. That way recognized the place of Scripture as the main source of Christian doctrine, but Scripture as mediated through the theological reflection of the fathers of the Church, the early creeds and the continuing liturgical tradition enshrined in *The Book of Common Prayer*. This approach to theology differed both from the direct appeal to the Bible typical of Protestantism and the exaltation of ecclesiastical authority believed to be typical of Roman Catholicism.

I think, however, that the Oxford Movement can be seen as part of a wider stirring that was happening in other areas outside

England. It was a protest against the dry propositional theology of the eighteenth century, whether that took the form of deistic rationalism, Protestant biblicism or Roman Catholic scholasticism. If this is correct, then one would see as a parallel to the Oxford Movement the new style of German theology associated with Schleiermacher, who stressed feeling and intuition. The comparison would hold only up to a point, for there is in Schleiermacher a streak of subjectivism, not found in the Oxford Movement, and Schleiermacher also lacked the Oxford apostles' veneration for antiquity. Nevertheless, during the years of his studies in Germany, the young Pusey had discovered Schleiermacher, and had apparently found some things in him that excited his sympathy. There is a comparison too between Newman and another critic of rationalist theology, Kierkegaard. Again, the comparison is valid only up to a point. Newman had a strong feeling for the Church, Kierkegaard did not, and declared himself an individualist. Both of them held that religious faith is more than an intellectual assent, and calls for something like a leap of faith.

Newman puts it this way:

> He who has made us has so willed that in mathematics indeed we arrive at certitude by rigorous demonstration, but in religious inquiry we arrive at certitude by accumulated probabilities – inasmuch as he who has willed that we should so act, co-operates with us in our acting, and thereby bestows on us certitude which rises higher than the logical force of our conclusions.[1]

We may contrast this with a passage in Kierkegaard in which he disparages any attempt to prove the existence of God: 'for if God did not exist, it would, of course, be impossible to prove it; and if he does exist, it would be folly to attempt it'.[2] Reason, in Kierkegaard's language, makes a collision, and then one is faced with the decision of either taking offence and turning away, or of making the leap of faith. Here again the comparison is not exact, for Kierkegaard's position is more fideistic than

Newman's, and there is nothing in Kierkegaard corresponding to Newman's 'accumulated probabilities'. Still another comparison might be made with the Scottish theologian John McLeod Campbell, an almost exact contemporary of Pusey and a rebel against the rigid Calvinist doctrine of atonement. Especially his teaching that the atonement is not a once-for-all event of the past only, but a continuing incorporation into Christ, has its parallels among the Tractarians.

One cannot dismiss these theological stirrings of the nineteenth century as 'romanticism'. This term has been applied to both Schleiermacher and the Oxford Movement, but it must not be allowed to obscure the intellectual acuteness found in these men. For instance, Schleiermacher's critique of the language of Chalcedon could well have been the work of a modern analytical philosopher.[3] The Oxford Movement began in intellectual circles, and however much its later phases may have moved into questions of ritualism, it has an intellectual foundation, and even ritualism can be traced back to that foundation. Keble was reckoned the most brilliant man in the Oxford of his day, Newman has an honoured place among the theologians and philosophers of the nineteenth century, while Pusey too was a man of very great learning, not only in Christian theology but in Hebrew and Arabic language and literature. The beginnings of the movement were literary and intended to appeal to the educated and the intelligent; the famous *Tracts*, which came to include not just brief statements such as would usually be called 'tracts', but lengthy volumes giving detailed theological treatment of various topics; the *Library of the Fathers*, which, in forty-eight scholarly volumes, made available a wide range of patristic texts, and did much to revive interest in patristic studies; and the *Library of Anglo-Catholic Theology*, which rescued from obscurity the works of great Anglican divines of the past. The amount of intellectual energy expended in the early years of the Movement is hard to visualize.

Let me now try to set out in more orderly fashion some of the leading characteristics of the theology which the Tractarians brought into being.

The first point is that for them theology stood in the closest connection with spirituality. This was not due to any anti-intellectualism, but to the fact that faith is an attitude of the whole person, not merely the assent of the mind to propositions. Theology cannot consist purely in argument and inference. If we turn theology into an abstract speculation, then we are in danger of becoming the 'great atheists', of whom Francis Bacon said that 'they are ever handling holy things, but without feeling'.[4] This was not what the Tractarians found in the fathers, who carry conviction not so much by subtle argument as by their candid and sincere expositions of the mysteries of faith. It reminds us again of John McLeod Campbell, who was fond of saying that the best defence of Christianity is to let it be seen in its own light.[5] The words in which Christian faith is expressed are not just logical units to be manipulated in accordance with the laws of thought. Every word is a mystery, pointing beyond itself to a reality which words cannot fully encompass. John Keble, who was for four years Professor of Poetry at Oxford, was well aware of this allusive character of language. Before he preached his famous assize sermon in 1833, he had published his book of hymns and poems, *The Christian Year*, which, like those of John Mason Neale and others, was a powerful means of spreading Tractarian theology. Such men rejoiced also in the allegorical interpretation of Scripture found in many of the Church fathers. It raised the question of whether the language of theology has more in common with poetry than with science, and surely no one would deny that both science and poetry are ways of expressing truth.

Admittedly, the allegorical interpretation of Scripture has gone out of fashion, and admittedly too the Tractarians were slow to come to terms with modern biblical criticism – only at the end of the nineteenth century did Anglo-Catholic theologians begin to take such criticism seriously. Yet it may well be asked whether critical theology and spirituality have not been allowed to drift too far apart. Some scholars think so. Andrew Louth, for instance, believes that the historical critical method may unconsciously bring with it presuppositions that may underlie the scientific method but which are not appropriate to the humanities, and he pleads for a new look at the allegorizing methods of the fathers.[6]

These considerations raise important questions about the nature of theological language. The Tractarians were equally suspicious of those liberals whose treatment was reductionist and who ended up by cutting down Christianity to a few religious and ethical commonplaces, and of Roman Catholic theologians who tried (as some Tractarians believed) to 'explain' a mystery such as Christ's eucharistic presence by the philosophical theory of transubstantiation. In both cases, there was a dissolution of the mystery and therefore of its spiritual power. Such theology no longer served spirituality, for it suggested that it had got to the bottom of the mystery and had thus taken away the sense of reverence, the feeling of the holy, appropriate to these mysteries. This does not imply that the Tractarians thought of mystery as sheer opacity or impenetrability, but as that which always transcends the reach of our understanding. There is always something going beyond, that is to say, transcendent.

Very typical of Tractarian theology, and closely connected with the problems just discussed and with the relation of theology to spirituality is the principle of reserve. As the term suggests, this means that one should not try to be too explicit in the statement of doctrine, but should hold something back. The principle of reserve became a matter of controversy, because some opponents of the Oxford Movement represented it as deliberate deception. They claimed that the Tractarians were not revealing their full intentions, so that they might gradually seduce their hearers into more extreme positions. A fairer estimate was that of R. C. Selby, who wrote that 'reserve is appropriate to fostering the reverence due to sacred things by withholding them until men are worthy of them'.[7] Newman himself wrote that 'religious men are very reserved, if only that they may not betray, if we may so speak, God's confidence'.[8] It was this reserve that made the early Tractarians suspicious of such overdefinitions of doctrine as they believed transubstantiation to be. Unfortunately, as time went on and Roman fever mounted in the Church of England, the principle of reserve tended to be forgotten, and among some of the enthusiasts there was explicit identification with Rome in everything. This was in the end to have harmful consequences in Anglo-Catholicism, for it tended to identify with the form of Roman Catholicism as understood in the mid-nineteenth century, presumably supposing that this would be permanent. Thus, when Roman Catholicism moved on to a new phase after Vatican II, those successors of the Tractarians who had unreservedly identified with an earlier phase found themselves isolated and looking like a survival from the past.

On the other hand, it was the same principle of reserve that allowed Newman in his controversial Tract 90 to place upon the articles of Religion a catholicizing interpretation which let them appear compatible with Roman teaching. His stated aim was to show that 'while our Prayer Book is on all hands acknowledged to be of catholic origin, our Articles also, the offspring of an uncatholic age, are through God's good providence, to say the least, not uncatholic, and may be subscribed to by those who aim at being catholic in heart and doctrine'.[9] The Articles, even if unconsciously, had preserved in a concealed form, the catholic truths.

Newman's interpretation of the Articles in Tract 90 appeared to his opponents a distortion and he was violently assailed. At a later time, in his *Apologia*, he justified his interpretation as follows: 'It is a duty which we owe both to the Catholic Church and to ourselves, to take our reformed confessions in the most catholic sense they will permit; we have no duties toward their framers.'[10]

Another way of understanding reserve would be to take it as a kind of halfway house toward the apophaticism or mystical silence at which some followers of the mystical way arrive.

The next principle to be mentioned is concreteness, and this too follows from points that have been mentioned earlier. Christian faith is not founded on abstract speculations, but on historical events and historical influences. It is always embodied in concrete realities, and must not be dissipated into some diffuse spiritual essence. The Church is itself a visible historical reality. This teaching brought the Tractarians into conflict with the Calvinists, who taught that the true Church is the invisible Church, the body of the faithful scattered throughout the world, the body whose number and membership are known to God alone.

Many of the major theological emphases of the Tractarians flow directly from this conception of the Church as a visible historical body, involved in the course of human history. Among these emphases is a doctrine of apostolic succession which already appears in John Keble's assize sermon at the very beginning of the Oxford Movement. The issue which the sermon raised was that of authority in the Church. The Church of England was by law established as the national religion, and the sovereign of the realm was (and still is) governor of the Church. The close association of Church and state has long been a feature of the English nation. Although John Keble challenged the right of the state to interfere in the internal arrangements of the Church, neither he nor his colleagues thought of seeking to abolish the close association of the two. Indeed, the story is told that when J. H. Hobart, Bishop of New York and a 'pronounced high churchman'[11] who held a view of Anglicanism similar to Newman's own, actually met Newman on a visit to England, the latter expressed surprised that one could be both a Catholic Anglican and a republican! Even today, when the Church of England enjoys far more control over its affairs than it did in 1833, only a minority of the people would like to see the ties between Church and state completely severed.

But Keble was clear in his sermon that the ultimate authority in the Church is derived not from the state but from the apostles who had in turn received their commission from Christ. The bishops are the successors of the apostles and the Church is the whole body of Christians, united according to the will of Christ, under the successors of the apostles.[12] The same theme was taken up in that same year of 1833 by John Henry Newman in Tract 1, the first of the famous series. That tract was addressed by Newman to his fellow priests in the Church of England. On what did their authority as teachers and pastors depend? Not on the state, and their spiritual authority would not be diminished if the state withdrew its support, though Newman acknowledged that this would cause some problems. He went on:

> There are some who rest their divine mission on their own unsupported assertion, others who rest it on their popularity, others on their success, and others who rest it on their temporal distinctions. This last case has been, perhaps, too much our own. I fear we have neglected the real ground on which our authority is built.

He then states the doctrine of an apostolic succession in its traditional uncompromising form:

> We have been born, not of blood nor of the will of the flesh, nor of the will of man, but of God. The Lord Jesus Christ gave his Spirit to the apostles, they in turn laid their hands on those who should succeed them; and these again on others; and so the sacred gift has been handed down to our present bishops, who have appointed us as their assistants, and in some sense representatives.[13]

Newman acknowledged that not all his Anglican brethren would agree with this. The view has been caricatured, as if it advocated some merely material tactual succession. But this is a misunderstanding, a failure to recognize the place of the sacramental in catholic theology and practice. We come again to the conflict between the idea of the Church as a visible society living in history and the Church as an invisible spiritual body, only ambiguously related to the visible historical Church, where that which is visible is not exhausted by the visible and the material but uses visible signs to point beyond themselves to spiritual reality. Laying on of hands is indeed a visible act, but it is more. The act may have had several meanings in the early Church or in the Jewish community, but in particular it signified the bestowal of a spiritual gift; in ordination, the gift of a share in the apostolic ministry. An invisible Church is in constant danger of lapsing into a kind of docetism. Something of this has, I think, crept into contemporary ecumenical discussion. We sometimes hear it said that the true apostolical succession is succession in the doctrine of the apostles, the transmission of Christian truth from generation to generation. This is indeed part of what is meant by apostolic succession, but it does less than justice to the full meaning of the expression. We have to ask about who does the passing on, who receives what is passed on, what is the sign of the passing on. The transmission does not take place in a vacuum but in a community of persons where the episcopate is the outward and visible sign of a sacramental act. It was their sense of the concrete and historical that led the Tractarian fathers to stress the importance of apostolic succession understood in terms of persons and a community of persons rather than as the abstract transmission of doctrines and formulae.

We could say that Newman and catholic-minded theologians thought not only of ordination as a sacrament, but of the Church as a whole as a sacrament. I doubt if any of them used this precise expression, but it has, of course, had considerable vogue in the Roman Catholic Church since Vatican II.[14] The Church has the nature of a sacrament because it is a visible tangible body in history and yet it is, as Christians believe, a community of the Spirit instituted by Christ to continue his mission and ministry in the world. It has sometimes been called a continuation of the incarnation, while Christ has been called the 'primal Sacrament', the divine Word given a visible, historical, personal form. It is clear that this sacramental language about the Church leads to a very 'high' ecclesiology. This would have been more intelligible in the days of the early Tractarians, when the Church was often regarded by politicians as a mere department of the state, but nowadays we should hesitate to speak so freely of the Church as a continuation of the incarnation, and are more likely to be aware of the numerous and serious occasions when the Church itself falls short of its calling in Christ. The Church may be ideally the continuing presence of Christ in the world, but this is a role which needs more thought than it has had from either Catholics or Protestants. Or the language may be treated eschatologically. The Church may be the spearhead of the kingdom of God in the world, but is still only on its way toward its goal. Perhaps the most that can be claimed is that the Church gives us some glimpses of what both Church and world can become when there is a genuine response to Christ, an incorporation into the life of God, already anticipated in the New Testament teaching that 'believers are made partakers of the divine nature' (2 Peter 1.4).

Pusey was author of three tracts (Nos. 67–9) on baptism, adding up to a substantial treatise on the subject. This deserves to be noted, since it has been objected that the Tractarians concentrated their attention on the eucharist to the neglect of baptism. Drawing on his great knowledge of the fathers, Pusey taught a powerfully realistic view of baptism, speaking of 'the indwelling of the eternal Son in the man Christ Jesus, the reality of the communication of himself to us, the reality of the mystery of holy baptism, and thereby our being *in* him'.[15] This high view of baptism contrasts sharply with a popular view that was widely disseminated at the time and acquired something like an official standing through the notorious Gorham Judgement of 1850, the view which denies that there is any baptismal regeneration. If such a low view of baptism strikes us as strange today, that is some indication of how the views of the Tractarians have influenced the whole Church.

Pusey taught equally realistic views on the eucharist. These are contained in three sermons, preached in Oxford between 1843 and 1871. The arguments are based mainly on the early fathers of the Church, who used strongly realistic language about Christ's presence in the eucharist. The first of these sermons was judged by some of those who heard it to imply belief in transubstantiation, and one of my own predecessors in the Lady Margaret Chair, Dr Geoffrey Fausset, laid a formal complaint with the Vice-Chancellor. A committee of six doctors of divinity was appointed to judge the sermon, and they condemned it without even allowing Pusey to be heard. He was suspended from preaching before the University for two years.

Meanwhile, he was busy and supplied references to show that all the points he had made could be supported from the ancient fathers. As Pusey said, he would have been sorry if, through ignorance, his judges would have found themselves in the position of condemning Cyril of Alexandria, when they thought they were condemning Edward Bouverie Pusey![16] In fact, Pusey explicitly rejected the doctrine of transubstantiation because, as we have noted already, it offended against the Tractarian principle of reserve.

I have confined myself to the earlier years of the Oxford Movement, but the theology evolved in these years contained the seeds of the later developments, including what was called 'ritualism'. It flowed very readily from the beliefs of the early Tracterians about the limitations of language when we try to speak of sacred mysteries. The early ritualist priests who were in many cases working in industrial parishes among people of little education, were very clear about what they were doing. People who might have difficulty in understanding theological ideas could be led into the same mysterious truths by action and gesture, music and colour, and all the accompaniments of ceremonial. This all follows from such interlocking concepts as reserve, symbolism, sacramentality and incarnation itself. Critics of the ritualists failed to recognize that it was the same sensitivity to the deeper significance of our embodied human existence in the world that drew these ritualists into the great industrial cities of Victorian Britain to share their vision with the people there.

essays. Ramsey's life was rooted in prayer, worship and a sense of the reality of God, yet all this was tempered with a sense of humour which prevented it from ever degenerating into pomposity or unreal pietism, still less into the dogmatism which has unfortunately characterized some bishops.

What kind of theologian was Ramsey and what did he contribute to the stubborn questions that were so hotly debated during his time? I think it would be fair to say that he was thoroughly Anglican. In one sense, there is no such thing as an Anglican theology. At the time of the Reformation, there was in the Church of England no dominant theological figure, no Luther or Calvin or Zwingli who imprinted his distinctive mark on the thinking of the new form of Christianity, as had happened in most of the countries that had experienced a reformation in the sixteenth century. The leaders of the English Reformation at the time of the Elizabethan settlement, theologians such as John Jewel and then his most famous *protégé*, Richard Hooker, were opposed to extremists among both the Roman Catholic and the Calvinist factions in the Church. They were not introducing a new religion but simply continuing the ancient catholic faith that the country had known for nearly a thousand years since Augustine, and even since before him. The English reformers did indeed believe as did their continental counterparts that some abuses had crept in and needed to be corrected, but they visualized a restoration of what they believed to be the pure faith and worship of the undivided Church of the early centuries. They aimed at a form of church that would retain the essentials of Catholic Christianity, at the same time making that church as comprehensive as possible to include the majority of the English people, though some groups remained and still remain 'dissenters'.

This conception of the Church of England as both catholic and inclusive earned for it the description of 'the Middle Way' (*via media*), an expression popularized by Cardinal Newman in his Anglican days before his departure for Rome. The same conception profoundly affected the kind of training that was given to the clergy in the centuries after the Reformation and, to some extent, even today. Those studying for the ordained ministry were given a thorough grounding in biblical studies, reflecting that new sense of the importance of the Scriptures common to all the reformers of that period. Biblical studies have been important in the Church of England ever since, and the Anglican contribution to these studies has been quite outstanding, less radical perhaps than the German, but no less scholarly. What, however, was distinctive in Anglican theological faculties, was the high place given to patristic studies, contrasting with the neglect of these studies in the neighbouring Scottish universities, where a Calvinistic ethos tended to jump over the centuries from the New Testament to the Reformers and from there to modern theology. Also important in Anglican training was the study of liturgy, which ensured that the academic aspects of theological training were not separated (or at least, not too widely separated) from the practice of religion. Liturgy is the living vehicle in which the Church's faith and way of life find expression and we recognize that Christianity is much more than a 'belief-system'.

The Church of England's *Book of Common Prayer* enjoys among Anglicans a respect not far behind that accorded to the Bible. Along with all this went an interest in history, in the trials, mistakes and triumphs of the Church through the centuries, bringing with it a sense of respect for the Church and a healthy, though not uncritical, pride in its past.

Although there may not be a distinctive Anglican theology, in the sense of a specific body of doctrines that distinguish Anglicans from other Christians, there is at least a distinctive way of going about theology. It is based on the Scriptures, as the original witness to the events on which Christianity is founded, on tradition as the unfolding of the understanding of those events in the corporate mind of the Church, especially in the ecumenical councils and the eminent theologians of the first five centuries, and finally on reason and conscience as people of each new generation sought to incorporate these truths into their own experience.

It was this kind of training that Michael Ramsey received in his student years at Cambridge and Cuddesdon, and on the whole he remained true to it. The first book in which he expounded his theological views was *The Gospel and the Catholic Church*. It was published in 1936 and led to his first academic appointment at the University of Durham. It remained his best book and also one of the best commendations of Anglicanism in existence. Even the title is very Anglican. It expresses the conviction of the Church of England that the Bible is central in Christian faith, yet at the same time it sees the Bible in the context of the Church and believes that it is to be read as the Church reads it and not according to individual preference.

In defence of this thesis, Ramsey reminds us that in the patristic Church, it was not so much continuity in doctrine that determined the catholicity of any particular local church. At least equally important, if not more so, was the need to show that the bishop had been consecrated in a succession of bishops having their origin in the Twelve, whom Jesus had chosen himself for a leadership role in his movement. But, in spite of his criticisms of individualism, neither Ramsey nor the Church of England generally has been strict in pursuing aberrations in doctrine and practice, and the commoner complaint has been excessive tolerance in such matters. Ramsey was certainly against individualism in religion, but not in a negatively repressive way. More important was his affirmation of the corporate nature of the Church and the probability that its collective wisdom outweighed the ideas of individuals.

Neither Ramsey nor the Church of England would have attempted to 'police' the thought of theologians, as sometimes has happened in the Roman Catholic Church, but the stress laid on the fathers and the liturgy in theological education has ensured that Anglican theology has never become a free-for all, so to speak.

A few quotations from *The Gospel and the Catholic Church* will make clear to us the salient points in Ramsey's theology,[1] for instance, 'the fact of Christ includes the fact of the Church' and although in this book he stated them quite explicitly, they were implicit as a background to all his other teaching and writing. First, there is the central importance of the Church, the community of the faithful, the corporate entity within which all Christian experience takes place, and faithfulness to which is the norm for testing the authenticity of any proffered theology. For Ramsey, it was indeed true that 'there is no salvation outside of the Church' (*nulla salus extra ecclesiam*). Primarily, as is clear even in the title of his book, Ramsey has in mind the catholic Church, as it had existed in the early centuries, but again we have to understand him in an affirmative rather than an exclusive sense, and I think he had learned this from the great Roman Catholic ecumenist, Yves Congar. Although we look back (perhaps through rose-tinted spectacles) to the Church of the past, whether the New Testament Church or the Church of the fathers, as the ideal, the norm of catholicity, Ramsey believed that the fullness of the Church is still to come in the future. In a conversation in New York with Cardinal Suenens, the Belgian Primate, these two leaders envisaged a wider conception of catholicity, in which there would be combined a strong adherence to tradition with a generous recognition of what those who have deviated from tradition may yet bring to the future. To quote:

> On the one hand, we must insist on the preservation of certain norms of the Church's catholicity, once given and never to be abandoned, such as the creeds, the tradition of episcopal ordination and the offices of bishop and presbyter as effectual signs of the givenness and continuity of the Church. But we have also to acknowledge that in various ways these gifts have been on occasion abused, and a better use of them can be learned from others.[2]

But let us return to *The Gospel and the Catholic Church* for a fuller exposition of Ramsey's understanding of the inseparability of gospel and Church. Christianity, he tells us, is not a solitary or individual matter. The Church is not an optional extra in Christian faith, not something that is added on because, from a practical point of view, it is good for Christians to associate and work together. Let me repeat that in one of his strongest utterances, Ramsey declares: 'The fact of Christ includes the fact of the Church.'[3] The same teaching had been given centuries earlier by Augustine of Hippo as was now coming from the successor of Augustine of Canterbury, namely, that there is one Christ, who is both the Head and the body. Jesus Christ was indeed an individual human being, but his place in Christianity includes the community that he inspired and grew up around him. This is a doctrine that has been restated by scholars in the United States, particular by the biblical scholar, John Knox, especially in his book, *The Church and the Reality of Christ* (1962), where he makes much of the idea of a 'Christ-event', the idea that the beginning of Christianity lies not only in the birth, ministry, death and so on of the individual Jesus of Nazareth, but on the whole community which came into being with and around him, called by Christians the 'body of Christ'. Ideally, this body continues the incarnate being of Christ on earth and in history, and it is this fact of the closeness of Christ and his people that allows Ramsey to say that the fact of Christ includes the fact of the Church, and enables Knox to say that the Pauline phrase about the Christian's 'being-in-Christ' is not to be understood as the Christian's inward private or mystical relation to Christ but more simply to 'being-in-the-Church'. Paul is sometimes, because of the special circumstances of his conversion and apostolate, regarded as an individualist or even a rebel in the Church, but this is not Ramsey's reading of the situation. He reminds us of Paul's struggle to assert his apostolic authority over the church at Corinth where, it appears, the eucharist had developed into a disorderly mêlée (I have heard Ramsey quoting one of his Cambridge teachers who described the eucharist at Corinth as being like a 'bump supper' in a Cambridge College), and likewise we find him criticizing Luther for prizing so much the initial individual experience of justification and conversion that he failed to recognize the need for the discipline and order of the Church as the sphere in which Christians are to grow into the fullness of their faith.

But Ramsey insisted not only on the Church as included in the fact of Christ, but also on the basic structures of the Church, as recognized universally among Christians for centuries of its existence, and still by the great majority of Christians today. It was the Church as described in the Chicago–Lambeth Quadrilateral, approved by the Lambeth Conference of 1888, the Church as resting on the foundations of the Bible, the sacraments and the apostolic ministry represented by the episcopate. He was very clear about this: 'We are led to affirm,' he declared, 'that the episcopate is of the *esse* of the Church.'[4] To illustrate his point, he again summons Paul to witness: 'Paul the apostle is part of the structure, not by his eloquence or distinction or personal gifts, but by his *office* as apostle, he represents to the local communities the fact of the one universal *ecclesia* in which they die and live; "Paul called to be an apostle unto the church of God which is at Corinth" (1 Cor. 1.1–2).' What Paul is doing is turning around the order of priorities in which many theological debates have been allowed to take place and many of the debates between Christian theologians and their philosophical or other secular critics. He is accepting that the language of academic theologians is a second-order language and that to understand Christianity, one has to go back to what we may term the 'raw material' of the Christian experience. We have already seen in this book that there are many experiences in life, even experiences which are not in themselves 'religious', but which lend themselves to a religious interpretation. The point I am making here, the point I believe Michael Ramsey was making, was that these experiences are at the root of the matter, and our interpretations, whether religious or anti-religious, are preceded (or not preceded) by the experiences and therefore already contain in themselves some understanding or knowledge which, if we may use the expression, 'we have known in our bones' and are now trying to bring to conceptual expression.

Let me add some further examples. Kierkegaard writes: 'Only through the consciousness of sin is there entry to Christianity, and the wish to enter it by any other way is the crime of *lèse majesté*.' At the other end of the spectrum, it may be an experience of the sublime, a vision of Jesus Christ, for example, that induces the feeling of the *mysterium tremendum fascinosum* and its accompanying awareness of the presence of a transcendent reality. Though such experiences seem to be more readily evoked in some persons than in others, Ramsey was correct in stressing the corporate nature of Christian experience. It would be interesting to know whether it was sin or the sublime or something quite different that led him into his own conviction of the truth of Christianity, but whatever it may have been, it was no passing or solitary emotion but his adherence to a corporate entity within which the initial experience could grow and be nourished and be properly interpreted.

Eckhart and Heidegger: Two Mystics

The title of this chapter announces a strange juxtaposition – Eckhart (1260–1328) and Heidegger (1889–1976). We might use of Eckhart the description applied to Spinoza, 'a God-intoxicated man', for he saw God in everything, lived, moved and had his being in God. Heidegger, on the contrary, is often regarded as a spokesman for modern secularism. He has been called by some an atheist, and in his extensive writings, he has little to say about God. Yet a sympathetic reader of Heidegger cannot fail to be aware of a religious spirit in his writings. As against the superficial view that he was an atheist we may set the view expressed by Hans-Georg Gadamer in his memorial address at the time of Heidegger's death: 'It was Christianity that pro-voked and kept alive this man's thought. It was the ancient trans-cendence and not modern secularity that spoke through him.'[1] Heidegger himself tells us in his *Letter on Humanism* that he is neither a theist nor an atheist. He explicitly dissociates himself from the atheism of Sartre, but he leaves the question open as to whether there is a God or even what the word 'God' means: 'Only from the truth of Being can the essence of the holy be thought. Only from the essence of the holy is the essence of divinity to be thought. Only in the light of the essence of divinity can it be thought or said what the word God is to signify.'[2]

These cryptic words show us that we must be very careful in using words like 'theism' and 'atheism', or in classifying persons as theists or atheists *tout court*. I doubt if either Eckhart or Heidegger can, strictly speaking, be called a theist. For theism, in the sense in which the word has been used in Christian theology and in western philosophy, refers to a God who is understood principally in terms of his transcendence. He is creator of the world, above and beyond it, but in traditional theism there has been very little recognition of God's immanence in the world. Neither Eckhart nor Heidegger conceived of God in the traditional one-sidedly transcendent way, and this may account for the superficial and inaccurate opinions that Heidegger was an atheist and Eckhart a pantheist. They both believed in a Reality which, I would say, could properly be called 'God', because belonging to a higher level of Being than the creatures or even the whole created universe; but they also believed that the creaturely levels of existence are intimately embraced within the higher ultimate Reality, and probably they would both have said that they are essential to it. I do not think that they confused God and the creatures, but they could not conceive God without the creatures. In Heidegger's case, what could Being mean or how could we know anything of Being, were it not somehow manifested in the multiplicity of beings? In Eckhart's case, could we properly speak of God unless there were also souls into which God's word could be born?

However, we have so far not indicated any definite link between Eckhart and Heidegger. But I believe we are on the track. I used sometimes to play a game with my students, by quoting to them a sentence or two from some well-known philosopher or theologian, and asking them to identify the author of the quotation. An example of such a sentence is this: 'The ultimate Reality is not all things, and not any single one of them; it is the principle of all things. How then do all things come from this one ultimate? It is because there is nothing in it that all things come from it; in order that beings may be, the ultimate is not a being but the begetter of beings.'[3] Who said this? It sounds like Heidegger, or it even sounds like Eckhart. The truth is that these words come from Plotinus, in Book V of the *Enneads*. I believe that the underlying link between Eckhart and Heidegger is that they both have their roots in the neo-Platonist tradition. Certainly they have both moved a long way from Plotinus, the founder of that tradition, but some fundamental characteristics have persisted. In my book, *In Search of Deity*, I tried to trace in outline the development of what I called 'dialectical theism', sometimes called 'panentheism', a doctrine of God which recognizes both the 'ontological difference' between God and world and their intimate bonding which is based on a deep affinity of Being and beings. This doctrine was first given clear expression in the West by the pagan philosopher Plotinus; his thoughts were later incorporated into Christianity by many of the later Christian fathers, most notably perhaps by Dionysius called the Areopagite, then continuing in a variety of forms through John Scotus Eriugena, Meister Eckhart, Nicholas of Cusa, Leibniz, Hegel, Whitehead and Heidegger. That is the historical stream to which Eckhart and Heidegger belong.

This historical stream of neo-Platonism, though it is philosophical and intellectual, has also a mystical element. The mystical element is sometimes more, sometimes less, evident in individual writers in the tradition, though one might say it is the culmination of neo-Platonism. Plotinus himself developed one of the most comprehensive philosophical schemes ever produced by a human mind. By a process of emanation, everything that is has emerged from the One, the ultimate Reality that, so to speak, overflows itself and gives being to the entire realm of beings in all their multiplicity and diversity. This is the *exitus*, the going forth from the origin. But the beings bear within themselves a 'memory', as it were, of their origin and seek to return to the One. In conscious intelligent beings such as members of the human race, this 'memory' is the mystical quest, the return or *reditus* to the source. This is not simply an intellectual or philosophical quest, not a high-powered metaphysic, for it comes to a point where there must be a 'leap', as it has been called, a point where the intellectual striving gives way to a receptive thinking. According to his biographer Porphyry, Plotinus achieves this leap four times during the years he was teaching in Rome. It seems to be an austere kind of mysticism, a mysticism which dispenses with imagery, and in particular with the erotic imagery reported by some mystics. This mystical element appears in both Eckhart and Heidegger, and in both of them it has the same austere character. I need not argue that Eckhart was a mystic, for this is something that has always been recognized, and his quest for an encounter with God is described by him in his own writings. But to claim that there is something corresponding to this in Heidegger does call for some justification. There are two passages in particular from the Heideggerian corpus that show us something of this mysticism or quasi-mysticism on his part.

The first passage is in his lecture, *What is Metaphysics?*, his inaugural lecture at the University of Freiburg when he was inducted to the philosophy chair in 1929. It is a masterly lecture, full of irony as well as of insight. He raises the question about the subject-matter of philosophy. What does a professor of philosophy teach in a modern university? At first sight, the whole field of investigation appears to have been pre-empted by other disciplines, the particular sciences, either natural or humanistic. Physics claims the phenomena of matter and energy, biology the realm of living things, history the unfolding of humanity in its manifold activities, even mental life has been claimed by psychology, and so on it goes. What is left for the philosopher? Heidegger's ironical reply is: 'Nothing.' So he proposes to lecture on nothing (though he didn't sit down and lapse into silence at that point). But 'the nothing' – *das Nichts*, an expression also used by Eckhart, and traceable, we have seen, back to Plotinus – turns out to be more than mere negativity or absence of being. It has been said that *ex nihilo nihil fit*, 'out of nothing, nothing is made', but Heidegger on the contrary claims: *ex nihilo omne ens qua ens fit*, 'out of nothing every being, as a being, is made'. Heidegger's claim is to be understood as parallel to that of Plotinus, quoted above: 'The one ultimate reality is not all things, and not any one of them. It is only because there is nothing in it that all things come from it: in order that beings may be, the ultimate is not a being but a begetter of beings.' In other words, from the point of view that sees only the beings (and this would include the view of the special sciences) this ultimate is dismissed as nothing. But how can we have any knowledge of this nothing? Indeed, is it possible to know that which can be called 'nothing'? Heidegger does not claim any leap of faith or any mystical union. Instead, he appeals to a phenomenon which he had already introduced in *Being and Time*, published twelve years earlier and looking back to Kierke-gaard and Augustine – the phenomenon of what Germans call *Angst*, usually translated into English as 'anxiety', or 'dread', though in Heidegger it means rather the state of being 'not at home with oneself' and is the primary example in Heidegger of a 'mood' or 'state of mind' which gives one an understanding not of a particular situation but of the general precariousness of one's being-in-the-world. According to Heidegger's description, *Angst* is closely connected with finitude, guilt and mortality. It is through this experience of *Angst* that we gain some under-standing of 'nothing'. He writes that in this mood of anxiety, the many beings that confront us in the world lose their separ-ateness and their individual identities. 'All things, and we with them, sink into a kind of indifference. The only thing that remains and overwhelms us while the beings slip away is this "nothing". *Angst* reveals nothing.'[4] It is interesting to note that he uses the word *Scheu* (awe) to describe the feeling we have when confronted with this nothing, a feeling (if you like) of the numinous, as if it were a direct perception. One may also ask whether this sinking into indifference of the multitude of things and phenomena is not related in some way to Eckhart's *Abgesch-iedenheid* (detachment, disconnectedness), or to the common mystical claim to see things in their totality.

The relation between anxiety and mysticism in the passage which I have been trying to disentangle is enigmatic and ambigu-ous, but I think that there are other passages in his writings which imply a different and more affirmative view of the role of moods and states of mind in throwing light on human exist-ence as a being-in-the-world.

I have in mind what Heidegger has to say about thinking. He makes a distinction among various kinds or levels of thinking. 'Calculative thinking' is probably the commonest kind of think-ing. It is a mode of thinking in which the human mind treats the beings encountered in the world as objects to be understood, eventually to be exploited, in the interests of the thinker. Heidegger includes science under this heading. This is the kind of thinking that dominates in the age of science, and that has gained a leading role in the modern western world. Even so, it is not universal, for most of us do not think of other people as exploitable objects, though in industrial societies we sometimes come close to such depersonalized ways of thinking. Another kind of thinking is that of the poet – he may be thinking of objects, but they are objects of admiration, objects endowed with meanings that go beyond use and exploitation. Heidegger himself in the course of his career has come to describe himself as a thinker rather than a philosopher, and to stress the closeness of philosophy to poetry rather than to science. He calls this kind of thinking 'meditative thinking'. It is not aggressively investigative, but listens, so to speak, receptively for the voice of Being. Meditative thinking is like the contemplative thinking of the mystic. We can also see that it has resemblances to the ontological intuitions that come with those states of mind which awaken in us an awareness of some aspect of our being-in-the-world.

Heidegger, following Kierkegaard, takes *Angst* as the typical ontological mood. This seems to be a negative mood, when we are aware of the ontological difference, the realization that the ultimate Reality, Being, is of a different order from the beings. But Heidegger also allows for more positive relationships – thankfulness to Being for the gift of finite being, the sense of enjoying the favour of Being, the sense of belonging to Being. To express this, Heidegger takes up the saying of Parmenides – *to gar auto noein estin te kai einai* – (usually translated, 'Being and thinking are the same'), which invites comparison with the claim sometimes made by Christians that in the prayer of the Christian, it is not the Christian who prays but the Holy Spirit who prays in the Christian.

Paul Ricoeur demands to know why Heidegger and Kierkegaard have chosen anxiety as the typical ontological mood. Is there some personal individual reason for this? Why not claim that joy is the most authentic as the state of mind that best illuminates our being-in-the-world? That could be the beginning of a very long argument that might in the end prove inconclusive. But a quick provisional answer is just the fact that the vast majority of people regard their lives as precious and do their best to stay alive. At any rate, the persons we have just been discussing have all believed that the ultimate Reality – God, Being, whatever name we use – does not depend on the cleverness of our arguments but is accessible in ways that are more akin to prayer, meditation, thankfulness. 'To think critically,' writes Heidegger, 'means to distinguish constantly between that which requires proof for its justification, and that which to confirm its truth demands a simple catching-sight of and taking it in.'[5]

Some of Heidegger's clearest statements on these matters come in his book, *Discourse on Thinking*. The German title is *Gelassenheit*, a word familiar in the mystical vocabulary, and meaning something like 'collectedness' or 'serenity'. Part of the book consists of a dialogue in which there take part a teacher, a student and a scientist. Let me quote:

Student: How do we awaken collectedness?
Teacher: Say rather, to keeping awake for collectedness.
Student: Why not, to the awakening?
Teacher: Because on our own we do not awaken collectedness in ourselves.
Scientist: Thus collectedness is effected from somewhere else?
Teacher: Not effected, but let in.[6]

In the situation described in this excerpt from Heidegger, nothing is forced upon the person who receives collectedness, but it is not something gained by his or her own effort. It is not 'effected' in him or her but is more in the nature of a gift, so perhaps there is even an element of synergism. A gift has not only to be bestowed but to be accepted, normally with gratitude. It would also be true to say that the situation which Heidegger describes bears comparison with such religious experiences as revelation, encounter, recognition of a divine presence, or with such specific experiences as Eckhart's near identification of the soul with God or God with the soul, or Eckhart's birth of the Logos or Word in a human soul. Or, to stretch the net a little further, with Kant's claim that sometimes the human mind is seized with an experience of the sublime, not something that it can prepare or devise for itself, or something at its own disposal, but something that overwhelms with its truth and reality, and we must remember that in Kant, as well as in the mystics, God and the finite soul are sometimes hard to distinguish from one another (see below, pp. 202–6). We should remember too that the experiences mentioned are not usually instantaneous. Taken together, they constitute something like a cumulative case for believing that there are ways to the knowledge of God other than through reasoning, but we should not think of them as flashes of illumination, for instance, sudden conversions. These often prove to be evanescent, unless they are strengthened and renewed by regular religious practices.

We can now see how it has happened that Heidegger and Eckhart have been charged, the one with atheism, the other with pantheism. Both charges are, I think, mistaken. The charge made against Heidegger, that he is an atheist or even a nihilist, has been answered by Heidegger himself. He claims that it is based on a misunderstanding of his use of the word 'nothing'. The difference between Being and the beings, the 'ontological difference', is so wide that Being is bound to appear as nothing to those whose attention is fully taken up by the beings of the world. Only when the beings have sunk to nothing does the nothing encounter us as an altogether different and higher reality than that of things, what is adjudged by the positivist to be nothing in the literal sense of 'no thing'. It is an altogether higher reality, the condition that lets the beings be. But we cannot describe it. That is why Heidegger is reluctant to use the word 'God' and why Eckhart talks about passing beyond the Trinity to the divine Essence, a kind of wilderness in which all distinctions have disappeared. Some mystics talk about the 'God beyond God', as does also Paul Tillich in mid-twentieth-century theology. In the absence of all distinctions, it seems hardly to matter whether we call this Ultimate, Being or Nothing

(No-thing). 'Pure Being and pure nothing are the same' (Hegel). In conjoining Being and nothing, we see a further evidence of the connection of Eckhart and Heidegger with the neo-Platonist tradition. This is the doctrine of the *coincidentia oppositorum*, the conjunction of opposites, most fully expounded by Nicholas of Cusa. In the realm of finite beings, the conjunction of opposites would mean the end of logic and of rational thinking, for it would offend against the basic law of non-contradiction. But Nicholas claims that these laws of thought which apply in the realm of finite things do not apply on the level of the infinite, as can be seen from the treatment of infinite numbers in mathematics. Heidegger likewise claims that his arguments do not infringe the laws of logic when our thinking is concerned with Being. Even Nicholas Cusanus could hardly go beyond the following declaration by Heidegger: 'Being is both utterly void and most abundant, most universal and most unique, most intelligible and most resistant to every concept, most in use and yet still ahead of us, most reliable and most abyssal, most forgotten and most memorable, most mentioned and most reticent.'[7]

The imageless mysticism of Eckhart and Heidegger culminating in the Being which is at the same time the Nothing has come out of the western philosophical tradition, but has a close parallel in some forms of Buddhism. The great Buddhist shrine known as the Boro-budur is built on a hill in Indonesia, and the hill is ascended by a pilgrim path which leads upward through the various levels. On the lowest level, the path is bordered by statues of the Buddha in plain view. On a higher level, the statues are partially hidden from view. The climax comes when the pilgrims reach the summit and nothing meets their gaze but the empty sky. Perhaps I should simply say, 'Nothing meets their gaze'. Or should it be, 'Being meets their gaze'?

An interesting link between Eckhart and Heidegger is the fact that both of them seem to teach that there are times in human history when God or ultimate Being comes close and addresses human persons, and times when God is distant, apparently absent. A similar pattern may show itself in the lives of individuals. Heidegger believed that we are living in a time of the forgetting of Being, a time when human energies are entirely taken up with things, with the beings. This alienation from Being has been with us since the time of the Enlightenment. Heidegger was specially impressed with the poetry of Hölderlin, a contemporary of Hegel who kept returning to the theme that the divine or the holy has somehow withdrawn from contact with the human race. In a striking phrase, he wrote: 'The Father has turned away his face.' Why should this be so? Is it simply our fault? Is it our greed, our materialism, our aggression and violence, that have shut out God and the spiritual dimension of life? Or are there deeper influences at work? Heidegger believed that human agency can neither drive out the sense of the Ultimate nor bring it back at a time when it has faded. Being itself may either draw near again or continue to absent itself, we can only await its appearing, though we may try to open ourselves for it. This was the message which Heidegger left in an interview with German journalists from the magazine, *Der Spiegel*. Both his death and the publication took place in 1976, and the title given to the article was a phrase which Heidegger used in the interview and had been frequently used by him in the later years of his life: 'Only a God can save us.'

We may compare these ideas of Heidegger about the presence of Being alternating with periods of absence with some similar ideas in Eckhart. I think that among the many sermons of Eckhart, my favourite is one on a text from the Gospel of John: 'A little while, and you will no longer see me, and again a little while, and you will see me' (John 16.16).[8] In his exposition of the text, Eckhart says: 'The vision and experience of God is too much of a burden to the soul while it is in the body, and so God withdraws intermittently, which is what Christ meant by the saying, "a little while and you shall not see me". But his departure is not final. Again, a little while and we shall see him.' Eckhart's explanation is that if God were there for us all the time, we could not in our finitude sustain this constant presence, and in any case we would have no incentive to seek him. But if God withdraws himself, we bestir ourselves and begin to look for him. If he remained hidden for too long, we might give up the search in despair. But the promise is that we shall see him again. This dialectic of presence and absence, we might say, is part of the pattern of the spiritual life, God's love affair with the human race.

It might be objected that although there is a broad agreement between Eckhart and Heidegger in their experience of God's presence or absence, the former is specifically Christian in his orientation, the latter is not, or, at least, not overtly so. So we find Eckhart, in what he says about God's presence and absence, basing himself on some specific teaching of John's Gospel, whilst Heidegger's appeal is of a very general nature. This is indeed a significant difference between them, but it should not be exaggerated. Mysticism is a form of experience which manifests itself differently in association with particular religious traditions. Christian mysticism, Buddhist mysticism, neo-Platonist mysticism, are all different, yet there are similarities of form and pattern that are discoverable, recurring through the differences.

Neither Eckhart nor Heidegger would be considered strictly orthodox Christians, but they were both within the Christian tradition, and this, I think, may be seen if we consider their views of incarnation. To begin with Eckhart, one might think that he did not lay much stress on incarnation, for does he not advocate a direct breakthrough of the soul to the very essence of God, a breakthrough in which no mediators, not even the Persons of the Trinity, seem to have a part? Yet we have also to note a remarkable parable which he tells:

There were a rich man and his wife. Then the wife suffered a misfortune, through which she lost an eye, and she was much distressed by this. Then her husband came to her and asked, 'Madam, why are you so distressed?' Then she replied, 'Sir, I am not distressing myself about the fact that I have lost my eye; what distresses me is that it seems to me you will love me less because of it.' Then he said, 'Madam, I do love you.' Not long after that, he gouged out one of his own eyes, and came to his wife and said: 'Madam, to make you believe that I love you, I have made myself like you. Now I too have only one eye.' This stands for man, who could scarcely believe that God loved him so much until God gouged out one of his own eyes and took upon himself human nature.[9]

Of course, even in this parable, Eckhart touches only lightly on the incarnation. He is concerned more to tell us about the nature of God as a God who is loving enough and humble enough to take into himself creaturehood. The parable depicts a particular event which leads the mind to a universal truth that God is not simply a transcendent Being external to the created world, but one who also indwells the creation, sharing its life and suffering. This is not, as some have complained, a lapse into pantheism on the part of Eckhart, but an attempt to reach a balanced or dialectical understanding of God as both over us and within us, a view of God common to both Christian and non-Christian mystics.

Something very similar is true of the philosophy of Martin Heidegger. What he calls 'Being' is not another specific being in addition to those that make up the universe, nor even the 'Supreme Being', but rather the Power of Being that lets all things be. The expression which Heidegger sometimes uses for this ultimate level of Reality is simply, in German, *Es gibt*, which means in English, 'There is' or more literally, 'It gives'. This seems to me highly compatible with the Christian teaching that God is love. The mystical strand in the human experience of being-in-the-world does not lay claim to infallibility, and still leaves unanswered questions, but it does have a good claim to bringing us as close as we can get to coming to terms with the mystery of existence.

The Continuing Relevance of Kant

Immanuel Kant has a good claim to be considered the greatest western philosopher of modern times. Today (in spite of those who talk about an ill-defined 'postmodernism'), our thinking is in the main still determined by the insights of the Enlightenment, and these insights found a comprehensive and balanced expression in the works of Kant. Even where nowadays we might question some of the Enlightenment tenets, we find that Kant was ahead of us. A good illustration of this is the optimistic view of the future of the human race, as taught by Lessing and others. Against these, Kant held that there is a radical tendency to evil in the human being. He wrote:

That the world 'lieth in evil' is a plaint as old as history ... More modern, though far less prevalent, is the contrasted optimistic belief, which indeed has gained a following solely among philosophers and, of late, especially among those interested in education – the belief that the world steadily (though most imperceptibly) forges in the other direction, to wit, from bad to better; at least that the predisposition to such a movement is discoverable in human nature. If this belief, however, is meant to apply to moral goodness and badness (not simply to the process of civilization), it has certainly not been deduced from experience; the history of all times cries too loudly against it.[1]

But this independence of mind, by which he challenged a widely held conviction of his contemporaries, Kant derived from the

Enlightenment itself, for in his essay, 'What is Enlightenment?' he had written: 'Dare to know! Have the courage to make use of your own understanding – this is the motto of the Enlightenment.'[2] So Kant was no slavish follower of the current fashion of thought. He dared to be enlightened about the Enlightenment itself, and perhaps this was especially the case in problems of religion. The problems I have in mind include the relation of natural theology to the theology that claims to be founded on a particular revelation, and the question of how far religious belief originates from a reality beyond ourselves and how far it arises out of the constitution of our own human nature. These are problems that are still with us. Indeed, it was when reading some of the work of Robert Scharlemann that I decided it might be worthwhile to go back and look again at what Kant had said on some of the issues.

The first of the problems I have just been mentioning is that of the relation of a so-called natural theology to a so-called revealed theology. I have put in the qualification, 'so-called', because it seems to me that there is no hard and fast distinction between the two. A natural theology almost inescapably incorporates ideas from revelation and may even appeal to a general revelation, while a revealed theology is only revealed if its revelation comes to us in events accessible in space and time. But though it would be difficult to make the distinction altogether precise, it is a distinction commonly made, and clear enough for most purposes.

As is well known, Kant had in his *Critique of Pure Reason* severely criticized the traditional natural theology on the grounds that it had transgressed the limitations of human reason to the phenomena of the world of space and time. By offering 'proofs' of the existence of God, it had strayed into the off-limits realm of transcendence. When Kant came to write his late book, *Religion within the Limits of Reason Alone*, then, as the title indicates, this was intended to be an exposition of religion founded on reason, not on a particular revelation, and he believed that it had the possibility of becoming the universal religion of the future. So, in one sense of these slippery terms, this rational religion expounded a natural, not a revealed theology, but this rational religion could not be the natural theology that he had tried to discredit in his first Critique. So we have to make our distinctions more precise. (1) There is natural theology in the old sense, using natural human intelligence to prove God's reality, but rejected by Kant because it went beyond the limits of reason. (2) There is revealed theology, basing itself on the Bible and the Church, but rejected or at least rendered doubtful by the Enlightenment because it relied on authority. (3) There was Kant's new religion within the limits of reason alone, offering itself as a replacement for both the old natural theology and the official or ecclesial theology based on revelation.

In the second edition of the religion book, Kant himself explained in the Preface how he understood the difference between a rational and a revealed theology. He compared the two types to two concentric circles. The larger of the two circles is revealed or biblical theology and this contains all the historical and doctrinal material out of which Christian theology has been constructed. The rational theologian or philosopher of religion must set aside all this material so far as it is concerned with the particular details of the supposed revelation, and extract from it its timeless essence, by which Kant understood its moral teaching. This moral teaching is capable of being derived from rational principles alone. Here we may note that Kant considered the main (or even the sole) value of religion to lie in its inculcation of moral sentiments. We have noted that moral principles are, in Kant's view, derivable from our own rationality, so if religion is (as he seems frequently to say) of value only as a support for morality, religion too must be derived from reason. Thus, although rational religion is latent as the essence of Christianity, and can be disengaged from its doctrinal and historical trappings, Kant visualizes a time in the future, possibly the distant future, when rational religion would be completely separated from the particularities of Christianity or any other concrete historical faith. In Kant's testimony, there is, strictly speaking, only one religion, which is rational religion, but many faiths, such as Christianity, Judaism, Islam and so on.

Certainly Kant leans heavily in the direction of a purely rational or natural theology, yet he never quite shakes off the Christian revelation, and perhaps does not want to do so. In fact, he is very ingenious in showing how various items in the revelation and in the system that has grown out of it can all be understood as symbolic representations of the truth. But it is this rational or natural religion that is important to him, and he sees Christianity as valuable only to the extent that it embodies rational religion. To support this view, Kant has to wrench Christianity out of its historical context, denying its connections with Judaism. He declares that 'completely forsaking the Judaism from which it sprang,' Christianity was 'grounded on a wholly new principle' and 'contained from its first beginning the seed and the principle of the objective unity of the true and universal religious faith'.[3] But surely to say this is to acknowledge that Christianity is indeed a revelation, a genuine leap forward in understanding the meaning of faith. The truth seems to be that even Kant is having difficulty in delimiting the border between the natural and the revealed.

He tells us: 'We need no empirical example to make the idea of a person morally well-pleasing to God our archetype; this idea as an archetype is already present in our reason.'[4] But when he tells us in more detail what the content of this archetype is, we read:

> This ideal of a humanity pleasing to God (hence of such moral perfection as is possible to an earthly being who is subject to wants and inclinations) we can represent to ourselves only as the idea of a person who would be willing not only to discharge all human duties and to spread about him goodness as widely as possible by precept and example, but even, though tempted by the greatest allurements, to take upon himself every affliction, up to the most ignominious death, for the good of the world and even for his enemies.[5]

What is described here is no bare moral ideal, no archetype reached by abstract reasoning, but an unmistakable allusion to the concrete historical figure of Jesus Christ. So there does seem to be some important revelation here. The empirical example is not so dispensable as Kant had suggested, and it cannot be dismissed as simply auxiliary, in the sense that it has led human beings more quickly to a vision of the moral ideal than their own reasoning processes would have done.

This confirms the belief that natural religion and natural theology are not opposed to revealed religion and revealed theology. On the contrary, each side seems to require the other. Although we have begun from Kant and the claims of rational religion, I believe we would have come to a similar conclusion if we had begun from Barth and the claims of revelation.[6] The reason for the convergence of the two positions is clear. How could we ever recognize a revelation as revelation unless we had some innate capacity for so recognizing it, some archetype already in the reason, to use Kant's terminology? And how could such an archetype ever impinge upon us and become a guiding principle for human life, unless it had appeared in flesh and blood and in historical actuality?

These considerations bring us to the second of the three problems mentioned near the beginning of this chapter – the problem of God and his relation both to the world at large and to the human race in particular. Although Kant denied that the traditional 'proofs' of the existence of God are sound, he was not an atheist. God, however, does remain elusive in Kant's philosophy. Probably for much of his life Kant thought of God in a way that was typical in the eighteenth century, that is to say, after the manner of the deists. This deistic God was conceived as a transcendent being beyond the world. He had created the world and given it in the beginning both the laws of nature and the moral law, and then left it to its own devices. The natural world was seen increasingly as a self-regulating system, and the idea of God became increasingly superfluous, at least as far as the natural world is concerned. So Kant's evaluation of the traditional natural theology was negative. But it was not entirely so. In his criticism of the argument from design, he claims that it gives some evidence of a divine architect. The moral law fared better, and became for Kant the point at which human life does encounter transcendence. But we hear echoes of both the natural and the moral laws in the famous words inscribed on Kant's tomb in the cathedral of Königsberg: 'Two things fill the mind with ever new and increasing wonder and awe, the oftener and the more intensely we meditate upon them; the starry heavens above me and the moral law within me.'[7]

The quotation shows us something that was typical of Kant's mature thought, namely, that the moral law within was presenting itself alongside the starry heavens as that which made the deepest impression upon him and excited awe and wonder. So his rejection of the traditional proofs for the existence of God was balanced by new arguments based on the facts of morality. But the relation of God to the moral life remained somewhat ambiguous in Kant. On the one hand, he was strongly opposed to any form of heteronomy, that is to say, the view that the moral law is imposed by any agency outside of the human person who is subject to that law. 'So far as morality is based on the conception of man as a free agent who, just because he is free, binds himself through his reason to unconditioned laws, it stands in need neither of the idea of another Being over him, for him to apprehend his duty; nor of an incentive other than the law itself, for him to do his duty.'[8] But in spite of his insistence on the autonomy of the human moral agent, Kant in his later writings seems to suggest that religion teaches us to see the moral law as a divine command. For instance, in what is virtually a definition of religion as he understood it, he says: 'Religion is morality in relation to God as Lawgiver.'[9] Furthermore, if we recall Kant's belief that there is a radically evil tendency at work in human nature, he acknowledges the need for some kind of conversion experience, or for the need of divine assistance or grace. And although he has great difficulty in accommodating such an idea, he notes the weakness of our nature in the face of moral demands. Yet he is well aware that to acknowledge this weakness contradicts some of his strongest Enlightenment convictions.

If we are willing to extend our view to the very end of Kant's career and to take into our reckoning the *opus postumum*, we find an attempt to resolve the difficulties. The work in question was put together out of a very large number of fragments left by Kant at his death. The idea of God which emerges from these fragments is very different from that of the distant God of deism which appears to underlie most of the writings in which he mentions God. He seems at the end to have moved very far in the direction of an immanent God, or perhaps one should rather say that he strives, in paradoxical language, to speak of God as both immanent and transcendent, both within and without. So we find the following expressions are all given a place:

> God must only be sought *within* us . . . God is not a being outside of me. The proposition, 'There is a God', means no more than, 'There is in human reason, determining itself according to morality, a Supreme Principle'. There is a Being in me, distinguished from myself as the cause of an effect wrought upon me, which freely – that is, without being dependent on laws of nature in space and time – judges me within, justifying or condemning me; and I, as man, am myself this Being, and it is no substance external to me, and, what is most surprising of all, its causality is no natural necessity but a determination of me to a free act.[10]

What do we make of these remarks? Commentators have differed in their interpretations. A few have thought that it represents a retreat by Kant from even the attenuated theism which had formerly been part of his philosophy. But a more plausible explanation is that here we have an attempt to supply the dimension of the immanence of God, previously missing. Moreover, this change in the conception of God is at the same time aimed at resolving the conflict between the existence of God and Kant's cherished belief in human autonomy. Clement Webb, in his study of Kant's philosophy of religion, has this to say:

> [Kant] had always believed in God, and thought that faith in him was bound up with the moral life, in the living of which

alone man possessed true dignity, because in living it, and only so, did he attain to true personality. The difficulties of theoretically justifying this faith had produced that hesitation in the use of religious language, that meticulous caution in the indulgence of the religious sentiments, which is so apt to strike a certain chill into the readers of his early works. But now, at the end of his life, encouraged perhaps by the open immanentism of his younger contemporaries, he was prepared to repudiate more outspokenly the deism which had been so predominant in his youth – the deism which had taught a merely transcendent God who was supposed to be needed to explain the order of the world, but who was too remote from human concerns to be in any true sense the 'heart and rule of life,' and who was to be honoured rather by intellectual acknowledgement than by a strict life of duty.[11]

Can we accept Webb's interpretation of Kant in these matters? I think we do have to examine it more closely before we can agree that the views expressed in the *opus postumum* in fragmentary and paradoxical form have been rightly interpreted by Webb as meaning that Kant had eventually arrived at a view which could be properly described as a form of theism. Does it not look rather like a form of pantheism, in which the deistic conception of a God who is wholly outside of the universe and beyond the human race has been converted into a God who is wholly immanent in earthly realities, including human realities, and who would be at best a kind of world-soul? Or, in another possible interpretation, is God being conceived by Kant as no more than an idea or ideal originating in the human mind itself, a merely 'regulative' idea in his terminology, what in earlier writing he had called a *focus imaginarius*?[12] No doubt these points could be debated further, but I think that if one bears in mind that Kant is seeking to express a very delicate balance between what acts from within and what acts from without, and further that he is trying to do this in reaction against the exaggeratedly external God of deism, then Webb's interpretation is not an unreasonable one.

Where, however, one might have new doubts about Webb's reading of Kant is at the point where he claims, admittedly with some support from the *opus postumum*, that the God of whom Kant is now writing, is a personal God, and that Kant 'could now more fully than before recognize in the moral law itself, by which his religious emotions had always been most deeply stirred, God and (as he puts it now for the first time) his personality immediately revealed to the soul as the Supreme Reality'.[13] Can we read so much into Kant's words? Certainly one might agree that in moral experience (as Kant believed) the human being breaks out beyond the phenomenal realm to make contact with a reality which may rightly be called 'spiritual', and certainly too this reality was experienced by Kant as holy, that is to say, as charged with religious value. It evoked what he called *Achtung* ('reverence' or 'respect') in the moral agent.[14] But was it experienced as a personal reality? This is more doubtful. Kant's strongly rationalist mentality led him, like many other philosophers of religion, to distrust any anthropomorphic language about God. This very word 'God' carries, for those of us brought up in the Judaeo-Christian tradition, the connotation of a personal being, but for some devoutly religious people, the object of their worship may be conceived as non-personal, though presumably as suprapersonal rather than subpersonal. That is why I have elsewhere suggested that 'Holy Being'[15] is a more inclusive and neutral term than 'God', though it is an expression that would be used in academic discourse, not normally in liturgy.

But in fairness to Webb – and perhaps also to Kant – we have to take the discussion a little further. Is it possible to separate such ideas as law, morality, spiritual reality from the life of persons or of a community of persons? It is true that in the passages in which he discusses reverence, Kant tries as far as possible to disengage this feeling from its affective associations, and indicates that reverence is directed to law, rather than to a person or persons. But does law exist outside a community of persons, and here the discussion concerns explicitly moral law, not the laws of nature, where the word 'law' has a different sense? Can there be a moral law that has not emanated from a source that is at least personal, or, possibly, suprapersonal, if we can venture to speak of the suprapersonal? Can our reverence for moral law be detached from a reverence for its source? To put the question in another way, could we acknowledge as God or Holy Being an abstract principle of reasoning without locating that principle or its source in some spiritual Being conceived in a manner analogous to that in which Christian theology has traditionally conceived God?

That Kant seems to have acknowledged an analogy between God and the human being can be established by examining another passage in his book on religion. If we ask what he means by the 'archetype' of a human life 'well-pleasing' to God, he tells us that it needs no special relation from outside, but is something that we can discover through our reason. He does not, however, claim that we invented it for ourselves. It is part of the givenness of our human nature. The archetype of a life well pleasing to God is something that we discover as part of our original endowment as we move through life and increasingly discover who and what we are. In theological language, this could be expressed by saying that we are made in the image of God. Kant does not use that language, but surely the language that he does use has powerful echoes from the mythological accounts of creation in the early chapters of Genesis. Speaking of the archetype, he says, 'just because we are not the authors of this idea and because it has established itself in man without our comprehending how human nature could have been capable of receiving it, it is more appropriate to say that this archetype *has come down* to us and *assumed our humanity*'. Here he seems to take over the traditional theological language of incarnation.

But does Kant understand this only in the vague sense of a general incarnation in all humanity, a godward trend as at least a potentiality in men and women, or does he associate it with the concrete and particular incarnation which Christians have claimed to perceive in Jesus Christ? This question is one that cannot be answered with complete assurance. Kant said different things at different times in his life, some of them apparently inconsistent with each other. He believed that there is a radical

streak of evil in human nature, that can only be overcome by
something like divine grace, however much he may have disliked
that idea. When he tries to describe the content of the archetypal
human life, he does so in terms which obviously refer to Jesus
Christ (see above, p. 199). And there is one more point that
has to be considered. What did Kant mean by the 'sublime',
mentioned in the third and most neglected of his *Critiques*?[16]
He defines the 'sublime' as 'the name given to that which is
absolutely great, what is beyond all comparison great'. The concept was introduced in the context of aesthetics, but has been
extended to other subjects. Some postmodern philosophers of
religion have applied it within their branch of philosophy, and
perhaps Kant himself opened up this possibility. His words
about the starry heavens and the moral law as awe-producing,
seem to look very much like an experience of the sublime, of
that which 'overwhelms' the recipient of the experience and yet
'draws' him to itself. Kant's analysis has a close resemblance
to Otto's analysis of the numinous, which he resolves into
the *mysterium tremendum fascinans* as the heart of religious
experience. Such an experience may arise when logical arguments over the existence or non-existence of God have reached
an impasse, and it is more like a sense-perception than an argument. Could we say that Jesus Christ is an instance of the sublime, by which I mean that the historical figure proclaimed in
the Christian gospel is identifiable with the archetype of humanity which we already find within the mind? If so, we may be
coming into view of a reconciliation between the type of religion
and theology which claims to depend on the human mind itself
and the type which appeals predominantly to a revelation given
in history by God.

We have also reached the stage where we can proceed to the
third and last of the problems stated near the beginning of this
chapter, namely, how far religious belief originates from a reality
beyond ourselves, and how far it arises out of the constitution
of our own humanity. That is not an easy matter to decide. We
do seem to have a tendency to project our own experiences upon
persons or objects outside of ourselves. No doubt the reason

for this is chiefly to avoid responsibility. God, the stars, and nowadays society, are convenient entities on which to project the burdens which may lie upon our consciences. Here we may briefly consider the role of conscience. Popular theories explain conscience as the voice of society, or in Freud's terminology, the *superego*, which becomes internalized in our experience, and approves or disapproves of different courses of action according to the standards of the society in which we live. In earlier times, conscience was taken to be the voice of God. No doubt, there have been and still are many cases where conscience does in fact represent simply standards of conduct commonly held in contemporary society, and there are still many people for whom conscience is the voice of God, to be learned from the Bible or some other sacred book. But these views are simplistic, and conscience at a deeper level can be explained as the average sinful human being's awareness of the success or failure of the efforts made to conform life to that ideal archetype, as Kant called it, which is already given in the constitution of our nature and toward which we have an innate tendency to transcend, the highest level of development of moral and personal development for the human being. And although Kant, as a philosopher, eschewed as far as possible an overtly theological terminogy he is surely saying something very similar to what a Christian theologian, Karl Rahner, would be saying about 250 years after Kant: 'Christ has always been involved in the whole of history as its prospective entelechy.'[17]

The Problem of Religious Knowledge

It was in 1962 that I arrived in the United States from Scotland to take up the position of Professor of Systematic Theology in Union Theological Seminary, New York. The Seminary had arranged for me to make visits to other seminaries and colleges in the eastern parts of the country, so that I might meet colleagues working in the field of Systematic Theology and have an exchange with them.

So it came about that in the spring of 1963 I went to Washington, DC. Among the institutions which had invited me there was Howard University, at that time a virtually all-black community. I was kindly received, and among those whom I met was Professor James Deotis Roberts (b. 1927), at that time still in the early part of his career. We struck up a friendship which has lasted ever since, renewed from time to time by meetings in both the United States and the United Kingdom. So let me begin by saying how pleased and honoured I am to have been invited to contribute to his *Festschrift*, and to celebrate both his outstanding public achievements as a man and a theologian, and at the same time almost forty years of personal friendship.

During the course of that visit, Professor Roberts presented me with a copy of his early book, *Faith and Reason: A Comparative Study of Pascal, Bergson and James*. It was inscribed on the flyleaf: 'To Prof. John Macquarrie with the compliments of the Author. May 23, 1963.' We made the interesting discovery too that during a period of study at the University of Edinburgh, Deotis had at weekends served a church very close to my home town.

Later he was to gain fame through his contributions to black theology, but in those days black theology had not yet begun to have the influence which it was destined to attain. But I think it is important to remember that before he wrote his books on black theology, Professor Roberts had wrestled with one of the most stubborn problems in what we may call fundamental theology. In an age of science, there is a widespread view that unless beliefs can be substantiated by arguments analogous to those used by natural scientists, they cannot qualify as 'knowledge'. They are dismissed as mere 'opinions' or even, by some extreme critics, as utterances without any cognitive content. One of the most challenging questions that can be addressed to any theologian or preacher is 'How do you justify your claim to have knowledge of God, or of Christ, or of human destiny?' Just as the everyday applications of mathematics in our technological civilization depend on more basic work in what is called 'pure' mathematics, so the application of theology to social questions presupposes a prior engagement with what I have called 'fundamental' theology.

That is why I am claiming importance for Professor Roberts' early engagement with the problem of religious knowledge, and why in this chapter I shall concentrate attention on his book, *Faith and Reason*. The subtitle of the book informs us that Roberts will consider three important figures from the history of philosophy – Blaise Pascal, Henri Bergson and William James. These three thinkers are all quite different from one another, but they were all in agreement in believing that truth has forms that are neither attainable nor testable by the logical procedures of abstract reasoning, and that these include the truths of religion.

Pascal appeals to the 'heart'. Admittedly, this is a vague word, which we associate more with romanticism than with science. When Pascal declares that 'we know the truth not only by reasoning, but also by means of the heart, and it is in the latter way that we know first principles . . . the heart has its reasons of which reason does not know',[1] he seems to be claiming some kind of intuition or direct knowing, rather like a direct perception, yet a form of knowing of which only vague accounts are given by those who claim to have experienced it. Obviously we shall have to come back to it for closer examination. May we perhaps provisionally name it, 'mystical knowing'? Meanwhile, we should note that Pascal was not in the least anti-scientific, but one of the most eminent mathematicians and physicists of his day. At the same time, he believed that not all our knowing is rational and scientific. There are other important forms of knowing, and these too have a rightful claim to be considered knowledge. He mentions in the passage quoted in this paragraph 'first principles', and probably he was thinking of the axioms and laws of thought that underlie mathematics and logic, yet which cannot be proved but are simply accepted as implicates of the very act of thinking. Is Pascal claiming that there is some analogy between these first principles of thinking and the basic truths of religion considered as implicates of living as a human being? C. G. Jung, for instance, claimed that there are in the human mind certain privileged *a priori* ideas, including the idea of God. He called such ideas 'archetypes', and they are so far from needing 'justification' that they provide themselves a basis for truth. On the other hand, he thinks that when someone has constructed a proof of God's existence, he is very quickly assailed by questions about its adequacy, and ends up with more doubts than he had when he began.

Bergson, who belonged to the Jewish community in France, had a scientific background, from which he moved into philosophy. His studies had been in biology, and what specially interested him was the difference between instinct and intelligence in the animal world. Many forms of animal life 'know' how to build nests or webs or perform other complicated patterns of behaviour without having learned them, they do it 'by instinct', as we say. It seems that they inherit these behaviour-patterns just as other animals have developed specialized organs, but instinct and its transmission are only very imperfectly understood. Bergson contrasts it with 'intelligence' which reaches its highest development in man. To these two modes of cognition there correspond two contrasting ways of understanding time.

In science, time is quantified and understood on analogy with space. Like a cinematograph, it breaks up the sequence of events into a series of static pictures. Only in our direct experience of time as duration, as dynamic and irreversible, time as a flowing stream, so to speak, do we begin to understand the temporal. He used his conception of time to defend the freedom of the human will and then, in a broader application, to distinguish between the material and the spiritual realms.

In his most famous book, *Creative Evolution*, his studies led him to emphasize the importance of instinct as contrasted with intelligence, and he claimed to discern in evolution a driving force or creative thrust (he called this *nisus* the *élan vital*) in opposition to the widely held Darwinian view that the changes of evolution come about mainly or even exclusively from chance mutations. In later writings, the somewhat vague idea of a creative urge toward life approaches nearer to the traditional idea of God. When he made his will in 1937, Bergson included the words, 'My reflections have led me nearer and nearer to Catholicism'. But he foresaw the wave of anti-semitism that was about to flood Europe at that time, and to his credit he stood loyally by the Jewish people and identified with them.

Different from both Pascal and Bergson is William James. His philosophy is often called 'pragmatism', but this is a word that has deteriorated in recent years. It is now often applied to the actions of politicians who care little about moral principles and are interested only in practical measures that will realize their ends. That was not how James understood it. Certainly he believed that thought and action must go together, but he did not share the views of those (including many scientists) who believe that thought must be 'value-free', that is to say, uninfluenced by religious or moral considerations. By contrast, James believed that our thinking is true (though this can never be more than a matter of degree) when it enriches human life. 'Any idea upon which we can ride, so to speak; any idea that can carry us prosperously from one part of our experience to any other part, linking things satisfactorily, working securely, simplifying, saving labour, is true just for so much.'[2]

The truth of religion, therefore, is not to be settled by intellectual arguments but only by the test of submitting ourselves to what James calls the 'religious hypothesis', namely, that human lives are somehow continuous with a larger life from which they derive help. Here he is perhaps stretching pragmatism to its limits, to something like a metaphysical speculation, though one might say that the test of truth remains pragmatic. He speculates that the unconscious reaches of the self may form the link with this larger spiritual world. He writes:

> The further limits of our being plunge, it seems to me, into an altogether other dimension of existence from the sensible and merely 'understandable' world. Name it the mystical region or supernatural region, whichever you choose. The unseen region in question is not merely ideal, for it produces effects in this world. But that which produces effects within another reality must be termed a reality itself; 'God' is the natural appellation for the supreme reality, so I will call this higher part of the universe by the name of God.[3]

I am not wholly convinced by this argument, which seems to be a departure from James' pragmatic method through the incorporation of a strong mystical tendency. But he could defend his position on purely pragmatic grounds if indeed religion and the acknowledgement of God have been shown historically to be an enrichment of human life. Incidentally, the reader may notice the close similarity between Bergson's move from the *élan vital* to God and that of James. The two men were in fact friends and correspondents.

Professor Roberts states in his Preface that his three chosen examplars 'make a radical break from the position to which they object (the autonomy of the rational method) and the swing to the opposite view (the affirmation of intuition)'.[4] He was wise to choose three exemplars rather than only one, for it seems that 'mystical experience' is an expression which covers many different kinds of meetings with God and has received many names. Jesus and Socrates, from whom our explorations began, both claimed to hear the voice of God sending them out on their respective missions at the beginning of their adult lives, Paul speaks of 'spiritual discernment' (1 Cor. 2.14), others have had deep inner experiences which they have great difficulty in expressing. The *terrain* covered by all these spiritual experiences is extensive and has not yet been carefully mapped. Any account of it is bound to be incomplete and will perhaps remain so. Possibly Kierkegaard and Bultmann, despite their devaluing of the historical element in the Gospels and their distaste for metaphysical speculation, could be added to the three exemplars named by Professor Roberts, but these two additions would tilt the scales toward the 'by faith alone' position.

In the preceding paragraph, I have assembled a somewhat untidy and disparate collection of witnesses to the occurrence of what we are calling, in a broad sense, 'mystical' experience, some of them drawn from Professor Roberts' book, some from other sources. It is interesting to note that Roberts does not place his three mentors on an equal footing. He gives the primacy to Pascal and he believes that he does so with good reason. All three had written in positive and appreciative terms of mysticism, but (so far as one can make such judgements) perhaps only Pascal was himself a mystic in the fullest sense and what he wrote on the subject was based on his own experience and has a special authority.

Pascal did in fact claim to have mystical experience and went so far as to compare his experience with that of Augustine. Only someone supremely confident in the validity of his experience would have made the overwhelming claim that he made: 'Jesus Christ is the goal of everything, and the centre to which everything tends. He who knows him knows the reason for all things.'[5] This is such a bold claim that perhaps one is initially put off by it. Is not this pure subjectivism? Is this not the kind of utterance that sets people against mysticism? Perhaps it is. But possibly there are different degrees of mysticism, just as there are different levels of aesthetic sensitivity, of moral attainment and of intellectual ability. When I wrote a few sentences back that, among the three exemplars chosen by Roberts, 'perhaps only

Pascal was himself a mystic in the fullest sense', I seemed to imply that he may (as he claimed) have been a recipient of mystical experiences similar to those of Augustine, whereas Bergson and James, though well versed in mystical literature and well disposed toward mysticism, may not have known it with the same immediacy and intensity that was experienced by Pascal. And when one begins to consider such cases, one might believe that they are, shall we say, stages on the way to that full encounter with God which is, perhaps, granted only to a few. One might, of course, still raise the objection that an individual experience falls short of an assured scientific conclusion that has been publicly scrutinized and tested. Nevertheless, the fact that as well as the deep experiences of a Pascal or an Eckhart, there are less striking experiences such as the constant experience of a divine presence, as reported by the Scottish theologian John Baillie or the impressive spirituality of Archbishop Michael Ramsey, and that their experiences are by no means uncommon must increase the probability that there are indeed genuine experiences of an Other whose existence and characteristics are not known in the same way as the objects and even the persons we encounter within the world.

The word 'knowledge' does not denote just one type of experience. We have been thinking so far in this chapter of a kind of knowing which, in its fullest and deepest form, is probably quite rare, but it is not difficult to find analogies which link our everyday experiences of knowing with what we have been calling 'mystical' knowledge.

Among these everyday experiences of knowing, the clearest distinction which we all draw is between knowing things and knowing persons, and it is obvious that if there is such an experience as mystical knowledge, it is closer in its nature to knowing persons than to knowing things. Knowledge of things and their behaviour is called 'objective' knowledge, it is built on observation, it is usually from the outside, and it frequently has mastery over the thing as its aim. Knowledge of other persons, which may include objective knowledge about them, is nevertheless very different from objective knowledge. The other person is not an object, but a fellow subject, the knowledge of the two persons is reciprocal, each knower being also the known. As mentioned already, our knowledge of another person will normally include some objective facts about him or her (weight, age, height, appearance, etc.) but more than these facts, more than the whole description given in *Who's Who*, would be implied if someone said that he knew another person who had been named. To know someone as a person, one must have talked to him or her, have shared experiences, perhaps shared common interests. Yet however complicated and even illogical personal knowledge may be compared with objective knowledge, there is one important way in which it remains closer to our knowledge of things than mystical knowledge, namely, that whether we are knowing things or living persons, we can see, hear, address or otherwise have sense-impressions of whatever it is that we know, and this important link is (often, though not always) missing in any alleged mystical knowledge.

Yet I would still say that one's knowledge of other people is closer to mystical knowledge than to objective knowledge. Personal knowledge is not objectifying. Such knowledge cannot be tested in the same way as objective knowledge. We do not claim to *know* a person if we know a few facts about him or her. One person knows another only as he or she is known by that other, through to some extent sharing their lives. I am not of course denying that one may also have objective knowledge of a person and sometimes this is important.

We must also ask about self-knowledge. It seems quite likely that the knowing of one's self is subsequent to the knowing of the other, and that the young child knows its mother before it learns to distinguish its own separated selfhood. We are told that there is no I without a Thou. Yet once self-knowledge has been awakened, we can see that its roots lie in the basic fact that one exists and knows that one exists. Just as the laws of logic are *a priori*, possibly in the sense that they are implied in the very activity of thinking, so (as Kant and Jung seem to have believed) there are 'archetypes' in the human mind such as God and the ideal of a human person which are already implicit in the very mode of human existence.

Could one even venture to extend this possibility of a trigger to mystical knowing to the natural world? Suppose one becomes fascinated by the mere existence of a world, and asks the question of Leibniz, 'Why is there anything, rather than just nothing?' Even an atheist may be brought to something like a mystical experience by that question. Professor Eugene Long cites the sceptical philosopher J. J. C. Smart, who after claiming that he knew how any version of the cosmological argument for God's existence can be 'pulled to pieces by correct logic', confessed that 'I still feel that I want to go on asking the question ... that anything should exist at all does seem to me to be a matter for the deepest awe'.[6] Smart, on his own admission, does not find any answer to the God-question satisfying, even when it is based on 'correct logic'. So there must be something more than logic involved in such a question. Call this 'something more' mystical knowledge, though just to give it a name is not to explain it. Eric Mascall called it 'wondering contemplation' (see above, p. 55). It is to link it with a type of experience reported by sensitive individuals scattered through the world's religions and found even outside of a specific religious context. The experience is often associated with a feeling, in Smart's case with awe, which in turn is associated with the sense of the holy. Analogous also is the feeling of *Angst*, 'dread' or 'anxiety', as described by existentialist writers, notably Kierkegaard and Heidegger. Kierkegaard can speak also of the sense of sin as the way of entry into Christianity. The feelings or moods they mention are not mere fleeting emotions but have some cognitive content, a holistic awareness of one's existence as finite being-in-the-world. They are sometimes called 'ontological feelings'.

Such mystical knowledge is of a different kind from the detailed knowledge of the entities within the physical world explored by the natural sciences, and it can be neither validated nor discredited by the methods of science, not even by 'correct logic'. Yet the two kinds of knowledge are not in opposition to one another, and both belong to human experience, though in varying degrees.

To hark back to Kant who was discussed in the last chapter

(see especially pp. 206–7), reason and what may justly be called 'mystical' experience – he prefers to talk of experience of the sublime – are not totally different from one another. Rather, in the mystical or the sublime the outreach of reason is stretched to become aware of the supersensible, described also as the substrate of both man and nature. Because this is a holistic experience, it resists conceptualization, and out awareness of it comes through feeling rather than through understanding. We recognize something ultimate, something beyond the bounds of ordinary experience, the place where to use Kierkegaard's language, 'reason makes a collision', and either has to give up or seek a different way of thinking about the question.

Kant's idea of the sublime has had something of a comeback in recent years, especially among such postmodernist philosophers as Lyotard and Derrida. The English theologian John Milbank has also appropriated the idea of the sublime, though he finds it exemplified in Kierkegaard, Nietzsche and Heidegger rather than in Kant. Perhaps it appears too in Bultmann's christology, though this is offered with virtually no supporting argument. According to Milbank, in Kant 'the sublime or indeterminable was safely off-limits for the proper exercise of theoretical reason, which is confined to notions that can be "schematized" within space and time. In the second phase, sublimity is perceived to "contaminate" what is deceptively taken for finitude.'[7] As Milbank says, philosophers are not content to remain silent on the sublime or the mystical. They have searched desperately for ways to talk about that which lies beyond both reason and ordinary language. Even Derrida, for all his scepticism, seems to find a place for the sublime in his elastic concept of *différance*. These recent recoveries of the sublime add to the suspicion that postmodernism, in some of its manifestations, is a return to premodernism, which would then mean a recovery of the rights of reason together with a curbing of its more exclusive demands. It would be interesting to enquire how far Professor Roberts' early book influenced his better known volumes on black theology, but that would be too large an enquiry to begin here. What can be said is that Professor Roberts, in that early book on the roots of a mystical knowledge of God, was touching on problems that are still high on the theological agenda. These questions are linked to his transition to black theology. Roberts has firsthand experience of what it means to be black. This is not theoretical knowledge, but something he knows 'in his bones', so to speak. Perhaps this is why white 'liberal' theologians have such difficulty with black theology. At any rate, James Deotis Roberts has put back on the table some questions affecting the very foundations of our knowledge of God, and that in itself is an important achievement.

Notes

Chapter 1 Jesus and Socrates

This chapter was the Bevir Lecture for 1996, delivered at Eton College on 24 January. Hitherto unpublished.

1. Plato, *Apology*, 31.
2. Xenophon, *Memorabilia*, I, 1, 2.
3. Plato, *Apology*, 24.
4. *Apology*, 17.
5. *Apology*, 17.
6. Plato, *Crito*, 4.

Chapter 2 Wycliffe on Lordship, Divine and Human

Wycliffe died in 1384, and this chapter was a memorial lecture delivered at Wycliffe College, Toronto, to mark the 600th anniversary of his death. It was first published in the college journal, *Insight*, no. 17, Toronto, November 1984.

1. Herbert B. Workman, *John Wycliffe: A Study of the English Medieval Church*, Oxford: Oxford University Press, 1926, 1, p. 217.
2. Workman, *John Wycliffe*, p. 275.
3. The Latin text of *De Demonio Divino*, edited by Reginald L. Poole, was published for the Wyclif Society by Trübner & Co., London, 1890 (hereafter referred to in the notes as *DDD*). The text of *De Civili Dominio* (*DCD*), also edited by Poole and published in the same series, had appeared in 1885.
4. *DDD*, pp. 257–476.
5. See J. Habermas, *Erkenntnis und Interesse*, Frankfurt: Suhrkamp, 1968.
6. G. W. F. Hegel, *The Phenomenology of Mind*, tr. J. B. Baillie, London: Allen & Unwin, 1931, pp. 227–40.

7. William Temple, *Christianity and Social Order*, London: SPCK, 1976, pp. 50–1.

8. Peter L. Berger, *A Rumour of Angels*, Garden City, NY: Doubleday, 1969, p. 94.

9. *Determinatio de Dominio*, in J. Loserth (ed.), *Opera Minora*, Trübner, 1913, pp. 404–30.

10. *DDD*, p. 4.

11. *DDD*, p. 220.

12. *DDD*, p. 16.

13. *DDD*, p. 149.

14. *DDD*, pp. 199–235.

15. *DCD*, p. xxi.

16. *DCD*, p. xxi.

17. *DCD*, p. 1.

18. *DCD*, p. 47.

19. Martin Luther, *Three Treatises*, tr. C. M. Jacobs et al., Philadelphia: Fortress Press, 1982, p. 277.

Chapter 3 *Temple on Transcendence and Immanence*

This chapter was a lecture given at a conference in Trinity College in the University of Toronto in 1981, celebrating the centenary of William Temple's birth. It was first published in *The Experiment of Life*, ed. F. Kenneth Hare, University of Toronto Press, 1983.

1. Edward Heath in his foreword to Temple's *Christianity and Social Order*, London: SPCK, 1976 (hereafter *CSO*).

2. Edward Norman, *Church and Society in England*, Oxford: Oxford University Press, 1976, p. 280.

3. A. M. G. Stephenson, *Anglicanism and the Lambeth Conferences*, London: SPCK, 1978, pp. 161ff.

4. William Temple, *Nature, Man and God*, London: Macmillan, 1934 (hereafter *NMG*).

5. Owen C. Thomas, *William Temple's Philosophy of Religion*, London: SPCK, 1961.

6. *Temple's Philosophy of Religion*, p. 147.

7. Temple, *NMG*, p. 57.

8. *NMG*, p. 57.

9. *NMG*, p. 212.

10. *NMG*, p. 261.

11. *NMG*, p. 395.

12. *NMG*, p. 265.

13. *NMG*, p. 435.

14. *NMG*, p. 480.
15. *NMG*, p. 265.
16. *NMG*, pp. 269–70.
17. Pierre Teilhard de Chardin, *The Phenomenon of Man*, London: Collins, 1959, p. 35.
18. Temple, *NMG*, p. 75.
19. *NMG*, p. 478.
20. William Temple, *Christus Veritas*, London: Macmillan, 1924, p. ix.
21. William Temple, 'The Divinity of Christ', in B. H. Streeter (ed.), *Foundations*, London: Macmillan, 1920, p. vii.
22. Edward Caird, *The Evolution of Religion*, Glasgow: Maclehose, 1893, II, pp. 217ff.
23. William Temple, *Readings in St John's Gospel*, London: Macmillan, 1939, p. vii.
24. Temple, *NMG*, p. 486.
25. Temple, *CSO*, p. 112.
26. I have in mind some of the forms of 'liberation theology'.
27. F. A. Iremonger, *William Temple, Archbishop of Canterbury: Life and Letters*, Oxford: Oxford University Press, 1948, pp. 537–8.

Chapter 4 Moltmann and the Suffering of God

This chapter first appeared as an article in *The Expository Times*, in a series 'Today's Word for Today', *ET*, vol. 92, October 1980.

1. Gabriel Vahanian's book, *The Death of God: The Culture of our Post-Christian Era*, appeared in 1961.
2. His lengthy work, *Das Prinzip Hoffnung*, 1959, is now available in English (*The Principle of Hope*, 3 vols, Oxford: Blackwell, 1986).
3. Jürgen Moltmann, *Theology of Hope* (hereafter *TH*), tr. James W. Leitch, London: SCM Press, 1967, p. 43.
4. Jürgen Moltmann, *Hope and Planning*, London: SCM Press, 1971, pp. 178ff.
5. Moltmann, *TH*, p. 180.
6. C. Morse, *The Logic of Promise in Moltmann's Theology*, Philadelphia: Fortress Press, 1979, p. 95.
7. Jürgen Moltmann, *The Crucified God* (hereafter *CG*), London: SCM Press, 1974, p. 5.
8. *CG*, p. 208.
9. *CG*, p. 277.
10. *CG*, p. 277.
11. Jürgen Moltmann, *The Future of Creation*, London: SCM Press, 1980, p. 82.

12. *The Future of Creation*, p. 82.
13. *The Future of Creation*, p. 82.

Chapter 5 Mascall and Transcendental Thomism

This chapter was a Mascall Memorial Lecture, given at St Mary's Church, Bourne Street, London, on 15 November 1997, and first published in the *Tufton Review*, vol. 1, May 1998.

1. E. L. Mascall, *Christian Theology and Natural Science*, London: Longmans Green, 1956, p. 83.
2. Anthony Kenny, *Aquinas*, Oxford: Oxford University Press, 1980, p. 25.
3. Brian Horne, 'The Paradisal Dance', *Tufton Review*, vol. 1, May 1997, especially pp. 42–3.
4. E. L. Mascall, *Theology and the Gospel*, London: SPCK, 1977, p. 35.
5. Mascall, *Christian Theology and Natural Science*, p. 294.
6. E. L. Mascall, *Existence and Analogy*, London: Libra Books, 1966, p. 78.
7. E. L. Mascall, *The Openness of Being*, London: Darton, Longman & Todd, 1971, p. 61.
8. *The Openness of Being*, p. 141.
9. M. de Wulf, *History of Medieval Philosophy*, New York: Harper Torchbooks, 1959.
10. Étienne Gilson, *God and Philosophy*, New Haven: Yale University Press, 1941, p. 139.
11. *God and Philosophy*, p. 141.
12. Mascall, *Existence and Analogy*, p. 52.
13. *Existence and Analogy*, p. 79.
14. Karl Rahner, *Spirit in the World*, London: Sheed & Ward, 1968. This quotation and the one following are from the author's Introduction.
15. *Spirit in the World*, Introduction.
16. Emerich Coreth, *Metaphysics*, New York: Herder & Herder, 1986, p. 16.
17. F. D. E. Schleiermacher, *On Religion*, New York: Harper Torchbooks, 1958, p. 39.
18. E. L. Mascall, *Whatever Happened to the Human Mind?* London: SPCK, 1980, p. 16.
19. Bernard Lonergan, *Verbum*, London: Darton, Longman & Todd, 1968, p. 90.
20. Bernard Lonergan, *Insight*, Philosophical Library, 1970, pp. 635–6.

Chapter 6 Berdyaev: A Russian (not very) Orthodox Mystic

This chapter was originally a contribution to the symposium, G. O. Mazur (ed.), *Fifty Year Commemoration of the Life of Nicolai Berdyaev*, Semenenko Foundation, New York, 1999.

1. Hans Jonas, *The Gnostic Religion*, Beacon Press, 1963, p. 52.
2. Nikolai Berdyaev, *The Destiny of Man* (hereafter *DM*), New York: Harper Torchbooks, 1960, p. 23.
3. Berdyaev, *Dream and Reality*, London: G. Bles, 1950, p. 1.
4. Meister Eckhart, Sermon 23, in *Meister Eckhart: A New Translation*, New York: Harper Torchbooks, 1957, p. 204.
5. Thomas Aquinas, *Summa Theologiae*, I, 12. 1.
6. John Macquarrie, *In Search of Humanity*, London: SCM Press, 1982, pp. 10–24.
7. Berdyaev, *DM*, p. 25.
8. Paul Tillich, *Systematic Theology*, 3 vols. in one edition, Chicago: University of Chicago Press, 1967, especially I, pp. 186–9.
9. Nikolai Berdyaev, *The Beginning and the End* (hereafter *BE*), London: G. Bles, 1952, p. 9.
10. Berdyaev, *BE*, p. 17.
11. Nikolai Berdyaev, *The Russian Idea*, London: G. Bles, 1947, p. 253.
12. Berdyaev, *BE*, p. 111.
13. Jakob Boehme, *The Way to Christ*, New York: Paulist Press, 1978, p. 18.
14. Berdyaev, *DM*, p. 25.
15. For one view of the relation of Gnosticism to John's Gospel, see the commentary of Rudolf Bultmann, *The Gospel of John*, Oxford: Blackwell, 1971. On the question of a precosmic fall, see N. P. Williams, *The Idea of the Fall and of Original Sin*, London: Longmans Green, 1927.
16. Berdyaev, *BE*, p. 234.
17. *BE*, p. 42.
18. Berdyaev, *DM*, p. 45.
19. Berdyaev, *The Meaning of History*, London: G. Bles, 1936, p. 198.
20. Berdyaev, *Meaning*, p. 1.
21. C. S. Calian, *The Significance of Eschatology in the Thought of N. Berdyaev*, Leiden: E. J. Brill, 1965.

Chapter 7 Christianity without Incarnation?

Section (1) of this chapter began as a book review published in *Theology*, September 1977, and was then published in a revised form in Michael

Green (ed.), *The Truth of God Incarnate*, Hodder & Stoughton, 1977. Section (2) is a slightly revised version of my review of *Incarnation and Myth* published in the *Journal of Theological Studies*, 1978. Section (3) is an abridged version of a review article on John Hick's book which appeared in the *Church Times* of 29 October 1993 and given by the editor the appropriate title, 'If It's Metaphor, Handle It With Care'.

1. John Hick (ed.), *The Myth of God Incarnate*, London: SCM Press, 1977.
2. The contributors, in addition to the editor, were Maurice Wiles, Frances Young, Michael Goulder, Leslie Houlden, Don Cupitt, Dennis Nineham.
3. Frances Young, *Myth of God*, p. 29.
4. Leslie Houlden, *Myth of God*, p. 125.
5. Maurice Wiles, *Myth of God*, pp. 148ff.
6. John Hick, *Myth of God*, Preface, p. 9.
7. Maurice Wiles, *Myth of God*, pp. 161ff.
8. Wiles, *Myth of God*, p. 9.
9. Dennis Nineham, *Myth of God*, pp. 194–5.
10. Nineham, *Myth of God*, p. 195.
11. Maurice Wiles, *Incarnation and Myth*, ed. M. Goulder, London: SCM Press, 1978, p. 1.
12. Don Cupitt, *Incarnation and Myth*, p. 45.
13. Leslie Houlden, *Incarnation and Myth*, pp. 104–14.
14. Wiles, *Incarnation and Myth*, p. 7.
15. Cupitt, *Incarnation and Myth*, p. 36.
16. Wiles, *Incarnation and Myth*, p. 6.
17. Wiles, *Incarnation and Myth*, p. 8.
18. Wiles, *Incarnation and Myth*, p. 10.
19. C. F. D. Moule, *Incarnation and Myth*, p. 139.
20. John Hick, *The Metaphor of God Incarnate*, London: SCM Press, 1993.
21. *Metaphor*, p. 71.
22. *Metaphor*, p. 100.
23. *Metaphor*, p. 101.
24. John McIntyre, *The Shape of Christology*, London: SCM Press, 1966; much revised and enlarged, Edinburgh: T. & T. Clark, 1998.
25. *Metaphor*, p. 48.
26. See, e.g., my article, 'Christianity and Other Faiths' in *Union Seminary Quarterly Review*, vol. 20, 1964.

Chapter 8 The Legacy of Bultmann

This chapter was published in *The Heythrop Journal*, vol. 37, July 1996, as part of a special issue celebrating the eightieth birthday of Bruno Brinkman.

1. The Mandaeans were still living in Iraq a few years ago, but whether they have survived the Gulf War I do not know.
2. Rudolf Bultmann, *The History of the Synoptic Tradition*, tr. John Marsh, Oxford: Blackwell, 1963, p. 24.
3. Rudolf Bultmann, *Primitive Christianity in Its Contemporary Setting*, tr. R. H. Fuller, London: Thames & Hudson, 1956, p. 182.
4. Rudolf Bultmann, *Theology of the New Testament*, tr. Kendrick Grobel, London: SCM Press, 1952, vol. 1, p. 16.
5. James Robinson (ed.), *The Nag Hammadi Documents in English*, Leiden: E. J. Brill, 1977.
6. Rudolf Bultmann, 'New Testament and Mythology' in *Kerygma and Myth*, ed. H.-W. Bartsch, London: SPCK, 1957, p. 5.
7. See Clement of Alexandria, reported by Eusebius, *Ecclesiastical History*, vi, 14.
8. See especially J. A. T. Robinson, *The Priority of John*, London: SCM Press, 1985.
9. For an account, see R. Bultmann and K. Kundsin, *Form Criticism*, tr. F. C. Grant, New York: Harper, 1962.
10. The methods of form criticism are rigorously applied in *The History of the Synoptic Tradition*.
11. Rudolf Bultmann, *Jesus and the Word*, tr. L. P. Smith and E. H. Lantero, New York: Scribner, 1934.
12. *Jesus and the Word*, p. 13.
13. Bultmann, *History*, p. 40.
14. Bultmann, *Theology of NT*, vol. 2, p. 66.
15. D. M. Baillie, *God Was in Christ*, London: Faber & Faber, 1955, pp. 49, 52.
16. C. Braaten and R. Harrisville (eds.), *The Historical Jesus and the Kerygmatic Christ*, New York: Abingdon Press, 1964, p. 20.
17. D. F. Strauss, *The Life of Jesus Critically Examined*, tr. George Eliot, London: Swann Sonnenschein, 1906, p. 780.
18. For a detailed comparison of Bultmann and Heidegger, see my book, *An Existentialist Theology*, London: SCM Press, 1955.
19. Bultmann, *NT and Mythology*, p. 34.
20. *NT and Mythology*, p. 5.
21. H.-W. Bartsch (ed.), *Kerygma and Myth*, London: SPCK, 1954, vol. 1, p. 196.

22. Rudolf Bultmann, *Essays Philosophical and Theological*, tr. J. C. Greig, London: SCM Press, 1955, p. 280.
23. This passage appeared in the first edition of Melanchthon's *Loci Communes*, but was taken out in subsequent editions. Bultmann quotes it with approval in *NT and Mythology*, p. 99.
24. Bultmann, *Essays Philosophical and Theological*, p. 287.

Chapter 9 DuBose on Christ, Humanity and Evolution

This chapter is a slightly revised version of a lecture given at The University of the South, Sewanee, Tennessee, and first published in *St Luke's Journal of Theology*, vol. 31, December 1987.

1. Donald S. Armentrout (ed.), *A DuBose Reader*, Sewanee, Tenn.: The University of the South, 1984, p. 149.
2. *Reader*, p. 149.
3. *Reader*, p. 150.
4. William Porcher DuBose, *From Aristotle to Christ*, quoted in Dennis D. Kezar, 'Many Sons to the Father's Glory', Oxford University D.Phil. thesis, 1974.
5. DuBose, *The Soteriology of the New Testament*, New York: Longmans Green, 1923, p. 70.
6. *Soteriology*, p. 147.
7. *Soteriology*, p. 80.
8. *Soteriology*, p. 142.
9. Armentrout, *Reader*, p. 152.
10. DuBose, *The Reason of Life*, New York: Longmans Green, 1911, p. 19.
11. Armentrout, *Reader*, p. 151.
12. *Soteriology*, p. 4.
13. *Soteriology*, p. 9.
14. *Soteriology*, pp. 361–2.

Chapter 10 The Cosmic Christ

This was a paper read at a conference on 'Christ and the Cosmos' at Westminster College, Oxford, on 9 April 1994. Hitherto unpublished.

1. *The Daily Telegraph*, 4 April 1994.
2. Karl Rahner, *Hearers of the Word*, New York: Herder & Herder, 1969, p. 27.
3. Immanuel Kant, *Critique of Practical Reason*. The words come from the Conclusion, and are inscribed on Kant's tomb.

4. Blaise Pascal, *Pensées*, No. 17.
5. Stephen Hawking, *A Brief History of Time*, London: Guild Publishing, 1988, p. 119.
6. Irenaus, *Against Heresies*, IV, 38.
7. *Against Heresies*, IV, 38.
8. Origen, *Contra Celsum*, VII, 17.
9. Allan D. Galloway, *The Cosmic Christ*, New York: Harper, 1951, p. viii.
10. See J. A. Lyons, *The Cosmic Christ in Origen and Teilhard de Chardin*, Oxford: Oxford University Press, 1982.

Chapter 11 *The Pre-existence of Christ*

This chapter consists of a revised version of parts of my *Expository Times* article mentioned in note 5 below, together with new material.

1. Karl Barth, *Church Dogmatics*, III/2, Edinburgh: T. & T. Clark, 1960, p. 53.
2. Karl Rahner, *Theological Investigations*, 1, London: Darton, Longman & Todd, 1961, p. 184.
3. Niall Coll, *Christ in Eternity and Time*, Dublin: Four Courts Press, 2001.
4. *Christ in Eternity and Time*, pp. 178–9.
5. John Harvey, 'A New Look at the Christ Hymn in Philippians', in *The Expository Times*, vol. 76, p. 379, August 1965. My reply, 'The Pre-existence of Jesus Christ,' is in *ET*, vol. 77, pp. 199–202, April 1966.
6. Justin, *First Apology*, xlvi and lxiii.

Chapter 12 *Christology from Above and from Below*

This chapter is a revised version of a Jordan Lecture, given at Newman College, Edmonton, Alberta, and was published in the *Anglican Theological Review*, 1997.

1. Readers can find the texts, with background in formation, of Chalcedon and other early Councils in the two volumes, *A New Eusebius*, ed. J. Stevenson, London: SPCK 1957, rev. W. H. C. Frend 1987, and *Creeds, Councils and Controversies*, ed. J. Stevenson, London: SPCK, 1966, rev. W. H. C. Frend 1989, or, with texts in original languages, in *Enchiridion Symbolorum*, ed. H. Denziger, Herder & Herder (updated editions are issued periodically).
2. Karl Rahner, *Theological Investigations*, 1, London: Darton Longman & Todd, 1961, p. 149.

3. A. Grillmeier, *Christ in Christian Tradition*, vol. 1, London: Mowbray, 1975, p. 544.
4. These terms are discussed in my book, *Jesus Christ in Modern Thought*, London: SCM Press, 1990, pp. 393ff.
5. J. D. G. Dunn, *Christology in the Making*, London: SCM Press, 1989, p. 114.
6. Rahner, *Theological Investigations*, 1, p. 155.
7. Irenaeus, *Against Heresies*, IV, 38.
8. *Against Heresies*, V, 20.
9. Emil Brunner, *The Mediator*, London: Lutterworth Press, 1934, p. 276.
10. See Stevenson, *A New Eusebius*, 1987, pp. 261–2.
11. F. D. E. Schleiermacher, *The Christian Faith*, Edinburgh: T. & T. Clark, 1928, p. 374.
12. *The Christian Faith*, p. 64.
13. Wolfhart Pannenberg, *Jesus – God and Man*, London: SCM Press, 1968, p. 189.
14. D. E. Jenkins, *The Glory of Man*, London: SCM Press, 1967.
15. J. A. T. Robinson, *The Human Face of God*, London: SCM Press, 1973.
16. John Meyendorff, *Christ in Eastern Christian Thought*, Washington: Corpus Books, 1969, p. 64.
17. Rahner, *Theological Investigations*, 1, p. 185.

Chapter 13 Development of Doctrine

This chapter is a slightly abridged version of my contribution to the *Festschrift* for Maurice Wiles: Sarah Coakley and David A. Pailin (eds.), *The Making and Remaking of Christian Doctrine*, Oxford: Clarendon Press, 1993.

1. H.-W. Bartsch, (ed.), *Kerygma and Myth*, London: SPCK, 1953, p. 5.
2. Patrick Henry, *New Directions in New Testament Studies*, London: SCM Press, 1979, pp. 109–10.
3. Maurice Wiles, *The Making of Christian Doctrine*, Cambridge: Cambridge University Press, 1967, p. 167.
4. Karl Rahner, *Theological Investigations*, I, London: Darton, Longman & Todd, 1961, p. 150.
5. Maurice Wiles, *Explorations in Theology 4*, London: SCM Press, 1979, p. 24.
6. J. H. Newman, *Essay on the Development of Christian Doctrine*, Notre Dame, Indiana: University of Notre Dame Press, 1989, p. 171.
7. Newman, *Essay*, p. 185.

8. *Essay*, p. 189.
9. *Essay*, p. 192.
10. *Essay*, p. 203.

Chapter 14 *The Theology of the Oxford Movement*

This is a slightly revised version of a lecture 'Theological Implications of the Oxford Movement' given in the Church of St Mary the Virgin, New York, in October 1983, to mark the Sesquicentennial of the Oxford Movement. It was first published in J. Robert Wright (ed.), *Lift High the Cross: The Oxford Movement, 1833–1983*, Friends of the Oxford Movement, New York, 1983.

1. J. H. Newman, *Apologia pro Vita Sua*, London: Dent, Everyman's Library, pp. 186–7.
2. Søren Kierkegaard, *Philosophical Fragments*, Princeton: Princeton University Press, 1936, p. 31.
3. F. D. E. Schleiermacher, *The Christian Faith*, Edinburgh: T. & T. Clark, 1928, pp. 391ff.
4. Francis Bacon, *Essays*, London: Henry Parson, 1730, p. 98.
5. J. M. Campbell, *The Nature of the Atonement*, London: James Clarke, 4th ed., 1959.
6. Andrew Louth, *Discerning the Mystery*, Oxford: Oxford University Press, 1983.
7. R. C. Selby, *The Principle of Reserve in the Writings of John Henry Cardinal Newman*, Oxford: Oxford University Press, 1975, p. 22.
8. Newman, quoted by Selby, *Principle of Reserve*, p. 94.
9. Newman, Tract 90, quoted in E. R. Fairweather (ed.), *The Oxford Movement*, Oxford: Oxford University Press, 1964, pp. 150–1.
10. Newman, *Apologia*, p. 133.
11. W. W. Manross, *A History of the American Episcopal Church*, New York: Morehouse-Gorham, 3rd ed., 1959, p. 219.
12. John Keble, *National Apostasy*, Oxford: Rocket Press, 1983, p. 22.
13. J. H. Newman, quoted in Fairweather (ed.), *The Oxford Movement*, p. 56.
14. See Edward Schillebeeckx, *Christ the Sacrament*, London: Sheed & Ward, 1963.
15. E. B. Pusey, Tract 67, quoted in Geoffrey Rowell, *The Vision Glorious*, Oxford: Oxford University Press, 1983, p. 75.
16. Geoffrey Faber, *Oxford Apostles*, London: Faber & Faber, 1933, p. 434.

Chapter 15 Ramsey on *The Gospel and the Church*

This chapter is a revised and abridged version of the Levy Memorial Lectures, given at All Saints Church, New York, in January and February 1989, and published as a booklet, *Arthur Michael Ramsey: Life and Times*, by All Saints Church, New York City, 1990.

1. A. M. Ramsey, *The Gospel and the Catholic Church*, London: Longmans Green, 1936, See pp. 34, 54, 84, 126.
2. Archbishop Ramsey and Cardinal Suenens, *The Future of the Christian Church*, New York: Morehouse-Barlow, 1970, pp. 60–70 and 113–127.
3. *Gospel and Church*, p. 34.
4. *Gospel and Church*, p. 84.
5. Søren Kierkegaard, *Training in Christianity*, Princeton: Princeton University Press, 1944, p. 71.

Chapter 16 Eckhart and Heidegger: Two Mystical Testimonies

A lecture given at Plater College, Oxford, in 1989. Not hitherto published.

1. Hans-Georg Gadamer, Memorial Address in *Evangelische Kommentare*, vol. 10, 1977, pp. 204–8.
2. Martin Heidegger, *Über den Humanismus*, Frankfurt-am-Rhein: Klostermann, 1947, pp. 36–7.
3. Plotinus, *Enneads*, V, 2, 1 (Loeb Classical Library).
4. Heidegger, *Was Ist Metaphysik?* Frankfurt-am-Rhein: Klostermann, 7th ed., 1949.
5. Heidegger, *The Piety of Thinking*, Bloomington: Indiana University press, 1976, p. 26.
6. Heidegger, *Discourse on Thinking*, New York: Harper & Row, 1976, p. 61.
7. Heidegger, *Nietzsche*, vol. 4, New York: Harper & Row, 1982, p. 193.
8. Eckhart, *Sermons*, tr. R. B. Blakney, New York: Harper Torchbooks, 1957, p. 110.
9. Eckhart, *Essential Sermons, etc*, tr. E. Colledge and B. McGinn, London: SPCK, 1987, p. 193.

Chapter 17 The Continuing Relevance of Kant

This chapter was written as a contribution to a *Festschrift* honouring Professor Robert F. Scharlemann in 1992.

1. *Religion within the Limits of Reason Alone*, New York: Harper & Row, 1960, p. 15.
2. *Sämmtliche Werke*, Voss, 1867, vol. 4, p. 159.
3. *Religion*, p. 116.
4. *Religion*, p. 56.
5. *Religion*, p. 55.
6. Karl Barth, *Church Dogmatics*, III/2, Edinburgh: T. & T. Clark, 1960 p. 218.
7. *Critique of Practical Reason*, London: Longmans Green, 1927, p. 260.
8. *Religion*, p. 3.
9. *Critique of Judgment*, Oxford: Oxford University Press, 1928, Pt. 2, p. 131.
10. E. Adickes, *Kants Opus postumum*, Berlin, 1920, pp. 819–24.
11. C. C. J. Webb, *Kant's Philosophy of Religion*, Oxford: Oxford University Press, 1926, pp. 200–1.
12. *Critique of Pure Reason*, London: Macmillan, 1956, p. 532.
13. Webb, *Kant's Philosophy*, p. 201.
14. *Groundwork of the Metaphysic of Morals*, New York: Harper, 1964, p. 17.
15. See *The Mediators*, London: SCM Press, 1995, p. 140.
16. *Critique of Judgment*, Oxford: Oxford University Press, 1952. especially 'The Analytic of the Sublime', pp. 90–227.
17. Karl Rahner, *Theological Investigations*, 1, London: Darton, Longman & Todd, 1961, p. 167.

Chapter 18 The Problem of Religious Knowledge

This chapter was a contribution to the *Festschrift* honouring Professor James Deotis Roberts, Summer, 2002.

1. Blaise Pascal, *Pensées*, Paris: Garnier-Flammarion, 1973, pp. 90, 92.
2. William James, *Selected Papers in Philosophy*, London: Dent, 1917, p. 206.
3. James, *The Varieties of Religious Experience*, London: Longmans Green, 1952, pp. 506–7.
4. J. D. Roberts, *Faith and Reason*, Boston: The Christopher Publishing House, 1962, pp. vii–viii.
5. Pascal, *Pensées*, p. 48.
6. Quoted by E. T. Long, from Anthony Flew and Alasdair MacIntyre, (eds.), *New Essays in Philosophical Theology*, London: SCM Press, 1955, p. 46.
7. John Milbank, 'The Sublime in Kierkegaard', *Heythrop Journal*, vol. 37, no. 3, p. 298, July 1996.

Index